B

20. Mary
From Edith.

With fondest love.

1954.
6D4
1st OD
8-
B/h
6B

THE TURBULENT YEARS

An ancient fragment of Auld Reekie—through the Castle Battlements, showing, on the left, part of the lantern-tower of St. Giles' Cathedral, the Outlook Tower, in the centre, and the spire of the Tolbooth (St. John's) Kirk, at the head of the Lawnmarket

THE
TURBULENT YEARS

A PORTRAIT OF YOUTH
IN AULD REEKIE

by

Alasdair Alpin MacGregor

"The thoughts of my youth pursue me."

R. L. S.

METHUEN & CO. LTD. LONDON
36 Essex Street, Strand, W.C.2

First published in 1945

THIS BOOK IS PRODUCED
IN COMPLETE CONFORMITY WITH
THE AUTHORIZED ECONOMY STANDARDS

PRINTED IN GREAT BRITAIN

DEDICATION

STIRLING MELVILLE

MY DEAR STIRLING,

What happy accident, and at a time so calamitous in the affairs of mankind, should have set us across one another's path, after so many years? For this expression of fortune, we have to thank none other than one bearing the brave name of him, the memory of whose prowess is perpetuated in the Abbey Craig. It is remarkable that a chance line, in a hand then unfamiliar to me, should have inaugurated so much. Truly, there are many instances in which the lines have fallen in places more pleasant than I have deserved.

In memory's ear there still vibrates the music of those hours spent in your mystery chamber, where, over and over again, as you cannot but recall, we played Joseph Hislop's singing of *Requiescat*, until we had mastered it, and could reproduce, to our own satisfaction, all its subtleties:

> *Strew on her roses, roses,*
> *And never a spray of yew.*
> *In quiet she reposes:*
> *Ah! would that I did too.*
> *Her mirth the world required:*
> *She bathed it in smiles of glee;*
> *But her heart was tired, tired,*
> *And now they let her be.*

Do you remember our ramble about Windlestrawlee (I wonder how many Edinburgh folks are aware of the existence of this farm in their midst!) and the evening we wandered in the Thornie-bauk, and afterwards explored the mysteries of Leamy, and saw, in your old back-garden, the decayed apple-tree that once bore in such prodigence? I was moved not a little that evening by our visit to your old home, and particularly to the wee roomie where you, the studious lad whose application we envied, assumed the rôle of an eastern archimage, and conducted those experiments of yours, playing weird tricks with electricity, and ultimately producing those wireless contraptions that mystified us all at a time when broadcasting was still very much in its infancy.

And do you remember our lingering about Cramond, where a slice of river goes tumbling dizzily through Dowie's Mill? I still see those beeches, and scent the garlic that, crushed underfoot in our passage down-river, exuded a pungency in such marked contrast with the perfume of hawthorn, a-drooping in profusion. Mind our listening to the wood-pigeons' cooing, and our watching the house-martins, newly arrived from sunnier climes, picking up, at the water's margin, material for the nest we eventually found, half-built, under the eaves of the ruined outhouse? Ah! and that touch of sadness when we reached the tidal parts, so full of boats as derelict as Dowie's Mill, so beset with rusted ribs protruding from the mud-banks at the Almond's mouth, near the ferry we frequented in boyhood.

On all we did and saw during those crowded hours together, this past May, one could compile an appreciable volume. Here, in London, as I write, my imaginative feet are following, through the Hermitage of Braid, the burn so incontinent after that downpour we just escaped! Who would believe that there lay within our city's confines a place as melodious with bird-song as the Hermitage, as liquid to the ear with the falling of water when the shower, gathered together on the Hills of Home, reaches that steep defile among oaks and larches and those very tall elms?

And this brings me to the hills whence, throughout life, has come much of mine aid. I never beheld anything lovelier than the Pentlands that Sunday morning when, in such remarkable stillness, we sought the path leading over from Bonaly to the reservoir of the same name. I visualise those patches of warm reddish-brown, where blaeberry shoots, springing among the turf on Torphin, resembled vast oriental carpets spread out in the sun, as if for an airing. I see, too, the fleecy plume of train-smoke, away in the valley to the north—so far away that, for all the earth's tranquillity that May morning, we could hear no sound of thrusting shaft and rumbling wheel.

I do not know when, in all my experience of hills, I enjoyed among them a day more Elysian than that on which we crossed Threipmuir, climbed out from its marshy fringes by the steep avenue of beeches in bud of livid green, sun-filtered in May, to Bavelaw Castle, and then travelled the Green Cleuch with its stiles and guide-posts, until we arrived at the shining waters of Loganlee, and finally embraced the tea-pot at Flotterstane.

At times I pine for that peep of Turnhouse Hill, seen through the trees at Flotterstane—the peep prompting us to our survey of Rullion Green, as the sun declined. Did we not feel, yonder, at the

Martyrs' Stone, that in our veins, also, pulsated the blood of the Covenanters? I wonder why, in these days of such colossal battle-fields, so small a patch of ground, contested nearly three hundred years ago, and by so few, should still exert upon us an influence so alluring? Nigh three centuries of sunshine and shower seem not to have cleansed this spot of its sorrow. I have but to think on it to see, again, the water-ouzel winging across our track to search the lake's edge, and to hear, once more, the woes of the persecuted, mingled with curlew-call and the peewees' plaint, with the bleating of lambs, and the tinkle of rill spilling clearer than crystal. There can be nothing in God's great world more enchanting than a day on our Pentland Hills when, in time of king-cup and cuckoo-pint, wild cherrytrees in the copses send their fragrant flounces a-fluttering among the firs.

With all these recollections pressing in upon me as the typescript of this book goes to the printer's, it is not altogether surprising that I should desire to have our consociation—our *entente cordiale*—commemorated thus, in yet another instalment of this protracted Family Saga. Let it be not too long, dear Stirling, ere we again go a-Maying among the Pentlands, or a-straying into the recesses of Leamy and of the Thorniebauk. Some bond, unbreakable, ineffable, binds me to Auld Reekie's grey stanes, and to her hilly hinterland—the lure of lovely and beloving memories, and, perhaps, a secret sob for the irrevocable dead.

Aye,
ALASDAIR

PREFACE

WITH the publication of *Auld Reekie: Portrait of a Lowland Boyhood*, a heartless critic described this family biography of mine as a monument in dalliance. What will he say when he sees this fourth volume, and learns that there may even be a fifth? Yet, why should one not dally? In our striving for material values, we get to the end of our lives early enough, in all conscience, some of us having little to show for the passage of the years but a balance at the bank, and most of us having not even that.

It usually falls to the lot of sequels to dash the high expectations of those who have awaited them most anxiously. The next few months will tell whether this volume is to share in that lot. It may be urged that it comprises far too many trifling domesticities. But are not our lives much more completely absorbed in such than we, perhaps, recognise? The difference in my case is that, whereas the domestic existence of most people is a tepid affair, that with the Colonel was usually maintained at boiling-point.

In writing about one's relatives and closest associates, whether they be dead or alive, one naturally remains under *some* measure of restraint, for, as De Quincey wrote in his own *Confessions*, rather than inflict mortification upon near and loving kindred, "any kindhearted man will choose to mutilate his narrative, will suppress facts, and will mystify explanations". It is for the reader, rather than for the writer, to judge whether, in this regard, these pages show any trace of kindheartedness.

When I first contemplated this further encroachment upon the public's patience and indulgence, I proposed including a chapter or two on that part of my youth spent in trench warfare on the Western Front. In the light of contemporaneous events, however, the introduction here of matter relating to one's own experience in a *previous* war hardly seems apposite. Moreover, although so large a proportion of mankind is at present imbued with an inflexible passion to kill and be killed, there must be many who are heartily sick of reading and hearing about this colossal insanity, and all the concomitant evils and excesses it necessarily entails.

ALASDAIR ALPIN MACGREGOR

297, *King's Road,*
Chelsea, S.W. 3.
January, 1945.

CONTENTS

ILLUSTRATIONS

CHAPTER I

WHAT A MAN!

IT HAS not taken long to decide which of us—the Colonel or his unregenerate son—should occupy the proscenium as the curtain rises on the turbulent years of my youth. If ever true, it is doubly so in my case that any portraiture of the son would make pedestrian reading, were it divorced from the father, a character unusual and original to the last degree, at once so reasonable and so autocratic, so modern, yet hating modernity, so full of sympathy and of cruelty, of understanding and of intolerance, so gallant and so unchivalrous, lovable and detestable, superb and pathetic—withal, a nature so contradictory and complex as to engender in one extremes of love and hatred. Again the Colonel must have the stage largely to himself in these opening pages; and I am constrained to allow him as much of the spot-light as the medium at my disposal can generate, even at the risk of some small recapitulation.

And why not? Was it not he who made himself responsible for all the drama in which his wife and family were involved? And were there not innumerable occasions when his youthful and hyper-sensitive offspring would have sacrificed anything to have had him curb those passionate peculiarities he exercised with results so embarrassing?

This man, so truly remarkable, whose very good was turned by excess into folly and fatuity, was a specialist in the art of self-dramatisation. Himself in his middle sixties, he insisted on playing in my youth, or at any rate during that part of it not absorbed in warfare, a rôle as menacing as it was vital.

From infirmity of purpose the Colonel never suffered. True, he may have tilted at many a windmill in his day; but he certainly never did so in a half-hearted way. He was a man of action and of firm resolve. "Put your hand to nothing you do not intend doing to the very best of your ability," was one of the maxims he observed throughout life. This applied as much to the manner in which he carried himself, as to anything to which he put hand or tongue. He believed that one was committed, in honour, to an acceptable standard of efficiency, in whatever calling one pursued;

and he had the knack of ensuring that those associated with him exhibited, at any rate while in his presence, that degree of discipline he set for himself. Slovenliness he abhorred, whether in the matter of mind, or of dress or deportment. He would never allow any of his children to lean against anything. It looked unseemly. Might it not augur the beginning of a life of loafing? "Why do you wear your hair so long? You look shaggy and unkempt! You're like a colt—like a Goth!" This warning, uttered but once, was enough to guarantee my visiting the barber's with the least possible delay, if a 'scene' were to be averted. One had to be uncommonly presentient where the Colonel was concerned, to make life with him livable.

He was no dandy. On the other hand, he never permitted himself anything careless or slipshod. Up to within a year or two of his death (he lived to be eighty-four) he groomed himself to perfection; and even thereafter, when more dependent upon others, he strove valiantly to do everything for himself, painfully conscious that failing eyesight and stiffness of limb now made it increasingly difficult for him to maintain, unaided, that degree of spruceness for which, in his earlier days, he had been noted. His influence in this respect, added to that self-discipline imparted by Aunt Dorothy in doses less drastic, and perhaps more subtle, explains the fact (a singular one, I suppose it to be) that, at this very moment, I am wearing the only two collar-studs I have worn in my life, except on those few occasions when I have been obliged to deck myself out in evening dress. When I went to the war, I put these studs in a drawer containing an assortment of things to which I hoped one day to return. On demobilisation some years later, I extracted them from that drawer, and have used them constantly ever since, one for the front of the collar, the other for the back. My friends tell me that this record is sufficiently remarkable to be worthy of permanent commemoration, which explains why I am tempted to mention it here. True, I have seen many skits and humorous cartoons on stud-hunting, which lead me to believe that stud-losing is more prevalent than I could have imagined. Yet, in more than three decades of shirt-wearing, I swear that twopence is all I have spent on studs.

The Colonel's bearing, when in his prime, had been remarkable; and, even as a septuagenarian, he bore himself perfectly. Age never conferred on him the faintest suspicion of a stoop. As for his powers of physical endurance, they were immense. He was well beyond the allotted span before he confessed that the stairs in Auld Reekie's tramcars were beginning to get a little awkward and irksome. Nevertheless, his mere presence still arrested the attention of the most casual passenger on any pavement, or traveller in any vehicle.

* * * * * * *

Work performed perfunctorily by anyone professionally employed in this walk of life or in that, he would not tolerate. If, for instance, he engaged a cook (this, alas! being the sort of duty devolving on him, now that Mabel, our mother, had ceased to live with him) he did so because the applicant for this position in his kitchen—in his royal household, one might almost say—had assured him that she could cook. If, having accepted the 'situation' offered, and taken wages in respect thereof, it transpired that she could *not* cook, he soon had it out with her, magnanimously granting her a few weeks' grace during which he hoped she would either learn or depart. This probationary period was often one of dire embarrassment, if not actually of such culinary upheaval as might be reflected in an epidemic of indigestion. Many a good dinner was spoilt as much through nervousness on the cook's part as through genuine ineptitude.

A like standard was demanded of our outdoor employees. If a man came to us as gardener, it was because the Colonel, in seeking one, had taken him at his word when he averred that he had had some experience of gardening. Imagine what happened, then, when the garden failed to produce the crops, whether swedes or sweetpeas!

The languor of a certain gardener we had in our northern days, I well remember. He was the only employee whose services were retained, as if in open defiance of his incompetence. Why this leniency with Willie Robertson, we never knew. Nor could the Colonel himself explain, when Mabel asked why the garden proffered no blooms worthy of the rose-bowl. "He's a wonderful gardener," father used to say, " if only you allow him plenty of time. But no one has ever heard of a gardener who could do less gardening in more time than Willie Robertson!"

Long before the days of films, Willie had been noted in the parish as a slow-motion artist. Never in his life had he been known to bestir himself, as the Colonel was soon to discover. The laggard passage of a snail across his spade was sufficient to infect him

3

instantly with a spell of inactivity, during which it was his pleasure to contemplate the heavens and the earth, as he moved round, sunwise, in sluggish rotation, leaning heavily on his implement the while, lest he should stumble in the very slowness of his turning, and punctuating each of the thirty-and-two points of the compass by giving his moustache ends a long and loving twirl. Though our dreamy gardener was no more than middle-aged at the time of which I tell, it took him an unconscionably long time to complete just one circle. When in the execution of his horticultural duties, he was more addicted to this performance than to any other. So you may reckon how much he accomplished in a normal day.

With epithets none too flattering, the Colonel bombarded the impervious Willie, almost from the first day he delved in our Highland garden. Impervious he certainly was, which explains how he managed to remain with us for years! Not even wrath on our parents' part seemed capable of provoking the weary Willie Robertson to down tools and quit. Smug in the security of Struan Cottage, the family hearth so aptly named, where his elderly sister kept house for him, behind walls and windows scarcely seen for ivy, "far from the madding crowd's ignoble strife," he preserved, with native complacency, the tenor of his tardy ways, content to remain by his ain fireside whenever he felt disinclined to exert himself in pursuance of his calling.

I must tell you, by the way, that *weary* William had a soft side for *sweet*-William. Had he been left to his own devices, he would have stocked the entire garden with this namesake of his, to the exclusion of everything else. It possessed the virtue of requiring the very minimum of attention. And who would deny there's much in a name?

Even more rigorous and exacting was the Colonel when transacting business with professional people. Their status, in his view, demanded a higher standard of competence. In his dealings with them, he would not suffer anything suggestive of that ἄριστον μέτρον—that "excellent mediocrity"—so universally approved, and even adored. Feeble-mindedness was preferable to mediocrity. If he engaged the services of a solicitor, as he so often found himself obliged to do during the bitter and futile years Mabel and he wrangled by proxy, he did so because it was taken for granted that the solicitor advertised himself, by brass name-plate, as a person well and truly qualified in the law, and entitled, consequently, to be paid fees in exchange for good, sound, legal advice. Heaven defend him, however, when the Colonel found out, as he occasionally did, that the solicitor's knowledge of the law was faulty or inadequate, so that he, as client, was placed in a perplexing situation just when he imagined he had triumphed, fairly and squarely and finally! Faced with a disappointment so shattering, not even Demosthenes could have been more eloquent. Annoyance produced in our unpredictable parent anything but aphasia. It loosened his tongue, on the contrary, and to an extent anyone might envy when in straits.

Because he dearly loved a fight, the Colonel was an antagonist in the literal sense of the word. He often spoiled for contest, a tendency his children soon recognised, and judiciously respected, and which, I must concede, most of them appear to have acquired, probably through their upbringing in an atmosphere so heavily charged with the fumes of belligerence. No one ever trailed his coat with impunity where Colonel MacGregor was concerned: no one ever let slip the vaguest suspicion of challenge that he did not take up instantly, and push to its appropriate conclusion. Would one be justified, then, in saying he was quarrelsome? I think you will agree one would, after you have read the passages describing hereinafter the rages he staged from time to time.

*   *   *   *   *   *   *

Not only in life's mental and spiritual conflict did he excel, but also in the physical and athletic. In his college days, there was none who could compete with him at shinty, nor anyone in the length and breadth of India or Burma who surpassed him at polo, when in his prime. He was a terror in both fields, I have been told. As a student at Glasgow, he had acquired renown for his skill with the *caman*—the shinty-stick. Contemporaries of his used to relate to us epics of his prowess and puissance, nigh half a century earlier—how he was as successful in winning prizes as he was formidable in thrashing those who menaced him, or showed him discourtesy. I well remember the account an elderly clergyman from Islay gave us in our young days of an incident that occurred in the neighbourhood of the Broomielaw, that quayside promenade so beloved of Glaswegians a generation or two ago, and still the rendezvous of many of the Gaelic-speaking inhabitants of that vast city. The Colonel, then but a youth not long arrived at this metropolis from his native Hebrides, observed three stalwart students, all of them a year or two older than himself, approach with the air of mischievous intent. They were bearing down upon him in a way calculated to ensure that he would be obliged to step aside, cringingly, so as to allow of their passing, three abreast, along the narrow footpath then fringing the Clyde at this point. They deliberately bumped into him. Instantly, the blood of the MacGregors was surging through his iron frame. Casting aside his jacket, and spitting on his palms before rubbing them together in the manner implying serious challenge (our storyteller used to vacate his chair at this juncture, so as to impress us the more with an ocular demonstration!) he set about them. A few seconds later, all three of them were struggling in twenty feet of river, while father was calmly pursuing his way along the Broomielaw, as though nothing unusual had occurred. By the following day, news of this riverside skirmish had spread through every faculty of Glasgow University; and the great Professor Caird, not long appointed to the Chair of Moral Philosophy, directed him to stand up in the lecture-room to receive his commendation. Thereafter, as our agèd informant used to tell, every student feared and respected him, and sought his acquaintance.

This remarkable physical strength and prowess, which, by the way, he carried into his eightieth year, had stood by him in many a tight and hazardous corner—in desert and in jungle, in his mountaineering exploits the world over, on perilous seas, in brushes with frontier tribesmen. Let me recall but one such situation, to wit, his ascent of Popocatepetl's eighteen thousand feet, when its upper reaches lay encased in snow. Here is the pertinent passage from one of his own books:

"It was a far cry to the top of the mountain that looked so near when far away; and it was with bitter experience that we found out the effects of the recent snowfall. During the greater portion of the steep ascent, we sank very much more than knee-deep into the soft snow at every step. Our course was a very tortuous and zigzag one, and occasionally my foot would slip on the more hardened layers of snow beneath, and then I would slither down till the accumulating bank of snow put a check to my undesirable backsliding; while climbing up again was the most trying task of all. I tried snow shoes over my boots; but they were to me like the armour of Goliath to David, as I was not accustomed to them, and I had to take them off.

6

"To increase our discomfort, a gusty wind blew across the mountain, loaded with blinding snowdrift, consisting of hail almost as fine as the sand of the seashore. The cold also became very intense toward the higher altitudes, and, long before we reached the top, my hair and clothes became as stiff as pasteboard, and looked like a panoply of radiant armour, flexible only at the joints. I several times thought of giving up the venture as a bad job; and I am afraid I should have turned back with my task undone, except that I was determined that nothing should mar the voyage which lay in my power to prevent. But perseverance surmounts difficulties, and ten or twelve hours of this severe strain brought us safely at last to the crater of the famous Popocatepetl, which we found smoking and fuming away in great style.

"It was a fairly round crater, with a well-defined margin, and an upper and lower lip to right and left of us as we entered. Except in odd nooks and crannies, the crater itself was free from snow, on account of the fumes; but outside, and immediately round it, a solid rim of ice, two or three feet high, marked the margin where the fumes from the crater ceased to have any great influence. On the sharp edge of this boundary I cut my shin by slipping over it. . . . Stimulants are fatal to the proper endurance of prolonged hardship; and to take them, when the long labour is still before one, would be a mistake of the first order. But, once Kenneth and myself were safely seated on our bench of ice, we really thought ourselves entitled to a wee drap o' the crather, though we found this kind of crather made us only cold and uncomfortable."

Had I the space to quote the entire account, you might be as understanding as I sincerely hope I was when obliged, in later years, to deal with the rather extraordinary father who had performed several such feats long before I was born.

* * * * * * *

In so many ways does the Colonel remind one of the more dauntless of the Highland chiefs, as portrayed in art and in literature. You will have some notion of what he looked like when I assure you that, had Raeburn met him, he would have painted him as memorably as he did 'The MacNab', that superb portrait

7

of Francis, XIIth and penultimate laird. The Colonel in Highland garb, bearing himself with that carriage displaying the build of his mind as well as the athletic proportions of his person, would have made an admirable subject for any canvas, except that, in all probability, he and the artist would have quarrelled as to the pose to be adopted, and as to the rendering of certain features of which he truly believed himself to have a monopoly. The portrait, in consequence, might never have been finished. Nevertheless, he was a character not one whit less picturesque than any Highland laird in history. I, his elder son, am convinced of this, however far short of convincing my readers these and earlier pages of mine may have fallen. At times I see him as 'The MacNab': at times as Alasdair, Chief of the MacDonells of Glengarry, the subject of yet another of Raeburn's masterpieces. And how true of the Colonel were those words in which Sir Walter Scott described his friend, Glengarry! "He seems to have lived a century too late. . . . He played the part of a chieftain too nigh the life to be popular among an altered race." Of course, only the most intrepid would have risked likening father to either of these stalwarts, for he, assuredly, would have regarded it as a disparagement. After all, who was Francis MacNab but the drunken and impoverished head of one of the minor clans? And who was Alasdair MacDonell, for all his 'tail' of fearsome Highlandmen, but a man imprisoned in his own feudalism? Miserable fellows, both of them, when compared with Colonel MacGregor—Gaelic traditionalist—Bard of the Clan Gregor—inheritor of a warlike patronymic from no less historic a figure than Alpin, King of the Scots of Dalriada, that most ancient of our kingdoms—potential claimant to the throne of Scotland (then named Alba) through Alpin's son, Kenneth MacAlpin—worthy descendant of the freebooter, Rob Roy MacGregor, O!! Is it surprising we children grew up with the idea that the MacGregors were a race specially chosen, and set apart by God Himself, and that anything connected with the Hanoverian succession was but part of an impertinent imposture?

Truly, the Colonel had a good conceit of himself. Not once in all the years I had to deal with him did he ever exhibit a vestige of autophoby or modesty. On the contrary, his self-assurance bore him through the greater part of his life with an outward expression to be envied, perhaps, by those of us who are less blatant, and more reticent and retiring. He would underline, on

8

the smallest pretext, all his own superb qualities, and keep us informed on how high he stood in his own estimation. When one happened to be out walking with him, he seldom deviated from 'the croun o' the causey', as though he were entitled to the best of every thoroughfare, to the centre of every right-of-way, by reason of his MacGregor blood—by reason, too, of the tartan he carried with such distinction. By assiduous application to his vanities, he had convinced himself that he had the best height, girth, weight, proportions, and complexion in the world, though by what standards he adjudged these, we never knew. No attribute requisite to Grecian perfection was overlooked when a flood of rodomontade gushed from him. His eyes were the finest ever seen in a member of the human race. His nose was as classical as any could be. His mouth denoted firmness, and his chin that measure of determination without which no man could consider himself complete. In short, he believed that he epitomised what, in physical terms, was God's own idea of an upstanding mortal. Fortified in this conceit, he could be uncharitable, if not actually slanderous, when referring to persons whose features, in his view, fell short of his arbitrary requirements. *"He's* no great shakes!" was the mildest observation of a derogatory kind he ever made of anyone the least worthy of his criticism. The variety, as well as the intensity, of expression at his disposal, when he wished to censure, was as large as it was terrific. Indeed, his condemnatory powers were transcendent.

The Scots, I need hardly remark, are grand at bragging; and they have a singularly apt way of extolling their virtues and standards, especially when parleying with the English. One is reminded of the Scotsman who, in the course of conversation in an English railway compartment, was congratulated by a fellow-passenger on his country's achievement in having supplied England with two archbishops, simultaneously. Judged by Scottish standards, this was of trifling significance. At best, they were but the heads of a foreign kirk, where *Scotland* was concerned. "Nae doot, they'd hae the gift o' the gab," observed the Scotsman. "But, if they'd stoppit at hame, naebody wad hae thocht onything o' them!"

*   *   *   *   *   *   *

The Colonel read character largely by physical contour, which explains a bad nose, or protruding ears, or eyes too close to one another, or legs a fraction out of shape—how any one of these was sufficient to damn a fellow in his estimation. Ridiculous as all this may seem, he did know something of the brain, and could spot hereditary weaknesses, such as insanity—even the merest trace of them—in an instant, simply by looking at one. "Do you see this fellow coming toward us?" he might now ask me, rather temerariously, and certainly too audibly, as we walked the streets of Auld Reekie together. "Look at the forehead! Do you notice anything peculiar about the eyes? There's insanity in that family." After the lapse of a few minutes, he might continue with "Observe this woman's walk—this woman about to pass. Shall I tell you something of her history?"

To the uninitiated, this may sound nonsensical. Yet, father was seldom wrong in his diagnosis, as I have ascertained from subsequent knowledge and experience. One must admit his predisposition to exaggerate when discussing other people's defects, of course. But, in the main, he was uncannily accurate. His friend, the late Sir Thomas Clouston, a psychiatrist of international repute, used to say that he envied him this faculty. It was supernatural.

* * * * * * *

If there were one thing more than another the arbitrary and contradictory Colonel MacGregor detested, it was a fuss—except, of course, when he himself was creating it. I shall never forget an afternoon when he fell asleep in his armchair while smoking. His cigarette had dropped from the holder, and had fallen in between him and the upholstery. I smelt something burning and, on rushing into his study, found him enveloped in smoke and flames, unperturbed, and even a little resentful of my efforts to rescue him and quell the blaze. He was in no hurry to vacate his burning seat. He would do so in his own good time, and in his own good way. "Why all this fuss?" he enquired, while conflagration raged on every side of him. "What's all this disturbance? It reminds me of your mother? Good God! I've survived typhoons in the China Sea, sandstorms in the Gobi, shipwreck in the Pacific, snow-blindness in the Himalayas! Why, at the age of eighty, should I be expected to show alarm at a trifle like this?"

He was not the least concerned about the armchair. Nor did he seem to realise that, but for my timely entry, the entire house might have been ablaze. His sole contribution to the situation was a lamentation that the cigarette had eaten an ugly hole in his favourite knickerbockers!

No one will have difficulty in believing that such a man was fond of dramatising himself. When lacking pretext for so doing, the subject of his marriage, or of his health, could always provide the necessary incentive. Each winter he contracted (intentionally, the family declared!) a cough. Of this he used to make the very most, particularly when desirous of indulging in a bout of self-pity, or when he thought we were treating with indifference his age, his incipient infirmities, and all he had endured since the accursed day he had fallen for Mabel. The cough always led up to Mabel; and Mabel always led up to the cough. As topics for dejection, they were inseparable and unfailing. He thoroughly enjoyed the belief that this annual cough was in the nature of a penalty arising from his having stumbled into wedlock with such a woman. It was, in reality, nothing more than a touch of irritation, deliberately magnified. He smoked a pipe for twenty minutes each afternoon and evening, so punctually that you could tell the time if you heard him striking a match in his study, or knocking the dottle out on the topmost bar of the fire-grate at the conclusion of this mild and modest recreation. Two ounces of tobacco every ten days—and it had to be Player's Gold Leaf Navy Cut, and none other—was all he allowed his abstemious self. This was part of the code of restrictions he placed upon himself, so that there might be available a little additional money for his children's education. Anyhow, all through the winter he used to sigh, and, after a little exaggerated coughing, murmur in rueful accents: "Ah! Nothing has gone right with me since the day I met that ——, your mother! This winter will see the end of me!! I shall certainly be in my grave before the spring!!!" In these terms, and as a preliminary to a spate of imprecations as original as they are unprintable, he continued to warn his children of his premature departure, winter after winter, for about twenty years. It was to him, in verity, the *memento mori*, the audible emblem of mortality and human frailty. No skull, no death's head—nay, not even Bardolph's face—could have been so grim a reminder of life's brevity and uncertainty.

Who, not bereft of his senses, would be so imprudent as to question the pronouncements or challenge the authority of such a tyrant? Yet, for all his sting of tongue, when roused, and his wrath of countenance, he remained respected, as well as feared, by those who knew him but superficially, and even beloved by those who knew him well. He did not dream of restraining his combative impulses, for it never occurred to him that he *had* any. Most people with whom he had any contact, however, were ready to concede his finer qualities, making allowance for his impatience, intolerance, and concomitant excesses. At one time or another, they had probably seen him at his best, so overflowing with blandishment, gentle and considerate, so airy of step, when abroad on a day of mental sunshine and tranquillity, that scarce an egg would have broken under his feet.

It was tragic that innumerable quixotries should have diverted from more definite achievement a man so potentially endowed. There were always too many windmills to be tilted at.

The kindest explanation for his unpredictable behaviour, if not also the most reasonable, was his wife's, namely, that he was assailed all too often by brain-storms attributable to his having got a touch of sun during his protracted sojourn in the East. Be that as it may, this man, so obstinate in his prejudices and fanatical in his preferences, so full of faults and ludicrous vanities, so steeped in that intolerance born of megalomania, was certainly cast in the heroic mould. If you be familiar with Tacitus's writings, you may well imagine he was the sort of warrior Galgacus exhorted before engaging the Romans at Mons Graupius. "Let us demonstrate the kind of men Caledonia has set apart for herself!" he urged.[1]

But what a man!

---

[1] "*Ostendamus quos sibi Caledonia viros seposuerit.*"

CHAPTER II

MACGREGORIAN ETIQUETTE

THE STORY is told of an Eton boy who aimed a snowball at the headmaster, and hit him, whereupon the head summoned the boy to his room. "I should be sorry to have anyone think," he said, "that the headmaster of Eton was afraid to have a snowball thrown at him; but, as you hit me, I shall say no more about it. Had you missed me, however, you would have been severely dealt with for what was, in fact, an act of gross impertinence."

No one able to appreciate the subtlety of the headmaster's words should have any difficulty in appreciating the etiquette prevailing in the Colonel's extraordinary household. The code of conduct laid down for the government of his family comprised the oddest assortment of principles and inhibitions, excesses and contradictions, all of which, to a greater or lesser degree, had some bearing upon life's verities. Like the Laws of the Medes and Persians, to which Aunt Dorothy discreetly alluded from time to time when anticipating any recalcitrancy on the part of Iain or myself, this code stood immutable. It was never revised, never admittedly modified, so long as we were in the process of growing up. One or two of its minor measures quietly slipped into desuetude, however, as I passed from boyhood to youth. But these were never overtly repealed, lest occasion arose when their provisions might have to be invoked. On the whole, then, this code remained on the family statute-book, unaltered, from the moment I, the eldest of the Colonel's brood, emerged to inhale the atmosphere of this mad-hatter planet, until thirty-four years later, when I buried the ashes of its author at Balquhidder, beside the grave of Rob Roy.

If there were one commendable respect in which the Colonel differed from the subject of Raeburn's celebrated portrait, 'The MacNab', it was in the matter of alcohol. At his elbow there stood no nine-gallon tankard—no traditional 'bachelor'—such as that from which the crapulous Chiefs of the Clan MacNab quaffed with notoriety. The Colonel preferred at his elbow a few good books, a dictionary or two, and a selection from his own

Gaelic writings, to which he could refer as he felt inclined, so that, had Raeburn painted him, he certainly would not have done so as a bacchanalian sufficiently notable to ensure the portrait's transference (not altogether inappropriately) from Taymouth Castle to the offices of Messrs. John Dewar & Sons, in the Haymarket of London. Sobriety, therefore, only where the consumption of wines and spirits was concerned, was a marked feature of our home. Nothing intoxicating ever crossed its threshold, though one must concede that at times the Colonel's behaviour gave our douce neighbours reason to suspect otherwise. Not even in the festive season did we imbibe anything more potent than ginger-wine. Yet, we were happy to think there may have been a grain of truth in father's declaration that our wily grandmother (his mother-in-law, who now came to spend a few of her sinister years with us) had a bottle of something stronger hidden in her bedroom, to the privacy of which she resorted in her flagging moments. How, otherwise, the Colonel wondered, could one account for her schemings, her spells of unmitigated wickedness! As for himself, he did not require inward aid to facilitate his terrific transports. He could stage a thundering rage at a moment's notice, without artificial stimulant. And, in any event, though he must have consumed a fair amount of alcohol in his eastern days, he was now a teetotaller, partly as an example to his children, and partly for the reason that, had he not been, he could ill have afforded to educate them in a manner befitting the offspring of so remarkable a parent. Had there been added to his intemperance of temperament that derangement associated with the generous in-taking of drink, one dared not contemplate the ordeals to which the household might have been subjected.

By way of maintaining our opposition to everything savouring of the bottle, a catalogue of tragedy was recited to us periodically: the evils of strong drink comprised one of the most frequent topics for his family prelections. But, of all the grave reasons with which he supplied us, none appealed to me so forcibly as his reiterating that alcohol impaired the critical faculties. Backward though I was, these were just the faculties I was most eager to retain, and to demonstrate as opportunity offered. Even when in popular disgrace at the bottom of the class, I managed to function mildly as a critic, thus earning for myself many a resounding clout!

* * * * * * *

On the forming of good habits while we were still young, the Colonel expatiated *ad nauseam*. "Bad habits," he used to repeat, "are more readily acquired than discarded. In the words of Thomas à Kempis, 'He that doth not shun small defects, by little and little falleth into greater'."

Winking, for instance, was a habit he strongly deprecated. It was low and vulgar, and ill befitted children upon whom he had bestowed not inconsiderable opportunities. And so much did we conform to his wish in this regard that none of us ever cultivated the art, with the result that, when the 'glad eye' came into vogue, we found ourselves at a disadvantage in being unable to reciprocate in anything but the crudest manner. We were not aware in those days that winking had been permissible among some of our noble families—among the Balfours, at Whittinghame, for example. A. J. Balfour and his sister, Nora Sidgwick (a distinguished pioneer in women's education, and Principal of Newnham) habitually communicated with one another by this means. But I doubt whether the excuse that such conduct was usual at Whittinghame would have justified imitation by a member of the Clan Gregor! Who, after all, were the Balfours, the Cecils, the Salisburys, the Argyll Campbells, or any of the lineage frequenting the hearth at Whittinghame, in comparison with *us*, descendants of Scotia's ancient and warlike kings?

There was one habit, however, father was anxious every member of his family should form; and that was the habit of reading, marking, learning, and inwardly digesting anything regarded as wholesome literature. Iain had acquired this admirable disposition before he was five, which, to some extent, must have explained his early promise and brilliance. The habit did not attach itself to *me*, however, until I was more than *twenty*-five, wherefore I remained largely unlettered until I was about thirty.

"A love of literature will sustain you when everything else has failed. Where, in the name of God, would I be now, were it not for my literary interests?" This was one of the more familiar of the Colonel's interrogatories in his latter years. "In a lunatic asylum," he would respond, without as much as pausing to draw breath—"especially after your mother had ruined my life and dragged 'the Old Name' in the mire. Cultivate the habit of reading, my boy. You will never regret it."

When walking up and down the study of an afternoon, puffing quietly at his pipe, and incidentally wearing bare a large arc of carpet with his constant tread, so that it had to be reörientated with each spring-cleaning, he was peculiarly prone to deliver himself of such sound advice, and to give freely of his knowledge and philosophy. All his retired life (which, by the way, exceeded thirty years) and between the hours of two and four p.m., he had been a habitual peripatetic, as innumerable carpets testified. It was between these hours that one found him most amenable to reason, most accessible to anyone seeking mental stimulation, or guidance on one of the several themes upon which he pronounced with authority. When in this benevolent vein, he might have been Aristotle, pacing the Lyceum at Athens.

He was anxious, too, that what his children read should be good in form, as well as wholesome in content. From our long and dutiful reading of the Bible under his supervision, we already knew something about literary form. To him, proper appreciation of the virtue of form in literature was essential, since form, as Max Beerbohm remarked, is the goblet for the wine. "Be the wine never so good," he observed, "is not our enjoyment of it diminished if the hospitable vintner pour it forth to be lapped up by us from the ground with our tongues?"

As with the *written* word, so also with the *spoken*. The Colonel was just as insistent upon maintaining among us a high standard of speech. He trained us meticulously in everything relating to orthophony. A word misused, mispronounced, or misplaced instantly precipitated correction, if not also a sentence or two of rebuke for having forgotten what he may already have told one. Slang was anathema. So, too, was anything the least coarse or prurient. Nothing savouring of sculduddery—nothing smutty— was tolerated. The phrases father employed so persistently and authoritatively, when defaming poor Mabel, might look none too pretty, were I to reproduce them here. Yet, it never occurred to us that there was even a tinge of indecency about them. They certainly were offensive in the extreme; but the Colonel had the knack of being superlatively offensive without seeming the least obscene. It may have been the pureness of heart with which he appeared to use certain naughty words that, in our youthful minds, elevated them beyond all possible suspicion. Smut, to be appreciated, I am credibly informed, has to be conveyed by indirect methods—by subtle suggestiveness, by painstaking devotion to the *double entendre*. The Colonel was far too impatient, far too direct, to be bothered with such artifices. What he had to

16

The Colonel at sixty-seven

The eastern half of Princes Street (from Frederick Street, in the left-hand corner) as seen from the Castle

say, he said in forthright manner. I never once heard him give tongue to anything the least risky, all the years he and I had to put up with one another; and I well recall his castigation when any contemporary of his was foolhardy enough to embark on a naughty story in his presence. The story, I can vouch, was never concluded. Indeed, it seldom got beyond the first breathing-place. The Colonel's angry eye, together with the exaggerated clearing of his throat in preparation for vocal action in the event of the teller's persisting, saw to that! Perhaps you will regard me as an unmitigated prig when I confess that this is one of the few respects in which father and I were similar. My limitation in this connection (for by many, nowadays, it would be regarded as a shortcoming, if not actually as a serious handicap) certainly explains how I know only one little story that might be deemed the least improper; and I usually remember this titbit so imperfectly that, on the few occasions I have felt qualified to relate it, I have to rehearse it privately beforehand, to make sure I have not forgotten it. Even then, I make such a hash of it that no one sees the point.

*   *   *   *   *   *   *

Money matters were taboo in discussion. Neither a lack nor a superfluity of this fictitious and elusive commodity interested us much as a family. Financial dealings with friends were strongly deprecated. If they took place at all, there must be no more than a superficial reckoning, since nothing created bad feeling more readily. In the event of any such transaction, we had to assume something of the attitude adopted by our clan's hereditary adversary, the Earl of Breadalbane, who, when asked to render an account of the money voted to pacify the Highlands, declared that "the money is spent, the Highlands are quiet; *and this is the only way of accounting among friends*". To discuss incomes, whether our own or those of others, was bad taste. A man's worldly possessions were not allowed to influence us in our estimate of his worth. Only the truly vulgar, we had been taught, were impressed by that sort of thing. We had known some very rich people, and some very poor. It made not a whit of difference to us children into which category they fell. We made friends as readily with the one as with the other. In this regard, father's example was thoroughly democratic. In accordance with one of the outstanding traditions of the Scots, we were instructed in the

c   17

virtue of thrift, that national trait so many southerners mistake for meanness. The Scots have many faults, we must concede; but meanness is not one of them. As a nation, they are boundless in their generosity. If the Colonel suspected any of us of a hint of stinginess, or of what Tennyson calls "the narrowing lust of gold", he was swift to reproach. We had been made to realise that money was an obsession occupying far too great a proportion of our dis-proportioned lives in this worldly world.

Notwithstanding this, we were discouraged from becoming too familiar with the trades-people, and their progeny, who might want to play with us. Whether this was on account of our being the offspring of so worthy a father, or because of our descent, through Rob Roy, from King Kenneth MacAlpin, we never knew. Both reasons may have been operating simultaneously. That vast army of mankind, spending its time in wiles and guiles to get you to buy its multifarious wares, was much beneath us, socially; and the idea that the Colonel's bairns, through their lack of application to the excellent schooling provided for them, and with so much self-denial on his part, might finish up in this station of life, was reprehensible to him. Britain was already sufficiently a nation of shopkeepers without *our* threatening to swell those overcrowded ranks. Of course, it never occurs to those parents, who have such vain and vague ambitions for their children, that trade, in one guise or another, is the enterprise engaging the masses, upon which every class lives. The Services, the professions, all exist in the modern state by reason of the very trade and commerce gentlemen's sons were expected to eschew, and in point of fact did, until a few years ago, when altered economic circumstances made it necessary for them to modify their traditional class pre-judice as a means of gaining a livelihood. However, we must not overlook the social gulf between wholesale trade and retail. The latter—well, socially speaking, it was in the hands of much the inferior species of humanity in the Auld Reekie of my youth. The gradations of mankind were so numerous within a stone's-throw of us, that only a magician knew where to draw the line between this person and that!

The topic of money recalls, incidentally, the Edinburgh custom of broadcasting coin after weddings. I do not know whether it exists elsewhere in Scotland, or whether it is peculiar to the Scot-tish Capital and her more immediate environs; but, anyhow, it was one which many an Edinburgh youth has had reason to appreciate. Even Iain and I, for all the sternness of our upbringing and the emphasis laid on etiquette, were sometimes tempted to avail ourselves of any little revenue that might accrue in this way. Father deemed it most improper, however, that sons of his, in company with other children of the neighbourhood, should be seen hanging about a tenement entry or garden-gate, waiting for the emergence of a newly married couple, in the feverish expectation that, as bride and bridegroom drove away on their honeymoon, either the bridegroom, or the best-man acting on his behalf, might observe the custom of distributing largesse among the urchins thus assembled. This was done by flinging out on the street, at the moment of the couple's departure, a handful or two of coppers. "Pour oot! Pour oot!" was the recognised exhortation on such occasions. If the best-man had not flung out a sufficient sum, the more persistent might follow the old growler bearing the couple to the station, until the exasperated bridegroom appeased them by pitching out of the window all the small change he had. No marriage in Auld Reekie was considered 'classy' where someone or other did not observe this gratuitous disbursement; and failure to comply with it stimulated a wide range of abusive choruses as the couple drove away and the wedding-guests dispersed. And, since our father had done his best to bring us up nicely, often warning us of the evil influences that might attend the consorting with guttersnipes, our returning home with a penny or two from an after-marriage scramble was looked upon with such disfavour that we felt reticent about disclosing the source of any small wealth thus obtained.

* * * * * * *

In a home so ridden with discipline, punctuality was insisted upon. As I have told you elsewhere, Iain and I had to be out of bed o' mornings the instant the Colonel called, just as we had to be within reach when, of an evening, he summoned us to prayers. The Admirable Iain, when he had a little private reading to do, or when philately, his particular specialty at this time, required some extra attention, was often abroad before daybreak. And very conceited he was about his early-rising, a predisposition that has never come *my* way. Although the prospect of attending school five days a week hung about me as a nightmare, often rousing me prematurely to realisation of the mental and corporal consequences of lessons unlearnt, the urge to *rise* seldom assailed me.

19

In later years I have always concurred most heartily with the Chinese sage who attributed all the cardinal virtues to the man disposed to remain in bed when most of mankind insists on being up—the man who is prone to lie as long as he likes, and think. Bed is a splendid place to lie and think in. I do all my serious thinking in bed, which explains in some measure how I often do not rise until ten!! The early bird, we are assured from infancy, catches the early worm. The timely worm is not to be had by the sluggard. The best pickings of life, as I was being constantly reminded, would all be gone ere I managed to rub the sloth from my eyelids. And what of it? Who, in his wits, wants to spend his life in catching and amassing worms, even figurative ones? I have always been wary of those who make a Christian necessity of being up and doing. Up and doing what? Up and doing whom? Up and making money, and plotting mischief, while their neighbours are still in the bosom of Morpheus! A good deal of wealth, and much of the world's mischief, are made by those who are pleased and proud to be up and doing.

In boyhood and youth I was exhorted to remember the luminaries cited by so exemplary a father—Akbar, Beethoven, Darwin, Edison, Dr Johnson, Napoleon, Spenser, Wellington—who were satisfied with but four hours' sleep. When rousing me to the effort of living consciously, he often found occasion to remind me of these, and to repeat the dicta of Nelson and of Napoleon, the more to impress upon me the achievements of the wakeful. As if the example of men who spent their lives in giving battle of one kind or another meant very much to me! Nelson attributed his successes to the habit of being a quarter of an hour before the time appointed. Napoleon claimed that four hours' sleep was enough for any man, and that he never permitted himself any more. It is said that he could go days without any sleep at all, but that thereafter he slumbered deeply for twenty-four hours. But see into what disaster it led him! It carried him to Moscow and back, then to Elba, and eventually to St Helena! Surely, we are entitled to suggest that, had he been a little more slothful, there is no estimating the suffering and anxiety mankind might have been spared, and the dates wretched school-children would never have had to memorise! I once had the foolhardiness to make this observation, while the Colonel was in the throes of a discourse on indolence, and with a consequence you may well imagine. For reasons over which I would appear to have no control, I have never been able to join the early-morning throng of busybodies. Some guardian-angel, some elusive benefactress (may it not have been Persephone herself?) has endowed me with the priceless gift of sleep. I can sleep anytime, anywhere, at a few seconds' notice, so that no one can possibly appreciate more than I do the sentiment of Swinburne's lines—

> Thou art more than the day or the morrow,
> The seasons that laugh or weep,
> For these give joy or sorrow,
> But thou, Proserpina, sleep!

To his strict observance of punctuality, the Colonel made one exception; and even this exception, he might have argued, was but a design on his part to be in time. Once or twice a year, he accepted an invitation to lecture to some society on Indo-China, perhaps, or on his exploits among the Dyaks. A minute or two before he was due to put in an appearance in some hall a mile or more away, one might enter his study to find him seated there in beaming serenity. If we children, knowing the hour at which his lecture was due to begin, urged him to realise the time, he affected no concern. We always regarded this as queer conduct for one so punctual, and one so notoriously insistent that every creature under his sway should be punctual too. One evening, however, he rewarded my curiosity about his exceptional behaviour.

"Father, you'll be awfully late for your lecture!" I pointed out, on rushing solicitously into the study. "You are due there now; and the audience must be wondering what has happened to you!"

"Come in, my boy, and close the door!" he responded in confiding tones. "When you come to my time of life, you will realise that, if you turn up to address a meeting ten minutes *before* you are due to begin, no one will pay the least attention to you. If, on the other hand, you arrive ten minutes *late*, having deliberately kept them on tenterhooks in the meantime, they regard you with a greater measure of deference, if not actually with veneration. Always make a private arrangement with yourself to be a little late, if you wish to give the impression of your being more important than you really are."

Sound advice, as I can testify from personal experience. As Socialist candidate for the Hartlepools at a general election a decade or so ago, my agent had accepted, on my behalf, an invitation to address a mass outdoor meeting in support of the candidate in the adjacent constituency of Seaham, in his campaign against my quondam friend, Ramsay MacDonald. The car sent to convey me from a meeting of my own electors to the heart of the Seaham coalfields broke down on its way to pick me up. The meeting was due to begin at 3 p.m. I did not reach the scene until nearer four. But my lateness—not intentional, as in the Colonel's case whenever he had to address the learnéd of Auld Reekie—assured for me the most terrific ovation from an audience of over twenty thousand miners and their families. Ah! There's an element of psychology in just the right amount of lateness, as father once explained!

*   *   *   *   *   *   *

To matters of health and hygiene the Colonel paid the greatest attention; and he viewed with gravity and scorn any infringement of the family health acts he had drawn up and passed, wholeheartedly, on our behalf. He was very strict, for example, in the matter of our night-attire and bed-clothes. Periodically, he lectured us on the hygienic reasons for never sleeping in garments worn during the day. From time to time, moreover, and without warning, he subjected us to a medical inspection. He required of us a standard of hardiness appropriate to the descendants of so sturdy and wiry a father, as also of so brave and warlike a race as the Clan Gregor. Like the Highland chiefs of old, he would have so inured Iain and me to hardship, had circumstances warranted or allowed it, as to have enabled us to drive a nail with our fists through a twelve-inch board. That was the sort of prowess for which he would have trained us, had we lived in Rob Roy's time. In point of fact, there were ways not very different, in which he did train us in fortitude and endurance. What of his wild encouragement when we were learning to swim? What of those interminable tramps on which he insisted we should accompany him? Each successive excursion he deliberately lengthened by half a mile or thereby, with the result that, by the time Iain and I were ten, we had become quite accustomed to an itinerary of a dozen miles and more. Father shared with Dickens the view that, in order to lengthen life, one should walk steadily, and with set purpose. "The wandering man knows of certain ancients, far gone in years, who have staved off infirmities and dissolution by earnest walking—hale fellows close of eighty and ninety, but brisk as boys."

At eighty, the Colonel was one such. He still retained the sound-ness of limb and endurance of foot that had carried him across deserts, and through jungle country where, for all our strides in travel, man has scarcely yet penetrated.

Conduct the least suggestive of scrimshanking was soon discoun-tenanced. *"No scrimshanking!"* was one of his more ominous moni-tions when he suspected son or daughter of complaining unduly of indisposition, in the hope of being granted even the briefest respite from school. This comical word, growled by a Spartan father, instantly bestirred us from our bed of feigned or imagined sickness. Indeed, at times it even urged us to attend school in a condition that certainly would have qualified our classmates for a few days' absence. But what could we MacGregor bairns do, with a medical officer constantly on the premises? We were denied even that breathing-space children are given while their parents wonder whether they should send for the doctor, and perhaps eventually do so, by which time at least *one* school-day has slipped by. No such loophole for us! If the complainant had not enlisted father's sympathy by 8.30 a.m., there was no alternative but to prepare for school, and depart undemonstratively, with the best grace one could muster in the circumstances. Behind any attempt we ever made at scrimshanking was the fear that father, with his uncanny —his almost diabolical—intuition, would detect the insincerity of our plea, and bundle us off after a stern chastisement.

To his regular habits he ascribed his health and longevity. This largely explained why he was so determined to regularise the lives of his children. Four score years were upon him before he lost a tooth; and I well remember the despondency that overtook him, and rested heavily on him for several days, when he discovered that one was getting a little loose. "Ah! I'm rapidly going down-hill," he would moan. "My very teeth are beginning to give way. This is what comes of marrying that —— who has ruined my life." Hitherto, his teeth had been a source of pride to him, especially when comparing them with those of people fifty years younger— dentures in most cases, he was appalled to discover. "What fine stuff I must have been made of! Every tooth in my head! Never known a day's illness! What a puny, sickly race we are breeding! Do you now realise the importance of forming regular habits, and of being nurtured on 'halesome fairin' ' like herring and potatoes and oatmeal?"

In our Auld Reekie days, bed-time always seemed the proper

hour for pranks, greatly to our guardian's annoyance. As a family, we were inordinately wakeful when reasonable folks wished to retire. Conversely, we were at our worst when the world of routine was waking to a new day. As you will have gathered, nothing but sheer necessity, short of a time-bomb, can arouse *me* from my beauty sleep.

One night at bed-time, following upon father's recapitulating the importance of personal cleanliness, Iain and I arranged a little scheme for deceiving him into believing that, in contravention of his ruling, I had gone to bed without removing my under-apparel. We placed the pillows in such a way as to give the impression that the bed was occupied by someone who had covered his head with the bed-clothes. While I hid under an adjacent washstand, the sycophantic Iain crept into the study, this time in *pretended* stealth, to inform father that I had retired with some of my daytime garments under my pyjamas. His suppressed fumings and fulminations could now be heard, as he sought his walking-stick. Without a moment's delay, he came stalking into the bedroom, followed by Iain, and grasping his stick as a man in danger might hold a lethal weapon when setting uncertain foot on territory fraught with perils unseen. He roared at me; but the thing in the bed neither moved nor answered. Now quite unable to restrain his wrath, he began forthwith to lash at it. Since the pillows gave no response, and he regarded my silence as defiance, his blows increased in ferocity. He did not desist until he noticed a large dip in the bed, as though he had broken his victim in two. On pulling back the bed-clothes to see how I looked after this onslaught, he was infuriated to find that he had expended his anger and energy on inanimate pillows!

"Where are you, you devils?" he yelled in tones that brought forth Jessie, our peacemaking sister, in her nightie, resolved to intercede for us if a thrashing seemed imminent.

With some trepidation, I crept from under the washstand. We all joined in hearty laughter as father withdrew from the scene, and Iain and I proceeded to re-make the bed.

"I suppose I was once young myself," we heard him mutter in a hoarse whisper, as he returned to the study to replace his walking-stick, which hung by its crook at the end of the mantelpiece, ready to hand when needed for corporal purposes.

You see, therefore, that humorous situations did arise in our home from time to time. But humour had to be taken in homeo-

24

pathic doses, and at infrequent intervals, since the Colonel discouraged it in more potent draughts. Like Adam Smith, he rather regarded it as "something which comes upon a man by fits, which he can neither command nor restrain, *and which is not perfectly consistent with true politeness*". A little humour went a very long way with him.

*   *   *   *   *   *   *

If there were one thing more than another in which the Colonel's regulations demanded a standard of high principle, it was that of abiding by one's word, however irksome the circumstances. He made us swear, as you already know, by the Grey Stane at Inch Cailleach, that symbol of Clan Gregor integrity.[1] Not that he himself always appeared to observe the golden rule this ancient slab denoted. In his transactions with the unfortunate Mabel, he seemed incapable, latterly, of realising when he had given her his word. Where she was concerned, his mind vacillated as often as did his mood, so that she found him unreliable. On the other hand, when dealing with his children, there was never anything but certainty in our minds that he meant what he said, and said what he meant. When *aware* that he had made a promise, nothing in heaven or on earth, nor any monster of the deep, would prevent him from implementing it.

Throughout childhood and youth, three classical instances of constancy, even unto death, were continually being brought to our notice, lest we should fall into laxity where our word was involved. "A MacGregor's word is his bond" was the household maxim in this context. It had been given very special prominence through his repeatedly calling to recollection the case of Alasdair MacGregor of Glen Strae, details of which I need not recapitulate here. "Alasdair, you must never forget how your namesake spared the life of his son's murderer, simply because, in granting him asylum, he had pledged his honour, the honour of an honourable clan."

The two other examples held up to us were of Biblical origin. We always felt sorry for the poor, little, ensnared ram, sacrificed by Abraham; and there were tears in father's voice as he came to

---

[1] "*I swear to ye, upon the halidome o' him that sleeps beneath the Grey Stane at Inch Cailleach!*" So swore Rob Roy when asked by the Bailie Nicol Jarvie whether, in the event of the Bailie's really making the proposed journey to the Highlands, he would soothfastly pay him back the siller he owed him (*Rob Roy, Ch. xxiii*).

those verses where Jephthah, returning unto his house at Mizpeh
after he had vanquished the children of Ammon, was met by his
daughter. So deep an impression had Jephthah's rash vow made
upon us, that we could repeat the pertinent passage by heart.
"And it came to pass, when he saw her, that he rent his clothes,
and said, 'Alas, my daughter! thou hast brought me very low,
and thou art one of them that trouble me: for I have opened my
mouth unto the Lord, and I cannot go back.' "

*   *   *   *   *   *   *

In drawing this cumbersome chapter to a close, I feel constrained
to tell you of the most heartless and thoughtless disciplinary action
the Colonel ever employed against me.

During the Battle of Menin Road—the Third Battle of Ypres,
as it is sometimes called—a young officer, whose battalion was
going into the line to occupy the position from which, owing to
the severity of our casualties, we were in process of being relieved,
crouched beside me near the shattered Cloth Hall, emptying his
pockets of things he felt he might never require again. The Germans were shelling Ypres heavily at the time, so that all relief and
transport were held up. Among the odds and ends he proceeded
to discard was a Green Envelope. "Here, Jock!" he said. "This
may be of use to you, now that you're coming out of the line, and
we're going in." I readily accepted the Green Envelope. When
the strafing had abated, we passed on our respective ways. He was
making for Hell Fire Corner: I was rejoining my company (or,
rather, such as remained of it) in temporary billets among the
dark, wire-netted cubicles inside the ramparts of Ypres, but a
dozen deadly yards from the Menin Gate. Seated on an empty
petrol-tin, with another such on my lap as a writing-desk, I began
to scribble a few lines to my father—in pencil, of course, and by
candle-light—just to let him know that, although I had not been
able to communicate with anyone for some time, I happened to
be alive, and was reasonably well. These lines I enclosed in the
Green Envelope, which permitted of one's saying a little more
than did the regulation field-postcard, on which the sender scored
out the printed sentences that, at the moment of writing, were in-
applicable. In weary handwriting, and in circumstances as difficult as they were perilous, I intimated that I was safe so far, and
that, on reaching rest-camp in the course of a day or two, I hoped
to write more legibly, and at greater length. In hurrying through

Poperinghe late that night, I posted the Green Envelope in the approved fashion.

A couple of weeks later, by which time we had moved to the Arras–Cambrai sector, I received from Colonel MacGregor a letter returning my Green Envelope, inside which was the untidy note I had scrawled by spluttering candle-light in the ramparts at Ypres. Across the face of it he had written "*This sort of letter not wanted here.*" He declined to be the recipient of such a scrawl!

I cannot describe to you the effect this manifestation of thought-lessness had upon a lad still in his teens, away in the trenches. It demonstrated clearly that even experienced campaigners in earlier wars had no conception of the conditions under which infantry regiments were operating in Flanders, in their four years' struggle to retain some semblance of a position on this holocaust of a Salient.

I never wrote my father again from the front.

Some months later, he came to visit me at a military hospital, where I lay with rheumatic fever, contracted through exposure. His first utterance, as our eyes met, was one of abject apology for his having impulsively returned my scribble from the battle-front. I was too ill to do more than indicate with a nod my accept-ance of his apology. Neither of us ever alluded to the incident again. Fortunately for me, I did not recover in time to return to the trenches for the German break-through in the spring of 1918.

CHAPTER III

AVIZANDUM

YOU MUST be wondering what, in the meantime, has become of Mabel. Truth to tell, she was now in London, four hundred miles away, gainfully engaged there in journalistic work. Some months prior to the family's departure for Auld Reekie under the Colonel's wing, she had proceeded against him in the sheriff court at Inverness, on alleged grounds of cruelty. She sought a legal separation, together with the custody of the children and commensurate alimony. The hearing, which lasted several days, created a sensation, especially in the Scottish Highlands, where father was so wellknown, and Mabel's charm and beauty had become proverbial. It should be remembered, furthermore, that this was at a time when most people would thole anything, rather than bring domestic dissension before the courts. Not so with Mabel, however. She felt she already had suffered too much at her husband's hands to boggle at recourse to any judicial channel through which she might be able to deal with so fanatical and unbalanced a man. And so to court went she.

With the details of this futile litigation I need not weary you. Suffice it to say that it merely exacerbated mutual hatred and mistrust, and eliminated, forever, all possibility of reconciliation. Resort to the law has an unerring trend in that direction, for the lawyers help you to say of one another things you ordinarily would remain silent about, and quite frequently things that would never enter your head.

It is hardly for me to say whether I think Mabel was justified in this move, or whether she had been ill advised, for I was but a laddie of ten when this ruinous public wrangle was instituted. Yet, I will go so far as to concede that she may have had more than a modicum of provocation. Her explanation for so serious a step I readily accept. Apparently, she and the Colonel had come to some agreement regarding the future of the children during her absence from the family fold, an agreement he now refused to implement. That he was conscious of his having gone back on any undertaking he had given, I would not care to say. "Should she want to see her children, let her return to them!" was the inexorable attitude he adopted forthwith. This Mabel declined to do, and not entirely without reason, since she regarded her husband as being in a temporary state of insanity, and her personal safety consequently in jeopardy, if she were to resume her place under his roof as wife and mother.

And, verily, in some danger of her life she was, for by now the Colonel had taken to loitering about the streets of Inverness, after dark, with intent as felonious—nay, as murderous—as any one could imagine. He was abroad with his army revolver, well and truly loaded, hoping to encounter her, or anyone whom he believed to be aiding and abetting her. Since the day he retired, this emblem of death had slumbered in an old trunk with the rest of his accoutrements. It was now ceremoniously resurrected; and I believe that, even yet, I could find my way without hesitation to the gunmaker's in one of the main thoroughfares of Inverness, whither I accompanied him, and where, with Mabel in mind, he purchased that small stock of ammunition which lay at the bottom of his despatch-box until after his death, and that I duly handed over to the Chelsea police when, with yet another outbreak of war, the authorities were anxious that private persons should not retain anything so potentially manslaughterous.

While still in this frame of mind, he, fortunately, took a step which certainly removed the likelihood of anything quite so tragic. One morning immediately after breakfast, he paid a visit to the burgh police station and asked to see the chief constable. In his anxiety that everything he did should be open and above board, he produced the revolver with which, as he now confessed, he hoped to lay low a certain person, who had not only blighted his life, but had dragged the proud and honourable name of MacGregor in the mire. Nothing but a well-directed bullet or two, in his view, could atone for offences so grave. (He was a grand shot, I may add—a marksman in his time.) His frankness saved the situation. The chief constable, a Gaelic-speaking Highlander like himself, pacified him, explaining that the effect upon his young children of the action he contemplated would be too frightful. Thereupon father acquiesced, agreeing to leave his revolver in the care of the police until such time as all danger of his resorting to a remedy so drastic was past.

In due course, "The MacGregor Case", as the newspapers termed it, went through its several days' hearing, with many irksome adjournments, and much acidulous evidence on both sides. Not since Prince Charles Edward's romantic and dramatic entry into Inverness, more than a century and a half earlier, had anything quite so colourful diverted the inhabitants of this quiet and comely Highland town. They crowded the public portions of the court-house, not sure whether their sympathies were with the young and dignified pursuer, or with the braw and bellicose defender. Their affections, their sense of chivalry, were sorely divided, as some of them have told me in more recent years. Should they allow their idea of Highland loyalty to a kilted, Gaelic-speaking Colonel in their midst, now fighting as much for the honour of 'the Old Name' as for anything, obscure the conviction that, at best, he must have been a somewhat trying fellow to live with? They were bewildered.

To everyone's disappointment, the sheriff deferred judgment at the conclusion of these unhappy proceedings. Hoping no doubt that, in the interim, the contending parties might find some sensible *modus vivendi*, particularly where the question of the children's custody was concerned, he took the case to avizandum, as Scots lawyers say.

"Avizandum!" the Colonel might be heard soliloquising in the study, during the next month or so, weary of the protracted suspense this legal procedure entailed. "Why the devil didn't the fool give judgment, and be done with it? He must know perfectly well what a —— she is, and that there can never be any compromise with her! AVIZANDUM, forsooth! AVIZANDUM! Ah! These lawyers!"

Yes! That unusual word again sent us children into a veritable stampede to consult (this time in secret, under the diningroom table) that unfailing family stand-by, *Chambers's Twentieth Century Dictionary*, the best dictionary in the world, as father used to say. Therein we read as follows:—"Avizandum: av-iz-an-dum, *n.* (*Scots law*) private consideration of a case by a judge before giving judgment."

This was but one of the innumerable legal words and phrases with which we became familiar at an early age, either through father's blusterings, or through his sorrowful monologues. There certainly could not have been much of the nomenclature associated with matrimonial causes we did not understand!

Mabel was more than a year in London, and her children a like period with the Colonel in Auld Reekie, before judgment was given. The sheriff found for the defender. Someone in the North wired the Colonel to this effect. In this wise, he retained the custody of his brood, and now set himself in terrible earnest to the task of educating us, and of bringing us up in the ways of valour and rectitude. All the law now required of him was that, in terms of this judicial separation, he should grant Mabel reasonable access to her unfortunate offspring. (The offspring, I might add, now had to go without this and that, until the lawyers' bills were paid.)

Some considerable time later, the postman delivered at the Colonel's door a small but heavy parcel bearing the Inverness postmark, and a superscription showing it to have been consigned by the police. This made us as curious about its content as we were afterwards disappointed, when, in our presence, father opened it, drew out the old revolver (with which Iain and I often played at Red Indians and cowboys thereafter) and proceeded to explain to us how he came to receive so odd a parcel. "I knew I wouldn't have been able to trust myself," he concluded. "If I hadn't had you children to consider, God knows what might have happened. The Unnameable One would have been dead, and I would have been hanged. . . . Ah! That a —— like her should have deserted her family, and besmirched the honourable name of MacGregor!"

By now the police authorities at Inverness thought all danger was past. It *was*, at all events so far as firearms were concerned. But the battle as to what constituted reasonable access had still to be fought.

CHAPTER IV

MABEL IN THE NORTH

"*RASHLEIGH* IN the North! Then the heather will soon be on fire!"

As a family, we were familiar with these ominous words through our knowledge of Scott's *Rob Roy*, and the faithful regularity with which we patronised a melodramatised version of it at the King's Theatre in Auld Reekie, when father's fanaticism for matters of race was at its peak. With the alteration of but a single word, these brief sentences were now to ring through the home, incessantly, for some days. It was a case of *Mabel* in the North! And the heather was well alight. She had arrived from London, not with any intention of resuming connubiality, but in order to comply with a statutory necessity, if she wished to retain at least the semblance of being a wife and a mother. We had not seen a sight of her for nearly three years. Her coming at this time was due entirely to something I, then a schoolboy of fourteen, had told her in one of my clandestine communications. Through my continually hearing the Colonel console himself with the assurance that he would soon be in a position to rid himself and his children of her, I wrote to her that, if she failed to visit us of her own volition within four years [1] of the date at which the legal separation became operative, she might find herself divorced without further ado, on grounds of desertion. My intervention was timely, since she had only a few weeks in hand. ("That just proves your love of mischiefmaking dates from quite early in your career!" was the heartless comment of a friend, to whom I related this incident recently.)

Of course, had father suspected my hand in this, he would have strangled me. I was quite grown-up, and he much mellowed by years, before I dared tell him of my complicity in it—my duplicity, I might term it, without libelling myself, for duplicity it certainly was. Even in the most trivial dealings with Mabel, he was convinced the Lord was on his side: conversely, anyone who, for an instant, questioned the rightness of his attitude toward her, or

[1] See footnote at page 36.

Scott Skinner, " The Strathspey King "

Alastair Sim (from the film, *Wedding Group*)

remained in touch with her after all that had happened, was in agency with the Devil.

Yet, the curious thing was that, though I conducted this secret correspondence with Mabel, she had already become, even to *me*, almost a mythical figure. Indeed, to all intents and purposes, she had travelled outwith her children's ken and concern. Only father's epigrammatical references and innuendos kept alive in us the notion that, sometime or other, we had had a mother, who was now living in England—in London, somewhere, we believed. To young persons in Scotland in those times, that meant a very large place, very far away. Mabel, in effect, was living in another country—living abroad, as it were. Even the letters she wrote me, her first-born, seemed but elusive exchanges, such as you might have received from a cousin several times removed, dwelling in the Antipodes—a distant relative about whom you had heard from your elders, but whom you were never likely to see. Those letters of hers were in the most beautiful handwriting you ever beheld. But they lacked reality. They were hardly the sort of thing an unloved son wanted from the mother he once adored. But by this time, possibly, all love was dead in Mabel. Love for children—*her* children—*anyone's* children. No! She had nothing of that in her make-up; and she has been frank with me in this admission. A sense of cold, calculated duty toward her children, however, she certainly did show in later years. But what child wants in its mother a sense of duty in place of a mother's love? (Yet, I wonder whether Mabel realises there exists in the world no one who understands better than I do just how repugnant to a woman of her temperament must be the formal bearing of infants! If so, she may well be conscious that there is still one fundamental bond of sympathy between us. In any case, enforced motherhood was not likely to improve matters where *her* marriage was concerned.)

Those letters I used to receive from her were so underlined and over-emphasised, so damnably business-like, that our correspondence petered out after about a year. Her partiality for underlining has continued with her all through life, and is one of the major amusements she still affords her children, even although they are now grown-up and, for the most part, married. None of us ever gets from Mabel a letter, the top lefthand corner of which (and possibly also the bottom lefthand corner) does not bear, in large writing, heavily underlined, one or more of the following notices :—

Immediate, Important, Urgent, Most Urgent—Please Forward, Private, Confidential, Personal. When you open the letter to find nine-tenths of it underlined, once, twice, and even thrice, you begin to wonder whether the remaining tenth does not comprise the really important passages! Knowing Mabel's flair for this kind of thing, we would not be the least surprised to learn that it was she who suggested the blackout warning seen in our railway compartments. "Before you alight, make certain the train is at the platform, and that you alight on the platform side." This looks uncommonly like her handiwork!

      *   *   *   *   *   *   *

Up to a point, my parents' legal separation—this divorce from bed and board, where Mabel was concerned, rather than deliverance from the shackles of matrimony—had worked as admirably as anything of the nature could, in such circumstances. At any rate, Mabel, already removed from her husband's control to the extent of some hundreds of miles, had now announced, through her solicitor, that she proposed coming North to see us. The mere thought of such a contingency evoked from the Colonel a muster of all the evil spirits that had beset mankind since the beginning of time. The very idea of such impertinence! In short, official notice of her intrusion occasioned a temporary aberration from sanity, such as had found expression, some years previously, in the burning of the tartan. This infamous woman, who, forsooth! now bethought herself of invading his new home, had entered long since on the way that leadeth to destruction. She was, irrevocably, on the highroad to hell, on the broadway to the deep, sunless abyss of Tartarus. Not until the Almighty had consigned her, forevermore, to that region, reputed to be as far below the ordinary Hades as the earth is beneath the heavens, would he feel safe from her intrusions. Why she insisted on travelling thither, *via Edinburgh*, he could not imagine. Yes! She was bound for hell all right—not any metaphorical or half-hearted expression of it, you must understand, but a real, good, blazing one, full of everlasting damnation and white-hot conflagration, super-charged with the suffocating fumes of brimstone. This creature (for by now she was as low as, if not lower than, the beasts of the field) whom he had once mistaken for a shepherding Amaryllis, innocent and tender, was nothing but a hell-born fiend, the reincarnation of the very serpent that, in like manner, had beguiled the unwary in the

Garden of Eden. How could he have endured life with a woman who, he declared, was as wily as that, who could assume as many complexions as the chameleon, and as many shapes as Proteus, that figure of antiquity so accomplished in aliases and disguises? Never was father more prone to revert to the primitive man in him than when invoking eternal punishment ("the most frightful idea that has ever corroded human nature," as Morley describes it) and heaping coals of vengeance on Mabel's hapless head.

Anyhow, invasion was imminent; and an invasion it truly was. No foreign army crossing the Border into Scotia ever precipitated greater upheaval in a northern home. Mabel's landing in Auld Reekie was accomplished with that strategy exhibited by Edward, Hammer of the Scots, when he marched to give us a good bashing. With Mabel, there was no hesitancy, no faltering, as in the case of Prince Charlie and his exiled adherents—no writing beforehand from a foreign country, in order to ascertain whether an invasion of the ancient kingdom was likely to achieve its purpose. She came direct to the kingdom's capital without an army, never doubting that her campaign would be highly successful. She was well armed, in that she had the law behind her. What Highland colonel in modern times, for all his courage and astuteness, could withstand *that* backing for long?

Some days before her arrival, and in the hope that British justice might still afford him a measure of relief, he consulted a clansman he had known for some years, through their mutual devotion to everything connected with the MacGregors. They were both members—nay, *directors*—of the Clan Gregor Society, the meetings of which they attended regularly and reverently. What the Colonel did for 'the Old Name' in his capacity as bard, the late John MacGregor, Writer to the Signet, 3, Coates Crescent, Edinburgh, did as treasurer, and as legal adviser in the administration of the bursary funds and endowments bequeathed to the Society.

Now, this was the question our Writer had to answer: 'Was there any method whereby Mabel could be denied access to her children?' At all costs, something must be done to delay, if not actually forestall, this intrusion, or at least render it as abortive as possible. "Evil communications corrupt good dispositions," he used to remind us, in Menander's words, when there appeared a likelihood of our seeing Mabel and of her seeing us. How could he guard against any such corrupting contingency?

Apart from the two John MacGregors, no one ever knew what

35

transpired at their interview. That they had had 'words', however, was certain. The obvious interpretation of the Colonel's attitude thereafter was that his clansman, having assured him he could not legally restrain Mabel from visiting us, acquiesced in her proposed arrival. This evinced a vein of treachery not to be tolerated in one carrying the tried and trusted name of Mac-Gregor! When, during the course of the next few days, the Colonel was informed that, in reply to a letter from Mabel's solicitor, his clansman had admitted her legal entitlement to access, and would make arrangements forthwith to see that it was granted, there remained but one word in the English language applicable to John MacGregor, W.S.—TRAITOR!! And the Colonel was unreasonable and impulsive enough to tell him so. That terminated their brief association as solicitor and client. Clan requirements, however, still necessitated their meeting occasionally, and for several years thereafter, at functions of the Clan Gregor Society. When they confronted one another at business meetings, and had, perforce, to sit in proximity, I believe they openly sneered at one another. As a matter of routine, each obstructed any proposal for the better government of the Society which the one had the temerity to make in the august presence of the other. This I was told a few years ago, and by another member of the directorate, who assured me that, thereafter, each conducted himself with the utmost independence. Whatever notion either of them expressed, he had to be prepared to defend it to the ultimate particle against his clansman's purely dialectical refutations.

So Mabel came, stayed some days, and departed, satisfied that her mission had fulfilled its purpose. She had rendered null and void all her husband's hopes of obtaining an easy divorce. Of her visit otherwise, I seem to remember little, except that she took an apartment just round the corner from us, and that a sense of resignation settled on everyone when she had gone.

[*Note:* From 1573 until recently, the period of absence for divorce by desertion was four years, although, by a judgment of the Court of Session, if the spouse returned, but did not submit to intercourse, the period of absence was not interrupted. The poor Colonel cannot have known this!]

CHAPTER V

JOHN MACGREGOR, W.S.

LET ME tell you more about John MacGregor, Writer to the Signet.

At the age of fourteen, he began to collect every press notice and every printed record of anyone of the name of MacGregor, and also anything even remotely connected with the name and clan, together with matter pertaining to members of other clans—to Robertsons, Stewarts, Campbells, Grants, MacFarlanes, MacLarens, Colquhouns, Menzieses, and the rest—with whom the MacGregors, in olden times, had had more immediate dealings. These he filed with remarkable diligence. He also picked up every pertinent document he could. At the Castle Menzies sale, held in Dowell's Rooms in the spring of 1914, he bought, literally, cartloads of old papers, because he imagined they might contain records of MacGregors in Glen Lyon and Strathtay. He had amassed quantities of old charters too. Even the most intricate of these he could read as easily as most of us read ordinary print.

Among his piles of documents were several concerning a filibuster of the clan, who went to Central America, where he made himself head of a tribe of Indians, described himself as "Prince Gregor", and accumulated something like a quarter of a million pounds. Our Writer, in his lifelong research, had actually picked up, in Vienna, one of the "Prince's" bonds with coupons attached, and also an oil-painting of him.

From his colossal collection he hoped, one day, to compile a monumental work on the Clan Gregor. But, as so often happens with the most fervent of collectors, he died without having accomplished this. Yet, during his earthly sojourn, he had given handsome publicity to 'the Old Name' through his innumerable contributions on the MacGregors and their affairs to the correspondence columns of any newspaper sympathetic enough to print them. In the John MacGregor Collection, to which we shall refer presently, he left his own monument, and one which any man might envy.

John MacGregor, be it known, had the loudest sneeze of anyone in Auld Reekie. The rafters of Parliament House often rang when someone, knowing his peculiarity, tempted him to a pinch of snuff. I have heard that on a memorable occasion he sneezed so violently, when in the Signet Library, that he all but brought the books tumbling from their shelves!

Despite his all-absorbing passion for things MacGregor and Highland, he found time to attend to his legal commitments. He was procurator-fiscal of the Lord Lyon Court; and he conducted a good, general practice before the Court of Session. He was a sound and cautious business man, with a large and influential clientêle. His specialised knowledge of Teind [1] Court law brought him work both remunerative and interesting.

*   *   *   *   *   *   *

By agreement between the Edinburgh MacGregors and the Glasgow MacGregors, the Grand Council of the Clan Gregor Society convened in Edinburgh and in Glasgow, alternately. This was a sensible arrangement, the Colonel thought, since it tended to minimise inter-city feeling. Notwithstanding mutual declarations of clanship and kinship, the centuries-old rivalry between Scotland's two principal towns was liable to break out at any moment, and on the thinnest of pretexts. Why should the Glasgow members (and they so given to running successful dances and whist-drives and good, whacking dinners, after the manner for which their great city is so renowned) be obliged to travel through to Edinburgh every month or so to out-vote an Edinburgh member's proposal that someone or other be invited to read a learnéd and abstruse paper on clan history, or weary them with those genealogical tables in which Treasurer MacGregor, W.S., specialised? Of course, had the two Edinburgh John MacGregors been even mildly amicable toward one another, they would have constituted a combination so formidable that the preferences of their go-ahead Glasgow clansmen, in order to have gained acceptance, would have required more tact and eloquence than their function-loving contingent could have mustered. The honorary bard, supported by the honorary treasurer, would readily have exploded the notion that the descendants of so royal—so *chosen*— a race needed whist-drives to keep alive 'the Old Name' and the indomitable spirit it signified. What had Kenneth MacAlpin, or Rob Roy, or the Dougal Cratur, known of such effeminate forms of entertainment?

*   *   *   *   *   *   *

[1] Tithe.

Some years ago, I had the temerity to engage our late treasurer in conversation on Princes Street, and to suggest to him that, in the event of his not being able to use the material which all Scotland—certainly, all Gaeldom—knew he had accumulated, he might be agreeable to placing at my disposal such of it as concerned Rob Roy and the Glengyle MacGregors. If he did not actually demur, he truly uttered no whisper of encouragement. And it occurred to me that, at the back of his mind, there may have lain some prejudice—some ineradicable vestige, perhaps, of the discord he and my father had had over Mabel's visit, a quarter of a century earlier. (MacGregors, like elephants, have long memories, when it comes to wrongs done them. Reared on the history of their persecution in olden times, and on the proscription of their name, they are swifter than most to resent an injustice.)

At his death in 1937, all his documents relating to the MacGregors were bequeathed to the historical department of the Register House—of the Scottish Record Office—at Edinburgh; while, in the accessions register at the Signet Library, you will find pages and pages devoted to books on Scotland, and especially on the Highlands and their clans, that once formed part of his vast library, and were donated under the terms of his will. His library should never have been broken up. What a pity that it could not have been bequeathed, like the MacGregor records, intact!

*   *   *   *   *   *   *

How do you think I learnt that our clan treasurer and recorder was no more?

Some months ago, while browsing in a secondhand bookshop in Auld Reekie's George Street, the proprietor, recognising me, came forward with a couple of books in his hand, and said: "These volumes might interest you." They happened to be copies of books written by the Colonel. Their condition was as fresh as when they left the binder's, forty or more years before. This made me curious. Where had they been all that time, to look so new?

"Can you tell me where they came from?" I asked.

"From a sale of books at a house in Glencairn Crescent."

Glencairn Crescent! The name was reminiscent, though I had no recollection of ever having visited anyone there. Yet, I soon recalled that that was where John MacGregor used to live.

"What was the name of the person who owned them?" I then enquired.

"Same name as yourself!" the bookman responded. "He was a W.S. But he would be a bittie before your time, of course."

"Before *my* time? Nonsense! You're referring to John Mac-Gregor, W.S., whose office was in Coates Crescent, but who lived in Glencairn."

"The very same," says he.

"I thought so," says I. "My father and he knew one another well; but many a year ago they quarrelled."

"Ay, you're an awfu' lot for quarrelling, you Heilan folk!" was the bookman's apt sally.

I have these books by my elbow now. In glancing through them, I readily visualise not only the extraordinary parent who wrote them, but another figure familiar to many thousands of Auld Reekie's inhabitants. I see John MacGregor, W.S., in Shandwick Place, or at the West End, or on Princes Street at lunch-time, stooping much beyond the weight of his years, his hands clasped behind him, carrying his umbrella where an animal carries its tail. The stoop had to be exaggerated in order to prevent the umbrella from trailing along the pavement.

*   *   *   *   *   *   *

The day our earnest and industrious clansman received so coldly my suggestion regarding his MacGregor papers, he never dreamed, nor did I, that a few years after his demise, *my* fingers were to be wandering through that great mass of material he collected and annotated with such ardour. And I do admit that, in looking through such of them as the few hours at my disposal would allow, I was moved more than once to a tear.

Nearly every query relating to the Highlands that came to Scotland during John MacGregor's active lifetime was referred to him; and, as a rule, he could give immediate answer from the records in his own possession. Canadians and Americans, anxious to trace their Scottish descent, invariably found themselves in communication with him. And this brings us to a curious coincidence. During the last war, two Canadian nurses, on the point of leaving for Britain, were asked by their grandfather, a native of Perthshire, to visit his birthplace, which, he said, bore the name of Nineveh. Having made fruitless enquiries at various libraries in Edinburgh, and consulted numerous gazetteers with as little success, they chanced to arrive at the S.S.C. Library—the Library belonging to the Solicitors in the Supreme Court, as so many of

Auld Reekie's legal luminaries of lesser candle-power are called. The authorities there failed to locate Nineveh for them; but it occurred to Dr Malcolm, the Librarian (now occupying a similar position at the Signet, close at hand) that the person to consult on such matters was John MacGregor, W.S. Whereupon he telephoned our clansman, who directed him to send the ladies down to his office immediately, where he would give them the precise location of Nineveh, for, as he added, "I'm probably the only person in Edinburgh who could tell them offhand." They went, and were duly informed not only on this point, but also on the matter of their own Highland lineage.

When Dr Malcolm related this coincidence to me the other day, I thought it very extraordinary. But, by an even stranger coincidence, when I left the Signet Library to resume my own researches amid the John MacGregor Collection, I happened to pull out a box containing a hundred or more miscellaneous papers. In dilemma as to where I should begin on them, I opened the pile somewhere about the centre, when my eye fell on a note in our seannachie's handwriting. The note ran thus:—

> "Among the stories I got in 1905 from Finlay MacIntyre in Gartnafuaran,[1] was one that in olden times the village of Strathyre was called Nineveh, and, upon my enquiring why, he told me it took three days to go round or through Nineveh, and there used to be three public-houses in Nineveh.
>
> "Today the Librarian of the S.S.C. Library telephoned that two Canadian military nurses were wanting information about Balquhidder. Would I see them? I agreed, and they called at the office and, on my asking what they wanted to know, one of them, Miss Harper, said her grandfather went to Canada from Balquhidder. He was named Malcolm Fisher, and came from a place called Nineveh. She never knew that that was the nickname for Strathyre. I wonder whether there was another person in Edinburgh who knew!—John MacGregor, 26/3/18."

A genealogical note on the back of the page showed that one of the enquirers was Miss Margaret Harper, Grandview, Manitoba, grand-daughter of Malcolm Fisher, who, as our clan historian was able to tell her, was born at Strathyre about 1813.

Glance at no more than the Inventory of the John MacGregor

[1] A farm near Balquhidder.

Collection, now lodged at the Register House, and get one of the officials to conduct you to the room where it lies, shelf upon shelf, beautifully and accurately docketed after the manner in which the Scots are unrivalled, and you will marvel at my clansman's industry throughout a busy lifetime. His painstaking and perseverance must have been colossal. Could any man have left to his love of clan and country a testimony more inspiring, more eloquent? I scarcely can convey to you what a revelation it was to me, the day I first went to see what these papers embraced. The donor's own index to the MacGregors occurring throughout them runs into three large folio volumes—a monument in itself.

It was strange that, as with the Colonel, and owing, likewise, to his fervid application to matters Highland, John MacGregor, W.S., should have so strained his eyesight as to have become almost blind in his latter days.

CHAPTER VI

OBSESSIONS AND PARTIALITIES

THREE MAJOR loyalties, amounting to obsessions, so coloured my father's life as to have coloured mine also. They were, in order of precedence, the Clan Gregor, 'the Forty-three', and 'the Forty-five'. The first of these, in addition to its embracing everything appertaining to the name of MacGregor, extended to all things even remotely connected with the Gaelic language, the wearing of the kilt, and the place of the bagpipes in human society. The second comprised the affairs of high principle for which Dr Chalmers had stood so valiantly and vehemently at the time of the Disruption. The third (between which and the second there lay a wide gap in the matter of relative importance) was concerned, in a somewhat romantic manner, with those issues bound up with Prince Charlie and his ill-starred adventure. There were, of course, as many loyalties of minor significance as there were partialities and prejudices.

The Colonel was a stickler for loyalty—loyalty to king and country and other conventional vaguenesses of like category. As descendants of Kenneth MacAlpin—*King* Kenneth MacAlpin, I must remind you!—all members of the human race enjoying the name of MacGregor were, in his considered opinion, doubly bound to respond at the king's bidding. As with the Light Brigade charging into the arms of death at Balaclava, it would have been discordant in *us*, if not indeed a mark of treachery, to reason why the government ordained this or that. It was incumbent upon us, on the contrary, to submit wholeheartedly to whatever hardship, inconvenience, or injustice the state decreed, having had our allegiance irrevocably pledged for us at least a thousand years before. Who were *we* to cavil, remembering the penalties that sheer loyalty had brought upon our ancestors? Nothing but fidelity explained how so many of our clansmen had been 'intercommuned' at the Mercat Cross of Edinburgh in olden times, or 'made short by the head', as the picturesque Scots phrase goes, or perhaps had dangled ignominiously from the gibbet on the sands at Leith, for all the world to see and heed. That special form of

43

boycott known as 'Letters of Intercommuning' had prevailed against many of our forebears, as father so often recalled. In terms of this ancient writ, the Scottish Privy Council warned all against harbouring or having any communication with those therein denounced, under pain of being held accessory to their crimes. Not by any means the kind of end likely to encourage in the Colonel's offspring that blind and primitive loyalty they recognised in their father!

Scarcely had I entered upon my youth when I saw through this silly acquiescence, through this antiquated conception of patriotism. It took me much longer to solve the least implex of the problems propounded by Euclid. I have never been a blind believer, an unquestioning follower of anyone, in anything, with the result that the family has always been somewhat exercised about my ultimate fate, and has gradually become reconciled to the prospect that I may conclude my life either in prison or in a penitentiary. The Colonel, on the other hand, like those who, of an earlier era, enjoyed the make-believe that the king could do no wrong, lulled himself into acceptance of the pretence that the chief of our ancient and noble race was every tittle as infallible as Stewart monarch or Catholic pope. Any suggestion of mine that MacGregor of MacGregor might also be human, and commit a blunder now and again, was repudiated by father, Bard of the Clan Gregor, as an expression of disloyalty ill-befitting a son of his. (The obvious explanation for any such lapse was, of course, that I had taken after my infamous mother!!) The mere heraldic fact that the MacGregors constituted the only clan of royal lineage, carrying the crown on their crest, and renowned for their feudal loyalty to whichever sovereign happened to be reigning, irrespective of the dynasty he represented, did not appear to me to warrant abstention from political criticism and even censure, though it may amuse you to learn that it was sufficient to restrain the Colonel, throughout the greater part of his life, from participating in public affairs, beyond the mere recording of his vote for a Liberal or Radical candidate. However, when his elder son joined the Labour Party and began contesting elections as a Socialist, he thought the time had come when he had better enquire what the Socialists' challenge to the *status quo* actually involved. At the age of seventy-five he found out. Consistently thereafter he advocated and voted for Socialism, contributing modestly to the party's funds, but only in the wishful assurance that Socialists were no more capable of disloyalty to king and country than he was as a MacGregor. Incidentally, he was an admirer of Shelley, and knew his *Ode to Liberty* by heart. I have often wondered since his death whether he fully realised the implication of the stanza beginning—

> *Oh, that the free would stamp the impious name*
> *Of King into the dust! or write it there,*
> *So that this blot upon our page of fame*
> *Were as the serpent's path, which the light air*
> *Erases, and the flat sands close behind!*

I think the answer is that he did realise, but would never have admitted it.

*   *   *   *   *   *   *

There is no end to the diversity of the things from which mankind derives enjoyment. Burns claimed, for instance, that he got as much pleasure from being in the secret of half the loves of the parish of Tarbolton as ever did statesman from being acquainted with the intrigues of half the courts of Europe. My father claimed that life divorced from his all-absorbing passion for Gaelic, his mother-tongue, would not have been worth living. Every day, and in every part of the world whither service or adventure had taken him, and frequently under circumstances none too easy, he read a chapter or two from his Gaelic Bible. To the day of his death, at the age of eighty-four, it was his proud claim that, after thirty years' absence in foreign climes, he returned to this country with a knowledge of Gaelic more extensive and authoritative than when he quitted his Gaelic-speaking home, wherein scarcely a word of English was ever heard, except when it was found necessary to make oneself understood to strangers, to Sassenachs. So annotated and emended was his Gaelic Bible at the time of his death in 1932, that no one but himself could decipher it.

For years he laboured at his Gaelic MSS., in the belief that he was doing something to preserve the ancient and dying tongue he loved so dearly. He was in the forefront of every effort to stimulate interest in it; and to this day his Gaelic writings and songs, as well as his innumerable contributions on Gaelic orthography, are regarded as outstanding by those best fitted to judge. For some time he insisted that our maids should be Gaelic-speaking, simply because he feared that, otherwise, the household might become too Anglicised. But, whereas Gaelic-speaking maids could converse with him in their native tongue, it soon transpired that there were other things to be done in the home, for which, in the main, they were largely incapable. Eventually he had to accept Mabel's dictum that the primary qualification for a maid should be domestic, rather than linguistic. This was a sore blow to him at a time when the survival of Gaelic, as a spoken language, dominated his life to the exclusion of matters of much greater import. "If only your father had given to the family's affairs a quarter of what he devoted to attempts to set the Thames on fire with Gaelic poetry," the unhappy Mabel used to say, "we would all be very comfortably off." Certainly, the time and energy he gave to controversy on Celtic matters in the columns of various newspapers might have gone in a direction more remunerative, if not also more abiding. The same is largely true of the time he frittered away in lamenting the downfall and desolation of the Highlands, and in being president, vice-president, honorary this and honorary that, of an endless number of societies and associations connected in some vague and aimless way with the Highlands, with the Gaelic language, and with Gaelic music—most of them organisations the main function of which, it would seem, was the mutual admiration or condemnation of persons most prominently connected with them. The vanity of the Gael is colossal; and this explains his readiness to take offence at trifles. I am reminded of the occasion when father declined to attend a lecture in London, given by a fellow-islesman, the most erudite of Highland authors and historians. The subject of the lecture was their native Island of Lewis. Father withheld his patronage because he considered the title of the lecture—*Peatland*—derogatory to their common birthplace!

It was a great pride to him that, during the last twenty years of his life or thereabouts, he was considered one of the foremost authorities on the Gaelic language. "I have been re-reading your father's Gaelic verses, and they give evidence of his possessing the bardic faculty in a very marked degree," an old and valued friend wrote me at the time of his death. "Their charity, their broad humanity, their high ethical tone, their love of country and kindred, their smooth-flowing style entitle him to an assured place among the Bards." Such a testimony from the living, after he had departed this life, was the tribute for which he had lived.

At one time his name was mooted for the Chair of Celtic at Edinburgh, where a vacancy was imminent. But the family held that the designation, Professor MacGregor, would not have suited a father so robustious; and we were afraid lest, in his unpredictable anger, he spoke to his students as he sometimes spoke to his own bairns, and perhaps chastised them with a good, resounding clout, thus bringing intolerable disgrace upon us all. He was not slow to remind us, however, that he was already entitled to be addressed in this high-sounding way. Had he not held an important professorial chair at Bombay, where, for some years, he was known as Professor MacGregor?

In his latter days, he secretly bemoaned what he knew to be inevitable, namely, that the Gaelic cause was already lost, and the language perishing, though he would not have made any such admission outside his own immediate household. Those turbulent years of youth I spent with him were punctuated by doleful monologues predicting this unthinkable state of affairs. I had to be an apt and attentive listener when he sought audience for his Gaelic jeremiads. Any hint of impatience or boredom on my part would have been irrefutable evidence of my unworthiness of so exemplary a father, and of a name as unimpeachable as Mac-Gregor. If I were within reach, it would also have earned for me a crack with hand or walking-stick, the more tangibly to mark both me and the occasion.

It was a dismal reality to him that not one of the Highland Chiefs could converse in the language of his fathers. And even such of them as had acquired a smattering exercised the same, not with its native flavour (for of that they were incapable) but with the accents, affectations, and effeminacies of England, where, in most cases, they had been educated. Nevertheless, he derived consolation from the reflection that *he*, at all events, had done everything possible to resuscitate this dying tongue. For this service he was sure that God would remember him when the time came.

The functions of An Comunn Gaidhealach he attended with unfailing regularity over a great number of years. The Mòd, held annually under its auspices, found him in attendance, either in the capacity of Gaelic adjudicator, or as a member of the audience listening to competitions for which one or two of his own songs had been chosen. The frequency with which his compositions were selected for competitive purposes was profoundly gratifying. It atoned in some measure for Mabel's default.

I remember a Mòd[1] in my early youth which I spoilt for him

---

[1] The assembly in Celtic Scotland corresponding to the Eisteddfod in Wales.

by a sudden attack of biliousness. The excitement of my accompanying him to Stirling for this great rendezvous had been too much for me, with the result that, for three days, I lay sick and feverish, on a hotel sofa, visited every now and then by my father, when able to tear himself away from those Gaelic competitions in which he was so engrossed. As it happened, some of his songs were being sung, and one or two of his protégés were competing. I shall never forget his returning to the hotel late one afternoon and kneeling by my couch of discomfort to tell me that a Lewis girl we knew (who had paid several visits to our home in Edinburgh, immediately prior to this great festival, in order to receive the necessary tuition from the Colonel himself) had won the Gold Medal of An Comunn with her rendering of one of the prescribed songs, both the words and melody of which were his own. This more than compensated for the inconvenience my bilious lapse had caused him. Indeed, he was now so delirious with joy and pride that for some days not even the thought of Mabel could assail him.

*　　*　　*　　*　　*　　*　　*

So fanatical was father's fervour for Gaeldom that he even insisted his children should bear Christian names of Gaelic origin, if not also of Clan Gregor association. There was no respect shown by *him* for the custom whereby the eldest son was 'named for' his paternal grandfather, and the eldest daughter called after her maternal grandmother. Throughout Gaeldom 'fancy' names (*i.e.*, those not already in local circulation) were taboo, and in all probability would have remained so, had Hollywood values not seduced us. Nowadays, there are scores of Highland Daphnes, Ednas, Cynthias, Rosemarys, and Pamelas.

Anyhow, the Colonel appears to have embarked on matrimony, having secretly reserved to himself the sole right to choose the names of any issue. I was called Alasdair for reasons with which my readers are already familiar. In any case, Alasdair went admirably with MacGregor; and there had been several Alasdair MacGregors among the noteworthy of our clan. The appropriateness of Alpin was obvious. It implied the very essence of Alba—of Scotland—the very patronymic of the earliest kings of Scots. What more befitting than Alpin, therefore? So the Alasdair and the Alpin were singularly happy on ancestral grounds.

My eldest sister was called Jessie after her *paternal* grandmother,

Seonaid (Janet) MacDonald. Iain (John) received his father's own name—the name of a score of eldest MacGregor sons in succession, according to the genealogical table as handed down, traditionally and orally, in the Outer Hebrides for generations— for centuries, in fact—the earliest of them recorded in no other way.

But Mabel, after much contention, did manage to interpolate O'Brien as Iain's middle name, in deference to our maternal Irish ancestry. Having scored this intermediary, though perhaps secondary, success, she was emboldened to attempt a primary one. So, while the fourth child was on its way, she was giving some consideration to what it was to be called, whether a boy or a girl. Hence Margaret, who also carries Mabel as one of her two middle names. "Margaret, forsooth!" the Colonel declared with feeling, immediately after the christening. "A damned English name! What the devil has a name like that to do with the Clan Gregor? None of *my* people was ever called by such a name! She ought to have been called Iseabal (Ishbel) after one of your Highland aunts!"

Little enough consideration for poor Mabel, who, to express it mildly, had now suffered the discomfort of bearing four children! But father must have his *quid pro quo*, even where Margaret's christening was concerned. If her mother insisted that Mabel should be one of her middle names, there would have to be a counter-balance with another middle name. And what better choice than Helen? That, after all, was the name of Rob Roy's wife, a woman as strong and commanding as Penthesilea herself. Not that he necessarily expected Margaret, when she grew up, to emulate this Highland Amazon in the savage observances of her day and generation. But it might be just as well to include in the family's list of names that of one so brave and historic! And there was another point: Helen must take precedence of Mabel. So, in the end, and after vexatious argie-bargie, she was duly christened Margaret Helen Mabel MacGregor.

How was father to live down this incongruity, this flaming indignity? Would he ever be able to purge the name of Mac-Gregor of this insult? Well, if there were another child, he would certainly do so. Indeed, there must be another child! So, in the course of laborious time, there arrived the fifth and final instal-ment of this ill-fashioned wedlock. She became Catriona Mairi MacGregor. The name, Catriona (the Gaelic equivalent of Kate,

Catherine, Kathleen) was eminently appropriate. There had been several Catrionas in our Hebridean lineage. Moreover, the scoundrelly James Mòr MacGregor, son of the doughty Rob Roy, had had an only daughter of that name, whose exploits astonished Scotland in the eighteenth century, and provided R. L. S., in the nineteenth, with the foundation upon which he made this lovely MacGregor name immortal.

Catriona (accent on the *second* syllable, please!) got her middle name, Mairi, in remembrance of a MacGregor aunt whom she had never seen. Catriona Mairi MacGregor! Surely you see father's hand in this! A choice so felicitous almost justified the birth of a child the acquiescent Mabel would fain have been without. With Catriona well and truly baptised after his own pattern, he was, as the Irish would put it, the happiest creature on the earth of the world. (You really ought to do something worth while, Catriona, with your looks, your intelligence, and a name as lovely as yours!)

*   *   *   *   *   *   *

Among the odd coincidences the Colonel used to relate were his meetings with fellow-Highlanders, or with their Gaelic-speaking descendants, in strange places and circumstances all over the world. The captain of the ship that rescued him when wrecked in the Pacific hailed from the same village in the Hebrides. They had been schoolboys together. They instantly recognised one another in mid-ocean, the one from the bridge, the other from the lifeboat. Gaelic salutations immediately ensued; and the passengers were curious to know to what nationality belonged the two stalwarts who could conduct so animated a conversation in the midst of raging seas.

It was seldom that a Highlander was not to be found at the various cantonment stations he knew, when serving with the Punjabis or with the Sikhs. Incidentally, the names of those stations, together with a good deal of the usual Anglo-Indian nomenclature current in British homes with Indian connections, were as familiar to us as were the proper names mentioned in the Bible—Dacca and Darjeeling, in Bengal, for instance; Shillong, in Assam; Lahore and Kashmir; Chaman, in Baluchistan; Jullunder, Umballa, and Ferozepore, in the Punjab; Bannu and Dera Ishmail Khan, in the North West Provinces, and so on.

In one of his own books father describes how, in the Jenolan Caves, he came upon a kilted Gael as fanatical on matters Highland as he was himself, whose grandparents had emigrated to Australia nearly a century earlier. He had never seen Scotland, the land of his origin. Yet, Gaelic was the everyday language of his home. To test the genuineness of the other's claim, they agreed that they should supply one another with the Gaelic for a calf—*laogh*—a word so difficult to pronounce that it is used as a criterion, a shibboleth. No one acquiring the language can ever render this word to the complete satisfaction of the native-speaker, unless he have a good dash of the Gael in him. (Try it, ye Sassenachs!)

Father's obsession for all things relating to Gaeldom certainly brought him interesting contacts. And I like to reflect that many of these have been handed on to me, his elder son, and that round them have gathered the most pleasant recollections and associations of my sojourn here on earth. In return for all this has meant to me, I could never repay him adequately.

Seldom was he happier than when in the midst of company exclusively Gaelic-speaking—which, by the way, recalls the story of three members of the Glasgow City Police, an inspector, a sergeant, and a constable, seated in a southbound train on the Oban–Glasgow line. They were returning to duty from their homes in the Hebrides, where they had been on holiday. Much to the annoyance of a Glaswegian crouching in a corner of the compartment, these braw Highlandmen told yarn after yarn in the Gaelic, and sang Gaelic songs to one another in rotation, without intermission. Their boisterous behaviour quite deaved the Sassenach fellow-passenger, whose ignorance of our ancient tongue precluded him from entering into the spirit of the journey. "For the love o' God, dinna come in here if ye're no' Heilan!" he exclaimed in exasperation, as the train drew up at a station *en route*, and another passenger sought to enter the compartment.

*   *   *   *   *   *   *

If the affairs of clan and of the Gaelic language took precedence in the home of my boyhood and youth, it is doubtful whether, at bottom, they influenced our lives as fundamentally as did 'the Forty-three'—the Disruption of 1843—when the Free Church of Scotland came into being. Father had schooled us ardently in the circumstances culminating in this breakaway, in the hard-

51

ship it entailed for so many, and in that ultimate triumph of conscience it vindicated so nobly. There was little use our knowing the Shorter Catechism if we failed to appreciate what the Disruption had stood for, and how it had permeated Scottish life throughout the remainder of the nineteenth century, and well into the twentieth. Indeed, it would be no inaccuracy to say that it still colours much of Scottish thought, although, in the main, the state of affairs the original dissenters deplored, and so courageously challenged, no longer exists.

"What, in one word, Alasdair, brought about the Disruption?" father might ask me, so as to ascertain whether I showed more intelligence in the matters on which he informed one so persistently and conscientiously, than in the curriculum maintained at George Watson's for the likes of me.

"Patronage, father!" I would reply, with a sneer calculated to prove that I, also, understood what the term implied in this special connection.

And what was it all about? The answer is that an inspired section of the Auld Kirk—the Established Church of Scotland—resolved to resist the practice whereby the patrons of livings "intruded", upon the congregations, ministers who were the sole nominees of the former. So far as the Established Church was concerned, the Court of Session had decided that a congregation had no power to reject the laird's nominee. If it found him unsuitable, it had to thole him gracefully, unless it could convince the Presbytery that he had at least one insurmountable defect, such as being club-footed, or "destitute of a musical ear", or given to "occasional exuberance of animal spirits". Such secondary shortcomings, of course, were cited only when the more obvious ones had failed to prevent the installation as the laird's presentee of one who, by this time, had probably been heard by the congregation, and pronounced by it to be "evangelically dead".

The question of patronage was now hotly disputed both in the Highlands and in the Lowlands. It involved a principle vital to those who believed in a free and progressive faith. The climax arrived when Dr Chalmers, followed by a large number of supporters, left the General Assembly in 1843 for another place of assembly, to form the Free Church of Scotland. Nearly five hundred ministers sacrificed their all at one stroke. Their livelihood gone with their livings; their children's prospects vanished; stark starvation facing them. Nothing remained but that courage born of conviction. These men had cast their bread upon the waters.

Though many landed proprietors refused to grant sites, a new and powerful church was afoot in no time. Churches, manses, halls, Sunday-schools, missions were springing up all over our northern land, so that a church, which had begun penniless, possessed millions less than half a century later, without patronage, and even in spite of it. Yes, they had cast their bread upon the waters, and received it after many days. The Free Church thus inaugurated attracted not only adherents from every class, but also many of the ablest theologians and preachers of the time.

I am as much a child of the Disruption as any Scot can claim to be the child of anything. My Highland forebears came 'out' in 'the Forty-three', just as our kindred were 'out' for Prince Charlie a century before. In father's view, this challenge to interference in a matter of the highest spiritual import was the most honourable episode in the long and troublous history of Scotland. This view he implanted in his children as soon as they were old enough to grasp anything at all. I regard it as a precious privilege to have been brought up in this stirring tradition. I revere it in a degree more intense than I do that of any other happening which has influenced my life. It is one of the greatest stories in the world. And to the United Free Church of Scotland, which ultimately evolved from it, I owe the very essence of my northern background.

*   *   *   *   *   *   *

And now a word or two on the Colonel's partialities.

High in his affection stood all members of the canine race. Their fidelity moved him. Like Socrates, he swore by his dog. When in genial mood, he often told us fascinating stories of doggie friends he had had in India and Burma.

He liked big, buxom women, chiefly because they possessed the qualities of the brood mare; and he believed it to be one of man's main purposes on this earth to breed and, if possible, found a family. On this, he and I never saw eye to eye. Consequently, it was with profound misgiving he learnt in his latter years that I had no notion of contracting a formal marriage, and of settling down in orthodox respectability to become a father, thus helping to perpetuate the royal name of MacGregor!

He loved ginger-bread, I remember, and could consume limitless quantities of it—ginger-bread with the pre-1914 constituents, I mean, for, like much else, it has never been quite as good since. Fish and shellfish made an especial appeal to his palate, probably because he had been so accustomed to them in the ichthyophagous home of his boyhood. The cask of herrings or the box of Stornoway kippers our cousins consigned to us periodically, was to be preferred to the most epicurean diet. A meal of tatties and herring, dished up in Scots style, might be deemed plebeian; but there was nothing he enjoyed so much. Only snobbery and ignorance, he contended, had displaced such wholesome fare from popular favour. Than the arrival of kippers from Stornoway, nothing was better calculated to produce a spell of amiability in our crazy home.

* * * * * * *

As one might have expected, a man so rigid in his formulæ had little time for the petty landlords of Scotland, especially those of the Highlands, who gave themselves airs and graces as enormous as they were intolerable. Much as he despised the new aristocracy of beer and tobacco, of iron, steel, and textiles, much as he deplored the rate at which these usurpers had bribed away their historic predecessors, he preferred them to the potty little Highland lairds, the *petite noblesse*, who possessed a few acres, but insisted on being called, not by their surnames, but by the place-names of their quite modest properties. In the Colonel's view, these mere nobodies, as he called them, had done much to intensify the snobbery of the Highlands, and to distort still farther that false sense of values prevalent among people who fall down before the shooting-tenant and his entourage as though they were a transcendent species of humanity.

A love of territorial titles forms an integral part of Scottish life, which reminds me of a story told by a whilom friend who, during the last war, lunched with the Earl of Glasgow aboard H.M.S. *Amethyst* in a South American port. The Earl was captain of the ship.

"What will ye hae?" he asked, turning to my friend, who was also a Scot, and who meantime scanned the somewhat sparse war-time menu. "I think I'd hae herrin', if I wes ye."

To this suggestion he cordially agreed, remarking that he had not tasted herring since last he was home in Scotland. Then followed the question of drinks. "Man, I'd hae a bottle o' beer. It gangs weel wi' herrin', ye ken; an' herrin' maun soom!"

This spate of the vernacular so surprised the guest that he complimented his host upon it.

"Man, what's the guid o' a terrrritorrrrial title," Glasgow replied, "if ye canna speak the language?"

In this context, Sir Seymour Hicks tells a good story of Sir Frank Lockwood, the man who defended Charles Peace. Lockwood's wife was a sister-in-law of MacLaine of Lochbuie. This Highland chieftain, who prided himself on his ancient title, as well as on the somewhat impoverished estate of Lochbuie, insisted on being referred to as Lochbuie, and not as Mr MacLaine. On one occasion, Lockwood and his wife accompanied MacLaine and his wife to a fashionable London party. The Lockwoods were amused to hear the footman announce the MacLaines as "Lochbuie and Mrs MacLaine". Following closely on their heels, Lockwood, who resided in Kensington, whispered in the footman's ear "14, Lennox Gardens, and Lady Lockwood". He and his wife were duly announced in these terms.

Lockwood was a man of considerable wit. He often told the story of a visit three ladies in mourning paid him at his chambers after Peace's execution. On being shown in by the clerk, they promptly informed Lockwood that they were his late client's mother, daughter, and aunt. Somewhat embarrassed, he asked them to be seated.

"I'm exceedingly sorry," he began. "But——."

Thereupon one of the three interposed with: "I fear, sir, that you misunderstand the object of our call. We have come to offer you our grateful thanks for the very successful result of the trial. We were all most relieved by the verdict."

CHAPTER VII

THE BAGPIPES AND THE KILT

"THERE WES acht o' us in Lucky MacKintosh's back-pairlour in the Canongate o' Edinburrie ae nicht; an' we wes a' playin' the pipes at wan time; an' we wes a' playin' different tunes; an', man, Ah jist thocht Ah wes in heavin!"

That, in a few words, epitomises father's idea of the grandest sound to which mortal man could hearken. Like so many Highlanders, he fervently hoped that he might be laid to rest to the strains of the bagpipes; and he arranged accordingly. To him, the prospect of there being no piper at his funeral spelt failure, if not actually ignominy. Any Highlander worth his salt, he claimed, made provision for a lament on the pipes at his committal. Some little time before his death, he was happy to learn of the request contained in the will of the Rev. Æneas Gordon, who, for fifty-two years, had been minister of the Fife parish of Kettle, and had just died. "I die a Highlander," ran a passage of the will. "I lived a Highlander. I have been indebted to Highland associations all my life. The last tribute of respect I can pay to my Highland ancestry is to be buried to the music of the bagpipes, which I beg my executors to provide, and to pay the pipers well." This wish his executors observed.

Father placed upon me, by word of mouth, a similar obligation, which I fulfilled. He was buried to the skirl of the pipes, played by an old friend, the late MacGregor-Murray, piper to the Clan Gregor. My reference to this in the dedication of one of my earlier books, however, brought me evidence of how touchy pipers can be about their profession. An infuriated piper somewhere abroad wrote me an indignant letter because he had read in this dedication that the Clan Piper headed the procession to the graveside, "fingering the coronach". *Fingering*, mark you! If that were not impudence, what was? A gross insult not only to MacGregor-Murray and to my deceased father, but also to the entire piping world! It explained why my correspondent declared that he would not provide house-room for a book which he had hoped to include among his favourites. Well, now, how do pipers

56

play, if they don't *finger* the chanter of their instrument? Again you see how ready the Highlander is to take offence.

Three generations of hereditary pipers, playing Highland laments, headed the funeral procession in 1933 of Cluny Mac-Pherson, Chief of the MacPhersons. There may have been an excuse for such an array on this occasion, however, since this picturesque laird had a castle and estates to give his funeral suitable background. (Ownership of property is still the most adequate of backgrounds, even in the Highlands.) Furthermore, Cluny was the direct lineal descendant of his namesake of 'the '45', famous in Highland story as one of the Prince's staunchest supporters.

Poor Colonel MacGregor had neither castle nor estates. Nor did he possess much in the way of property during his closing years. For this, both he and I had reason to be truly thankful. "Let me tell you, scholar," wrote Isaak Walton, "that Diogenes walked on a day, with his friend, to see a country fair, where he saw ribbons, and looking-glasses, and nut-crackers, and fiddles, and hobby-horses, and many other gimcracks; and, having observed them, and all the other finnimbruns that make a complete country fair, he said to his friend: 'Lord, how many things there are in this world, of which Diogenes hath no need!' And truly it is so, or might be so, with very many who vex and toil themselves to get what they have no need of." It certainly simplified the Colonel's latter days that he shared with Diogenes this sentiment about worldly possessions.

His interest in piping never waned up to the time of his death; and, albeit, so far as I remember, he never once played the bag-pipes during *my* lifetime, his knowledge of pipe-music was considered extensive. I shall not forget his pride of achievement when the compilers of a collection of wellknown pipe-tunes wrote to ask permission to include no fewer than three airs of his own composition. Imagine his delight when a presentation copy arrived with all manner of compliments, and he found it to contain not only these tunes of his, but also one *dedicated* to him, and bearing his name, composed by one of Scotia's foremost pipes-major!

*   *   *   *   *   *   *

On occasions the Colonel used to adjudicate at piping contests in Auld Reekie, in his capacity as an official of a piping society, the name of which evades me at the moment. (Could it have been the Caledonian?) How a man so notoriously impatient was able to sit out those interminable pibrochs, hour after hour, we never understood. The rendition of a single pibroch, you must realise, often took well over an hour; and it appeared to be a virtue in competitive piping to drag test pieces out as long and solemnly as possibly. We were convinced that father, by some primitive self-hypnotism, allowed himself to be so absorbed in pipe-music as to have forfeited all sense of time or of his earthly responsibilities. Wouldn't he have revelled in those ongoings in Lucky MacKintosh's back-parlour?

For all this, I had it on acceptable authority that he earned a reputation as a good, sound adjudicator.

As most of the competitors were obliged to work for their liveli-hood, these skirling contests had to be held on their half-day— on Saturday afternoons and evenings. I once made my way to a dingy, gas-lit hall somewhere in the Dalry or Gorgie district of Edinburgh, on a Saturday evening, to pick my father up after one of these protracted performances. On reaching the door of the hall, I was greeted by the mournful groans of a pibroch, played by an upstanding member of the Edinburgh Police Force, who, disporting full regalia to suit the occasion, strode up and down the platform at snail's pace, all but losing his balance at times for the slowness of his procession, especially when, in turning, he had to synchronise his footsteps and the music. Suddenly father's voice rang out above the whining strains, to the embarrassment of the competitor, as well as of those still to be heard. His son, mean-while, had hidden himself in darkness behind a cupboard door in a dusky passage, affecting to disclaim any relationship with the person roaring, in Gaelic, into the ear of a judge deafer than himself, making the observation that, if this were an example of the interest in pibroch, better for Scotland's reputation that it should never have been revived. (You will have noticed that deafness is no disqualification in an adjudicator of pipe-music: on the contrary!) This amused me, since I was wholly unaware that father had ever made any serious study of pibroch, or con-sidered himself the least competent to judge such a performance.

With every visit to this dingy and depressing hall, his ardour for the pipes increased. "Why in the name of God cannot you even play your own father's pipe-tunes on the chanter he gave you?" he would ask in sullen mood on his return, or whenever there arose anything to do with piping. The answer may be that his

58

zeal had stifled any budding enthusiasm in me. Yet, little did either of us imagine that, a year or two later, I was to be marching in and out of battle with a Highland regiment, to the strains of the most martial music in the world!

In the home, you may remember, the piano received but scant respect from the Colonel. Only as a very third-rate medium for Gaelic airs and pipe-tunes could he suffer it at all. Put to any other purpose, it was an effeminate instrument, a symbol of decadence. "The bagpipes, if you like," he used to remark. "But the piano—NO! NEVER! It may be suitable as a mild accomplishment for school-girls, but not for lads approaching manhood, and bearing the name of MacGregor." So ill did he think of it in our Highland days that, while Mabel played Chopin in the drawingroom, he would retire to the study, with malice aforethought, to hum Gaelic melodies in opposition. But, since Mabel could play longer and better than he could hum, he used to get restive, and then jealous, and then raucous. "Haven't you had enough of this Chopping fellow?" he would bawl, on entering the drawingroom, intent on interrupting her playing. "Give us a Highland tune or two! Why not let us have one of my *own* lovely Gaelic airs?"

*   *   *   *   *   *   *

A word or two on the wearing of the kilt, by no means the least important of the passions ruling the Colonel's life.

During many of his years in retirement, the kilt formed his principal article of apparel. Trews thereunder were scorned, since the wearing of them was not in the true tradition. It denoted degeneracy. Only namby-pambies and alien shooting-tenants, disporting tartans to which they had no right, wore these 'undies'. The kilt required no such unseen garment. Iain and I were quite big boys before we were allowed to desecrate our graceful Highland limbs with anything as English—as 'civilized'—as a pair of breeks. When we lived in Inverness, our bright kilts of MacGregor tartan rendered us kenspeckle within a radius of several miles. And we were resident in Auld Reekie at least a couple of years before father would allow of our wearing anything else.

Only when the kilt was worn at balls could trews be excused. Even then, they were taboo among kilted dancers belonging to our Highland regiments, whose evening-dress kilts were taped inside with elastic, that the whirling exertions of the reel might be undertaken in a manner reasonably seemly. One remembers a horrible incident, in this connection, reputed to have taken place in Edwardian days at a ball held in the Assembly Rooms at Auld Reekie. The elastic of an unfortunate subaltern's kilt gave way, with results that shook our city to her very foundations. For weeks this frontal attack upon the sheepfolds of respectability, though quite unpremeditated, was the chief topic of conversation, both in our West End drawingrooms and in our shops.

We were instructed never to refer to the single garment as kilts, as do so many of the uninitiated, to the disaffection of the more perfervid of the Scots. On no account should this article of clothing be pluralised, unless one be prepared to meet a heavy concentration of Scottish Nationalist ire.

It warmed the cockles of father's Highland heart to see anyone wearing the MacGregor tartan, particularly if he carried it well. He could never allow anyone displaying it to pass him without a word or two of conversation and commendation. He was liable to hold up any wearer, mainly to discover whether he had any entitlement to it—what connection, if any, he had with the Clan Gregor. The procedure whereby he intercepted the passerby was often a source of extreme discomfort to his offspring, when out walking with him. Woe betide the fellow who, in parading Princes Street in our tartan, could not claim closer kinship than that his maternal grandmother's great-aunt had been a MacGregor! One would have thought father had been directed by some crown authority to check up on matters of this kind, as do the revenue officials with coats-of-arms and the police with motor licences.

In father's opinion, very few men were qualified, physically and temperamentally, to wear the kilt as it should be worn. Nothing riled him more, therefore, than to witness the puny creatures who, without a vestige of claim to this emblem of the Highlands, disported it like vain cock-sparrows, when Balmoralism became fashionable in Scotland. One requires to have 'the leg for the kilt', as the saying is; and persons of volatile disposition are incapable of lending to it the dignity it demands.

The kilt at this time was by no means an uncommon dress among Edinburgh school-boys. Indeed, the young wearer sometimes found himself in popular demand. I remember a laddie who, simply because he wore a kilt, and a shabby one at that, was chosen for a kinderspiel version of *Rob Roy*, staged in an old theatre down in Stockbridge. His part, a non-speaking one, was that of a Highland ragamuffin. We envied him this distinction.

To-day, to a large extent, the wearing of the kilt, by adults, forms part of that farcical cult finding its noblest expression at Highland Games. There its devotees are mainly those pallid intellectuals and ineffectuals who, having not the remotest claim to any tartan, have gone to endless trouble, and often spared themselves no expense, to prove that some unlikely ancestor bore this or that Highland surname, thus entitling them to wear the appropriate tartan. Among the humbugs now displaying this dress in settings where the descendants of the ancient clans find trousers more convenient, if less picturesque, are many who have convinced themselves that they wear it in succession to an ancestor who did so in the time of Cromwell, if not even earlier, regardless of its having been unknown until the opening years of the eighteenth century. The tartan, of course, is much older than the kilt; and there is a page or two of history in every check of it.

Jacobites are particularly given to wearing the kilt. Yet, it is doubtful whether the Young Chevalier, though generally depicted in it, ever wore anything but breeches, until he appeared in the rôle of Betty Burke, when he donned the skirt provided by Flora MacDonald. At least one of the usurpers who, later, occupied his throne, wore it, however. I am thinking of George IV. Egged on by Sir Walter Scott, he got into the kilt to visit Edinburgh. And a kilt of Stuart tartan at that! Surely the Scots, with their sense of logic, must have recognised how paradoxical was the sight of a Hanoverian monarch in the romantic tartan of the dethroned!

The kilt has provided the more argumentative Scottish Nationalists in recent years with many a bone at which to gnaw. They argue as to how long it should be; as to whether the knees should be bared or screened; as to how much knee or how little. They cannot even agree among themselves as to whether all of them should wear it. The Duke of Montrose, who may be regarded as the leader of their movement, constantly appears in it, as to the manner born. On the other hand, the late Sir Alexander Mac-Ewen, who was provost of the tartan town of Inverness, and contested at least one parliamentary election as a Scottish Nationalist candidate, could not picture himself so conspicuously arrayed. But Compton Mackenzie, in every way an *ultra*-Englishman, wears it with the flair of a fanatical Highlander. And what of the Duke of Argyll, that hardy Chief of the Clan Campbell? There is nothing English about *him*! This believer in faun and faery, in spook and spunky, even cycles in the kilt along the shore-road between his castle at Inveraray and the offices of his factor, a mile or so away. He does his shopping in the kilt, and looks braw in it.

* * * * * * *

The fate of father's dress kilt and its accessories, such as tunic, plaid, sporran, dirk, and brogues, constituted one of the major griefs of his closing years. The entire outfit had been purchased in London, rather expensively, toward the end of the nineteenth century when, after his final return from the East, he was so popular in Scottish and Caledonian circles. As a septuagenarian he donned it but seldom. His girth was now an inch or two in excess of what it could cope with. So, for a year or two, it lay, undisturbed, in an old trunk under his bed.

One day shortly after the Great War, a rag-woman arrived on the doorstep, and tempted Jessie with offers for old clothes. What about father's Highland regalia? It had reposed so long among moth-balls in the trunk that its fond owner had probably forgotten its existence. The likelihood of his ever asking for it, she imagined, was now as remote as the possibility of his ever wearing it. For a shilling or two, the thoughtless Jessie gave it to the rag-woman.

Months passed. Then one day the Colonel, with his uncanny intuitiveness, took it into his head that he must see his precious kilt and its appurtenances at least once more before he died. He drew forth the trunk. As it scraped along the floor, a shudder as of an impending cataclysm visited the household. Those glorious garments, reminiscent of his splendour, were gone. Never again would he gaze upon them. Never again would he fondle them, and lay them back, affectionately, as he had done so often. When, eventually, Jessie mustered enough courage to tell how she had disposed of them, he entered upon one of the longest lamentations of his life. Job's tribulations were as nothing in comparison with what had already overtaken him in his first having married Mabel, and then having had by her a half-wit of a son like me. Now added to these were the loss of his kilt and the irreparable damage done to his dignity through Jessie's doorstep transaction. The humiliation that his lovely Highland raiment should now be lying in some Edinburgh rag-and-bone merchant's was intolerable. Despite all the woes and perils he had endured throughout his active life, despite all those calamities that had beset his path since Mabel first stumbled across it, he was now afflicted as never before. He

could not have mourned more deeply the loss of his dearest child.
If our unhappy mother were not his immediate theme, when he
sat bleating in his armchair during the next few years, the fate of
that kilt was. "And for a couple of shillings she gave away my
beautiful Highland dress to a rag-woman at the door. Ah! God!
That's what comes of marrying such a ——!"

So, as usual, the ultimate blame had to be laid to Mabel's
account.

CHAPTER VIII

AN INVETERATE MISCHIEF-MAKER

"TAKE HIM with you, constable! Take him with you! Ah, God! That I should have married his mother, and been cursed with a son who is no better than a common thief! That a son of mine, bearing the tried and trusted name of MacGregor, should bring such disgrace upon 'the Old Name', is more than I can endure! Take him with you, then, and have him sentenced and imprisoned!"

These devastating words, uttered by a fanatical father with every ounce of imputative emphasis when I was twelve or thirteen, lurk in my memory. But, in order that you may understand the full import of them, I shall have to tell you (in violation, I fear, of the proverbial injunction, *de mortuis nil nisi bonum*) a little about the wily Elizabeth, our Irish maternal grandmother, the most accomplished of mischief-makers, and prime mover in the plot culminating in the issue of these terrifying directions.

We had been but a couple of years in Auld Reekie when this human blight descended upon the family, adding yet another dilemma to my unhappy days. She had been living in semi-retirement in Suffolk when, by way of showing disapproval of her elder daughter's conduct in having left husband and youthful children, she suggested coming to us on a visit of indefinite duration. It seemed odd that the Colonel should have entertained for one instant the housing of his mother-in-law, and a Roman Catholic at that! Only her supposed hostility toward Mabel, our mother, could have explained that lack of apprehension with which he received her into a household as Presbyterian, as Calvinist, as ours.

No survey of the turbulent years of my later boyhood and early youth would be complete that ignored the wily Elizabeth's nefarious activities during her unsolicited sojourn with us. In all expressions of devilry, she was alarmingly puissant; and she seemed to taint, as with something sinister and devilish, everyone with whom she came into contact, and also everything she touched. Even when detected in some glaring falsehood or other improbity, or caught red-handed in her mean pursuits, she

64

Joseph Hislop as Rudolfo

A MUSICAL TRIO

1. The Bonnie George Campbell
2. Robert Burnett
3. George Short

exhibited not a grain of modesty. On the contrary, as though some primitive bloodthirstiness lay deep down in the fibre of her, and had to be allayed, she pursued her cruel course relentlessly, with but greater vigour and cocksureness, resolutely impassible where the finer feelings of mankind were concerned. The more one found her out, the more she assumed the rôle of an avenging Tisiphone.

"Set a thief to catch a thief!" she was in the habit of casting at me when favoured by an impressionable audience, though what application this adage had to the circumstances then obtaining, I seldom could see. She seemed to use it indiscriminately, trusting that, once in a while, it might be appropriate. To her repetition of it she added a semblance of learning by tacking on to it a Latin tag I have now forgotten. Had I been as confident in the Classics as behooved a lad of my years, I might have retorted in Quintilian's words, *Mendacem memorem esse oportere*: to be a liar, memory is necessary.

Let us look at the Evil One superficially for a moment. In appearance she was distinguished. She was of medium build, and in height a little taller than most people. She was beautiful to look at—quite unusually so. The shape of her head was so patrician that it lent her a distinction its *contents* certainly did not merit—unless it can be said that a head as full of malevolence as hers qualifies one for some such regard. She had charm, and grace, and a queenly dignity. She moved with an easy rhythm. The style in which she did her hair lent a touch of the picturesque. In point of age, she was better fitted to have been my father's wife than his mother-in-law. According to orthodox standards, one would have been justified in regarding her as tolerably well educated. She knew a certain amount about the arts. She was interested in painting, and possessed a good working knowledge of music. In the matter of English and Irish folk-song she was appreciably versed. Occasionally—very occasionally—she played the piano, and with a curious elusiveness, as though the faeries of her Green Isle were putting a fey quality into her finger-tips. She read well at sight, and had a perfect ear; and in the latter connection she was adept at sitting by the drawingroom fire, correcting my sisters as they practised certain familiar pieces after school hours. Judged by the frequency and persistence of her amendments, her repertoire, in her musical heyday, must have been extensive.

Furthermore, she was a most industrious needlewoman. In the making and mending of my sisters' clothing, there was more sewing in our home during her sojourn—more snippeting of scissors and snappeting of thread—than ever took place in the workroom of the celebrated tailor of Gloucester.

At times she gave the impression of having retained a little of the humour of her calf-country. Yet, even in her best moments, one detected in her the fear lest her most trivial *jeu d'esprit* should pass unnoticed, or, if noticed, unappreciated.

Finally, albeit she was the mother of three, and had nearly reached the allotted span when she came to us, she pretended to as little experience of life in the great, big world as has the ant when leaving the formicary on her nuptial flight.

Yet, the wily Elizabeth was the world's most perverted inhabitant, a woman remarkably efficient in all the works of uncharitableness, past-mistress in the art of mischief-making. In these barren fields, no one has excelled her. In the practice of misrepresentation, of heterophemy, there was never her equal. In every word she uttered, as in every activity in which she engaged, there was the suspicion that she had developed to perfection the *suggestio falsi* and the *suppressio veri*. An adept dissembler, the most plausible of liars, she ruled the Colonel's household by cunning and stealth.

Of her descent from one of the oldest families in Ireland, Granny, as we children called her, was intensely proud. She was not long in our midst, however, before I had reason to regard her as an unregenerate member of it. In temper and temperament she was peculiarly Irish, in the English sense of the term. Her temper (always worst when she appeared most affable) *plus* her faculty for mischief-making (now her principal occupation in life) made her a formidable foe, if ever one got on the wrong side of her. And once on the wrong side, never again on the right! There exists, I believe, not the faintest shadow of evidence that, during her long life of discontent and scheming, she ever did anyone a good turn, though it would be remiss of me not to take some cognisance of her devotion to my youngest sister, Catriona Mairi, then but a child. But, speaking by and large, she was of the type Edmund Burke had in mind when he pronounced that in the doing of good we are generally cold and languid and sluggish, and afraid of being too much in the right. The performances of malice and injustice, on the other hand, are in quite another style. They are effected, as

66

Burke remarked, with a bold and masterly hand. Without a doubt, the malice and injustice accomplished by the wily Elizabeth had a masterly swing about them. Whenever I am reminded that such a person once trod the earth, a cold shudder visits my spine, and I feel my lips forming, involuntarily, all sorts of naughty words. Add Elizabeth's schemings and cruelties to my unhappiness at school, and you have some conception what I endured until I 'listed.

That a person so dignified in appearance, so cultivated in demeanour, could have been as corroded at heart was startling. For some time her superficial merits, her surface culture, seemed to outweigh her more obvious defects. But deep down in the nature of her lay a malevolence artfully concealed at the outset of her visit. However, the longer she postponed her return to Suffolk (she alleged that she had a cottage by the sea at Southwold, where she frequently had heard the ghost-bells of churches long since buried beneath the sea) the better opportunity we had of experiencing her venom and criminality. At the end of a year or eighteen months, both my father and I knew much of her doings. Yet he, in his thoughtless and impatient way, either condoned or encouraged her cruel and insensate attitude toward me, the eldest of her daughter's motherless brood. The weariness occasioned by her long train journey from England had scarcely worn off before she decided to concentrate on me as the subject for her victimisation. All too soon I became, in effect, the family whipping-boy, the scape-goat in an ultra-Presbyterian home thridded through and through with the insidious threads of Jesuitry. The Colonel, already exasperated at my lack of application and consequent duncery, required little encouragement from the wily Elizabeth in the matter of inflicting upon me a good sound beating. She earned for me many a thrashing to which I was not entitled.

Her first serious essay into my affairs I well remember. At the close of the session at George Watson's, I had returned with a prize in geography—that worthless *second* prize, which I mentioned in my previous volume. To Granny it seemed preposterous to assume that so undesirable a grandson could possibly have gained such an award honourably. He certainly had not obtained it by his better intelligence. So, while I was away holidaying with the Goat-wife at the Hill of the Peats, she put it into the Colonel's head that I must have forged this award in some artful way, and persuaded him to institute enquiries in the appropriate quarter. Of anything so dastardly as forgery, I had never been guilty in my life, not necessarily because I then had any serious moral objection to the practice, but through fear of detection. I had read in the newspapers what the police did to offenders in this regard. But that a boy, who consistently had been the booby of the class, should arrive home with a prize, lay it on the table without passing as much as a syllable of comment on his achievement, was so extraordinary that, perhaps, even the suspicion of his having stolen it was excusable to a warped mind like Granny's. Anyhow, actuated throughout the greater part of her life by what Borrow calls pure brimstoneness of disposition, she delighted in doing one an injustice.

In due course, and in my absence at Aunt Dorothy's, a second report was submitted by the school authorities, endorsing the award of this prize in geography. The Colonel was an octogenarian before he volunteered the confession that our Irish grandmother had instigated his action in this matter, and that he was heartily ashamed of his participation in it. That the authorities had been approached in some connection or other at this time, I was aware, of course. How, otherwise, could it be explained that one day I accidentally found on the study mantelpiece a duplicate report, together with a covering letter referring to my paltry award?

*   *   *   *   *   *   *

Grandparents in those days were regarded with unqualified veneration, solely because they were grandparents. They might have been the very worst characters in the world, as many of them, doubtless, were. Nevertheless, they received obeisance. Often, as a matter of course, one paid to them a meaningless deference, though I would not have you deduce from this remark that I necessarily approve the cavalier way in which the youth of today treats parents and elders. No doubt, I myself reviewed the wily Elizabeth in the most favourable light when first she came in our midst; and I well recall how younger members of the family were able to sustain for her some degree of love and admiration until eventually they, too, had cause to fear her. As the eldest, I was the first to see through her, the first to experience the full blast of her evildoing. She was scarcely a month among us before she had contrived, by well-planned scheming, to make me suffer too much at a time when the Colonel's strong hands were already more than my framework and super-sensitive nervous system could bear.

In years more tolerable, I have oftentimes wondered how the Colonel was so long in discovering that she was the evil genius of the home. Had he not been so obsessed by his Gaelic interests, he might have 'rumbled' her sooner. It is true, however, that she was not very long with us before we could hear him soliloquising in his study. "There are mothers-in-law *and* mothers-in-law. But SUCH a mother-in-law!" Small wonder, he used to add, that he had found his wife so utterly impossible. "What sort of wife could one expect to find in the daughter of SUCH a mother-in-law?"

Soon Granny herself took to hearing fragments of these uncomplimentary monologues. She would eavesdrop at the study door on the chance of catching the less audible passages, or stop suddenly when tripping along the lobby, assuming the attitude one sees on a cat when she detects, in the garden, a rustling among fallen leaves.

As her visit dragged on, so did family drama. Latterly, her threatening to leave us—leave us *in the lurch*, as she hoped—was so persistent that we paid no attention to it. We soon accustomed ourselves to this habit of hers, realising that she had no intention whatsoever of going. She had enough sense to know that neither of her daughters wanted her, and that she had better remain where she was. As for her son, well, she appears to have abandoned him when he was but a child, with the result that, when he died a few years ago, I, who would otherwise have been his heir, inherited neither his landed estate, nor the six figures of cold cash he left.

When the Colonel, heartily tired of her continual threats to desert us, tried to persuade her to leave, she dug her heels into the carpet, and refused to budge an inch. "What? Leave my dear grandchildren with a madman like you?" she would ask. "What *would* people think?" A Roland for his Oliver, you must admit! Her determination to hang on after a fine scene with the Colonel, and neither speaking a syllable to the other for a week or more, made us children doubt the veracity of all her grandiose stories about the house by the sea at Southwold. How could any sane person, with such a fine house to fall back upon, tolerate the atmosphere in which she now lived? And once, when feigning preparations to quit, she dragged one of her trunks out of her bedroom in dramatic fashion (I can see those scratches on the waxcloth yet!) and left it lying across the front door, inside, the more to convince us that she was really going *this* time. When the Colonel returned in the dusk from his constitutional, he went a-sprawling over the trunk. He was furious. I can hear his language now, as plainly as I visualise those scratches on the waxcloth by Granny's bedroom door! On picking himself up, and in the hope of ensuring that she would really depart, he pulled the offending receptacle outside, and banged the front door on it. But again the wretched Elizabeth had no intention of leaving. She was far too comfortable with us, despite all these scenes and bickerings. 'Despite' is hardly the correct word here, however, since she *throve* on discontent. It was as essential to her existence as are peace and harmony to reasonable people. To my immense disappointment, she was abroad in the small hours, surreptitiously dragging her trunk back into the house, a fraction of an inch at a time. Disturbed by her creeping about, I rose stealthily to witness this drama, while the rest of the household slumbered. There she was, the wicked witch, tugging away at her trunk by the light of a candle placed on the floor just inside the doorway, flickering in the dark draught of night.

Henceforward, there was as much direct intercourse between the Colonel and his mother-in-law as existed between the Pythia at Delphi and the servants who swept out the temple. Where we children were concerned, the wily one became increasingly captious, affecting to take offence at the merest peccadillo. Frequently hereafter we heard father, as he recapitulated life's misfortunes in the sombre solitude of his study, repeat the Gaelic proverb giving expression to the tradition that Saint Columba would not suffer to remain on his Isle of Iona either a woman or a cow:

> *Far am bi bo, bithidh bean;*
> *'S far am bi bean, bithidh mallachadh.*
>
> *Where there's a cow, a woman will be;*
> *And where there's a woman, there will be mischief.*

These lines are usually quoted in a good-natured way, as applicable to the entire womankind. But not so when the Colonel resorted to them. He, on the contrary, found relief in taking them literally. Whereas there was no cow at hand to stimulate his recalling them, the most transient thought of Mabel, or the slightest irritation attributable to the wily Elizabeth, was more than enough to carry them to utterance, with very special emphasis on the latter line. "'*S far am bi bean, bithidh mallachadh!*" he would snarl. The truth of this, he maintained, he had experienced all too poignantly soon after he married Mabel; and now he was to realise it again, with undiminished bitterness, while his mother-in-law, a creature eminently proficient in all the cardinal vices, remained, importunately, under his roof.

*   *   *   *   *   *   *

Granny's conception of what constituted honour was well below par, as the following incident illustrates. At one end of the family sideboard there lay an old despatch-box which the Colonel had used on various missions in the East, and of which he was very proud. It had been with him in all sorts of queer predicaments. As related in one of his own books, a robber in Calcutta managed to break it open, and decamp with its contents. The despatch-box, battered and abandoned, was afterwards recovered by the Indian police, and restored to its owner, who had it repaired and again brought into service. It still bears the marks of the instruments employed on it by—

> "*a low thief of Calcutta,*
> *Who saw a man open and shut a*
> *Rich cash-box, and said*
> *To himself 'I'll be dead,*
> *If I don't steal the swag from the gudda'.*"[1]

In this trophy (for as such one might have been entitled to regard it) the Colonel kept his very private papers, some precious relics of oriental origin, a few rubies from Burma, chunks of silver ore from the mines of Mexico, and of gold from mines he had visited in South Africa and Australia, a service revolver and cartridges, a Gurkha kukri complete with sheath, and so on. It also contained, I remember, a huge bag of foreign coins and tokens he had collected in every part of the globe at a time when he had a notion for numismatics. Some of these had been handed to him during his travels by interesting people, such as the King of Siam and the Sultan of Johore. We children often wished in later years that each coin in this ponderous linen bag had been worth its weight in gold. There were so many of them that an equivalent number of sovereigns would have made possible many a venture upon which the family never had sufficient money to embark. The Colonel's entire resources, as you will have gathered from the companion volumes to the present one, were being devoted, in good Scots style, to his children's education.

Now, among the papers hid in the despatch-box from the eyes of mankind were all manner of weird passports granted to the

---

[1] Anglo-Indian for a gowk—literally, a moke, in Hindustani.

Colonel by various rulers and governments, in order to enable him to complete his journeyings into and out of many of the remotest corners of the world. And there was also a letter from the Prime Minister, informing him that a grant had been made from the Treasury for his literary contributions to the Gaelic language. We children noticed that our postmen became excessively deferential after the news had gone abroad that one of them had delivered at Colonel MacGregor's house a letter bearing, in big black letters in the bottom lefthand corner of the envelope, the words, PRIME MINISTER. Nowadays prime ministers are responsible for so many letters of one kind of another that no one pays very much attention to them. However, at the time of which I write, a communication from so important a personage was regarded as sacrosanct.

As children, we were never permitted to know what this particular letter was about. The Colonel disclosed the nature of it not even to his closest friends; and, knowing the petty jealousies stirring the hearts of his Gaelic-speaking acquaintances, it was not the least likely he would discuss it with *them*, or in any way advertise the Prime Minister's estimate of his contribution to the Gaelic cause. But one day our scheming grandmother, bent on discovering why her son-in-law had received this imposing document, and had not as much as mentioned to her his receipt of it, bribed me with two copper coins of the realm to procure for her the despatch-box key. (Oh, she was an evil woman, that maternal grandparent of ours!) For the ridiculous sum of twopence, paid in advance, I pledged my coöperation, and pawned my honour. Somehow or other, I obtained brief possession of the key. At this interval of time, I cannot recall precisely how. Dishonestly, I do admit. I stood by, while the wily Elizabeth opened the despatch-box, and extracted the letter from the P.M.; and I remember she was just completing her perusal of it when we heard, on the threshold, the Colonel's footfall. He had returned from his evening walk a few seconds earlier than usual. Granny became flustered, while I, her accomplice in this mean and temerarious act, kept my head. Replacing the letter and hurriedly tidying the contents of this iron repository, I locked it inaudibly, withdrew the key, assumed that air of calm and confidence said to be the specialty of hardened and habitual criminals, and quietly began to think out some means of getting the key back to where it ought to have been. No sooner had I succeeded in the final ordeal than Granny demanded the return of her twopence: I had failed to *remove* the letter, as I was now to learn had been her original design. Apparently, I had misunderstood the real purport of our nefarious collusion—the *conditio sine qua non*, so far as these paltry coppers were concerned. My reminding her of the precise terms of the letter (I had been looking over her shoulder as she studied it) in no way satisfied her. She wanted the letter in its entirety. She also wanted the return of her twopence, which by this time I had spent.

"What did the letter say about a grant?"

"It said, Granny, that a payment would be made in the course of the next few days."

It had always been this evil woman's habit to receive the postman when he called. The maids were strictly forbidden to answer the door when the ringing of the door-bell was followed by that deep, resounding warning issued by Edinburgh's postmen in the execution of their duties. *"Po-o-o-o-st!"* they call in garden, or in the well of tenement stair, as they approach with letters. On the pretext that letters were too important commodities to be entrusted to maids, who might be careless with them, or absent-minded, Granny was always afoot before the first delivery o' mornings. She liked to examine everyone's correspondence. But, spite her vigilance, some days later there passed into the Colonel's hands, unbeknown to her, a second letter from the P.M. Constantly threatened by her for the return of her quite modest bribe, and by this time tempted to turn king's evidence rather than continue in any collaboration of so dishonest and risky a nature, *I* managed to answer the postman's call when he brought the second letter. It happened to be about 10 p.m., on one of the very few evenings on which the wily Elizabeth ever went to the pictures. And it was some secret satisfaction to me to know that, thrice daily, she continued on the *qui vive* for a document already reposing in the old despatch-box.

On my return from war in 1919, by which time our Irish grandmother was well dead and buried, I confessed to the Colonel my complicity in this shabby business. It so affected him that, a day or two later, *he* felt constrained to clear up another unhappy matter, and had to endure a somewhat startling admission on my part.

With this prelude, then, we come more particularly to the incident inspiring those withering words with which this chapter opens.

CHAPTER IX

THE POLICE IS CALLED IN

NOW TO a juvenile malfeasance of mine in which, as *agents provocateurs*, the Colonel and this Irish harridan conspired.

When the former came in from his walks, it was his wont to discard his outdoor jacket for an old smoking one he wore in the house. On my return from school one afternoon, I accidentally brushed against the outdoor garment, as it hung in its customary place behind his bedroom door, and, in so doing, heard the joyous jingle of coin of the realm. I now shook the jacket a little, so as to locate the more precisely whence issued this inviting sound. In an external card-pocket concealed by a width of belt (the jacket was of the Norfolk variety) I found several coppers, to one or two of which I was tempted to help myself. Now, the curious thing about the little pocket was that, like the widow's cruse of oil, it seemed inexhaustible. The more coppers I took from it, the more did they increase in number, until one day the pocket contained money to the value of half-a-crown or thereabouts. By this time my furacious fingers had formed the habit of abstracting a modest percentage of what they found there. Once or twice weekly, then, I conducted my raid behind the bedroom door. In this wise, and never suspecting, I sustained myself in petty cash for some little time. It was, indeed, my sole source of revenue; and it almost appeared as though the Colonel were placing money there for my exclusive benefit, the way that brownies and faeries do nice things for people in the Highlands, never permitting themselves to be seen in the performance of their beneficences.

However, on my coming in from school one day, father followed me into the drawingroom to inform me, in portentous tones, that I was not to go out: a policeman was calling to interview me. My heart all but died within me, for I was overcome by an instant presension. My temples poured with perspiration. So unnerved was I that *"mes genoux se dérobent sous moi"*—my knees undressed themselves under me, to use Cagliostro's words when the Parisian crowd assembled about his apartment to congratulate him on the acquittal of the Cardinal de Rohan. In a state of collapse, I flopped on the sofa, a mass of moaning misery. Presently, a heavy footfall was heard approaching our front door, and the bell tolled ominously. In stepped Constable Fiddes—the dreaded Ginger—one of the more fear-inspiring of the policemen on our Bruntsfield-Morningside beat. I had a glimpse of him from the sofa of my desolation, as he passed with measured stride through the hall, toward the Colonel's study, deferentially carrying his helmet under an arm akimbo. He was being ushered in by the mischievous Elizabeth with her unshakable aplomb. Aye, and with a good hearty smack of sadistic satisfaction, one might add. Without loss of time, a private session was in conference in that study. Meanwhile, I writhed on the sofa in mental agony, a prisoner who could have escaped, but did not quite know where to escape to, aware that, sooner or later, hunger and cold would have compelled him to give himself up, either to the police or to the Colonel. I would not care to hazard an estimate of how long I suffered in this situation. It seemed a very long time, indeed, before anyone did anything. The suspense was too frightful. It enabled me at an early age to realise something of what the condemned endure while waiting to be killed professionally.

Suddenly the door of the study was opened, and a word of command summoned me to compear, in true Scots fashion, before this august tribunal. Trembling from head to toe, I entered, and was duly arraigned. The charge against me was one of organised and persistent theft, one of flagitious conduct that only a long term of imprisonment could expiate. "Great God in Heaven!" exclaimed the Colonel, by way of contributing to the situation his usual touch of melodrama.

I was not asked whether I pleaded guilty, or had anything I would like to say in mitigation. Any such formality was denied me. My guilt was taken for granted. I had entered by the wide gate, and travelled far along the broad way leading to destruction; and no mercy was to be shown me.

Turning to Ginger, the Colonel now delivered himself as premeditated. "Take him with you, constable! Take him with you! Ah, God! That I should have married his mother, and been cursed with a son who is no better than a common thief! That a son of mine, bearing the tried and trusted name of MacGregor, should bring such disgrace upon the Old Name! Take him with you, and have him sentenced and imprisoned!" I broke down in convulsive sobs.

75

"None of your crocodile tears!" my father demanded. "You have chosen the highroad to perdition. You're going to—PRISON!!"

I now had visions of my being led, manacled, through the douce streets of Edinburgh, under police escort, on my way to the Central Police Station in the High Street. There I would be formally charged, and spend the night in a cell, preparatory to court proceedings the following morning. O, that the darkness would fall, so that I might be transferred unnoticed!

By way of intensifying my terror, Ginger, acting in perfect concert with my father and grandmother (he had rehearsed his part with the wily Elizabeth that forenoon), began fumbling for his baton, though, why he should have required the assistance of so formidable a weapon in the apprehension and removal of a helpless schoolboy, no one explained. With exaggerated motions, this awesome weapon was now brought to light.

"Take him with you!" the Colonel again commanded, whereupon Ginger seized me by the shoulder with one of his big horny hands, at the same time dangling his baton over my head with the other.

"Well, constable, shall we give him another chance?"

"Whatever you think, sir," answered the accommodating Ginger, temporarily releasing his grip of me.

"Ah, no!" the Colonel uttered in fulminating tones, recanting at the suggestion of any weakness or indecision on his part. "Prison is the only place for a boy who pilfers from his father."

With a good thud, Ginger's arresting hand returned to my shoulder. Again and again this pretence at forgiveness was repeated: again and again I suffered release and re-arrest.

Then came the next stage agreed upon by these self-ordained inquisitors: Ginger now proceeded to make a jingling sound with something secreted in his hip-pocket. By slow degrees he produced a pair of handcuffs. As he feigned to affix these to my wrists, I uttered to God my *de profundis*, and swooned. Standing over me when I resumed consciousness were the three accomplices in this piece of devilish cruelty.

"Constable," I seemed to hear my father say, for the last time, "do you think we might give him just one more chance?"

In a state of collapse and dissolution, I was granted my final release. A few minutes afterwards, Ginger was pursuing his beat, while my father returned to his pipe in the study, where he continued to emit noises of despair. He had been cursed with a son who was a pilferer, as well as a dunce. Such unpardonable peccancy, if it were inherited, as he firmly suspected, could be laid nowhere but to Mabel's side of the house. This, verily, is what came of his having married so unworthy a woman. What better could be expected of her son?

And what of the impenitent Elizabeth? I was not long in discovering where *she* betook herself after my ordeal. She had gone out to poison against me some friends living near at hand, who hitherto had been quite fond of me—to warn them against me, as I afterwards learnt. She smutched my waning character right royally. The mother of that particular family, then a woman well over sixty, never spoke to me again, though for fifteen years thereafter I continued to visit that selfsame house once or twice weekly, except during my absence at the war. Yet, this queer lady, now so prejudiced against me that she never entered any room of her own home in which I happened to be with other members of her family, despatched a parcel to me every week I was on the Western Front, and even sent provisions to me at the military hospital in which I eventually found myself. All this gave me reason to suppose that she had forgiven me for any delinquency of which the wretched Elizabeth had told her, and would be her generous self when the war was over, and I returned to take up my life again within a few hundred yards of her. But not a bit of it. Whether through a sense of pride, or because her remission did not carry her as far, she never spoke to me again, and would cross the street to avoid me.

For a year or two thereafter, I was so ashamed of my offence that, rather than encounter Constable Fiddes, afoot in the execution of his duties, I would make tremendous detours through the city. No doubt, you have heard of people preferring to run the proverbial mile sooner than undertake something they dislike. I marathoned many a *statutory* one, rather than be seen by the vigilant Fiddes!

*   *   *   *   *   *   *

Henceforth, so far as Granny was concerned, I opposed her on every possible occasion, and mooned about the house with murderous intent. In what moment of inexcusable recklessness, I asked myself, did Nature permit the conception and birth of so unmitigated a jade. But it was not long before the Colonel

77

himself began to adopt toward her a somewhat similar attitude. Indeed, toward the close of her reign in Scotland, his hatred of her was so intense that he might have been a Kaffir required by tribal custom to be ashamed of his mother-in-law, and to spend the remainder of his life in avoiding her. He was now to find it a source of relief to allude to her as *'ave it wen it's 'ot*, for, although she spoke beautifully and (so long as her tongue could keep away from the acidulous) pleasingly, he enjoyed the delusion that she dropped her h's. It is possible, of course, that, like so many of her generation, she may have imagined that only the unlettered sounded the initial h in words derived from the French, and that it was therefore correct to speak of 'otel, 'ospital, and 'umour, and to insist, on the other hand, that, if one said *h*otel, one should also say *h*onest!

There was just one occasion, I believe, when father and Granny were involved in a squabble royal, and the latter did drop one h in her rage and excitement. Ever after, the Colonel branded her as an illiterate, as more Cockney than Irish, as someone whose origin was the slums of the East End of London. You will have observed it was his delight to assign to anyone meriting his displeasure all and every contemptible attribute, however little deserved. The subject of his antipathy must have, in the superlative degree, every fault of origin, of taste, every baseness of character. Those who knew Granny loved to hear her converse. They enjoyed the idiomatic niceties flavouring her delivery, little aware what potentiality for mischief lay behind her plausible tongue and comely exterior.

The Colonel now liked to imagine, too, that she imbibed secretly in her bedroom. How else, he used to ask himself, could her behaviour so resemble that of the Maenads of antiquity. He was positive that at times she became frenzied in the worship of Dionysus, though, to give this inveterate devil her due, I must add that no member of the household ever saw anything suggestive of crapulous habits, or even smelt the faintest whiff of alcohol. Anyhow, father derived no negligible satisfaction from his belief that he had diagnosed at least part of her trouble. At this time, as you will have gathered, there was nothing too incriminating for the one to say, however unjustifiably, about the other.

Granny was what is known as a *bad* Catholic, he was constantly reminding us. "It seems very extraordinary that she has been to Mass only once since she cast herself upon us some years ago.

It's all very odd to me," he would say. Had she been a *good*
Catholic, he often remarked after she had departed, one might
have been able to cope with her. "But such a renegade! Such an
apostate! And *I* married her daughter! Ah, God! What is this
blight that has come over my life?"

In our Calvinist household, we tended to regard the befalling
of illness or misfortune as God's way of getting His own back,
as one puts it in vulgar phraseology. So, when the wicked Elizabeth fell ill with erysipelas, and was hurried off in blankets by
ambulance to the fever hospital at Colinton Mains, it occurred to
me that this was definite proof that the Lord's hand was extended
to her in chastisement. This salutary manifestation of His displeasure I found very gratifying indeed, very satisfying. And I
cannot confess to having experienced the slightest twinge of
charitable commiseration for her, all the weeks she was absent,
nor even a particle of welcome when she returned. In any event,
she was scarcely back in the managerial saddle before she
reverted to her schemings.

*   *   *   *   *   *   *

Among the mails at Poperinghe, awaiting those of us who survived the Battle of Menin Road in 1917, was a letter from Mabel,
informing me that Granny had died, and that, in remorse on her
deathbed, she had repeatedly asked for me. News of her translation
was the best piece of intelligence I ever received at 'the front'. I
always feared that, if I should be so fortunate as to return from the
war, I, at the height of my turbulence, might have laid myself open
to a charge of manslaughter, so much did her cruelties and
injustices rankle. Death intervened. On learning that she was
gone, I tossed my 'tin hat' in the air in jubilation, and sent my
father a brief postcard congratulating him on his having outlived
her. How odd that I should have been killing Germans, 'somewhere in France' as we used to say, while there lay upon her
deathbed the woman who, as troops headed by a pipe-band
passed within sight of our drawingroom windows, on their way
to war, habitually taunted me, then a boy of sixteen, with
cowardice. "*You'll* never be man enough to go and fight!"
she would hurl at me, as she drew back the curtains on hearing
the strains of the pipes. As if the desire to fight and kill were
evidence of manliness!

When I rejoined the Colonel in Auld Reekie shortly after the

cessation of hostilities, one of the first things he did was to confess
to me his shame for the part he had played in that episode, so
many years before. My absence in the trenches had given him
time for sober reflection. He told me that Granny had put him
up to replenishing the supply of coppers, day by day. It had never
occurred to him that, by deliberately purveying temptation in this
way, he was aiding and abetting.

I now asked him how a man of his experience should have seen
fit to employ so drastic a method of dealing with a pilfering schoolboy. "But did it never occur to you, father, that, had you said to
me 'Look here, Alasdair! I know you are taking my pennies; and I
know you won't want to deny it. I would be so much happier if you
came and asked for one or two now and again,' it would have cured
me instantly? Surely you realise that the scheme you adopted is
the sort of thing that precipitates people into habitual crime!"

A few moments' silence followed.

"Is there anything else you would like to say, father, about that
unhappy delinquency of mine, now that you have brought it up?
How did you decide upon so senseless a plot?"

"The idea was that wretched woman's, your grandmother's,"
he replied. "We thought it would cure you."

"Cure a creature like me by resorting to anything so devilish?
. . . And were you satisfied afterwards that, by being accessory
in this way, you *had* cured me?"

To this the Colonel ventured no answer.

"Well, father," I concluded, "*I* have a rather unpleasant
counter-confession to make. Far from having cured me, you so
embittered me that I left your coppers entirely alone, and, for
some months thereafter, concentrated on your silver, and was
never found out. *That is my counter-confession.* . . . You see,
father, as Mark Twain observed, it is the simplest thing in the
world to control a boy. All you have to do is to call out the
militia, or summon a formidable member of the police force."

It was within my competency to have said much more. But I
could see that the Colonel was already confounded by this
dénouement. Indeed, for a moment or two, I thought he had had a
cataleptic seizure. Never before had I known him so motionless,
so inarticulate. He seemed incapable of comment; and neither of
us, during the remaining fourteen years of his life, alluded to the
incident again. This was the first occasion in our lives that there
seemed any likelihood of our ever understanding one another.

James Horne, Esq., M.A.
("Johnnie Horne" to Watsonians the world over)

Edinburgh Waverley. The western exit from the Waverley Station, as seen from the Mound, with the Waverley Bridge in the middle-distance, the North Bridge in the

CHAPTER X

THE BURGH POLICE COURT

I WONDER whether the incident I have just related instilled in me, in my early youth, a morbid and unwholesome interest in police matters! I do believe that, after my ordeal with Ginger, I derived some perverted satisfaction from hearing about, and even witnessing, the agonies suffered by others at the hands of the police. The pettiest of offences now engaged my attention in a way hitherto unknown to me. When the youths of the neighbourhood observed or smelt a lum on fire, I now shared with them that elementary excitement reaching its climax when the policeman arrived on the scene and, in the execution of his duties, strove to look as formidable as possible. So well do I remember our constables, perhaps suspecting some trifling misdemeanour as they passed by on their beat, trying to look as terrifying as they could! They reminded one of the stories told of the old Town Guard, members of which, for the most part, were Highlanders, selected because it was held that their uncouth mien filled with fear and awe the hearts of potential evildoers. In our youth, we believed a police constable was vested with summary powers to convict and fine, on the spot, the tenant responsible for the offending chimney. Auld Reekie's schoolboy population enjoyed the notion that he was entitled to extract, on the doorstep, half-a-crown for the first offence, five shillings for the second, and the statutory maximum of ten shillings for the third. On the fourth (so, at any rate, we imagined) he straightway marched the negligent housewife off to the High Street, where she lay in durance vile, until her husband arrived to bail her out. What happened to defenceless widows and spinsters in such straits, we never discovered. We assumed they had to thole their detention, and perhaps received some little compensatory treatment when they appeared before the bailie in the morning. We liked to hang about, therefore, on the chance that the fumigating offence the constable was investigating was the *fourth*. When the chimney ablaze was one of several huddled together at the top of some lofty tenement, and wreathed everything around it in

G
81

rolling fumes, he often had difficulty in finding the appropriate common-stair leading to the house to which the chimney belonged. Even then, he might have to use his sense of smell, and ring doorbell after doorbell, in his endeavour to locate the citizen guilty of infringing one of the city's statutes, and to collect, on behalf of the Watching and Lighting Committee, as we supposed, the statutory number of half-crowns, or to apprehend in the case of a fourth offence. Data as to when last this chimney or that had been on fire, and how frequently during the current tenancy, we believed he obtained by consulting the very special notebook he carried. We often saw him stop for a few moments in his circuit to enter in that black, ominous document notes we feared might one day be used in evidence against ourselves! I must say I derived no small pleasure in shadowing him as he hurried from one part of a tenement to another, in search of the culprit. At night-time, of course, the importunate chimney was more difficult to find, especially if, by the time the constable arrived on the scene, flames were no longer shooting from it. And this explains why some of Auld Reekie's more wily housewives waited until after dark before setting their sooty lums alight, thus dispensing with the service of the sweep.

* * * * * * *

By this time, the Colonel's gloomy picture of penury at the Scottish bar, and the absence of that influence at "the mart of Scandal", as Glenalmond described the Parliament House of Edinburgh in *Weir of Hermiston*—that influence without which success, in the commercial and conventional sense, is long deferred, if ever achieved—undermined my youthful ambition to tread it in wig and gown. So I now transferred my interest to the Burgh Police Court, near at hand, where I began to imagine myself one day in the rôle of burgh prosecutor, pursuing my duties *ad vindictam publicam*. Many a Saturday morning, after family-worship, you might have found me there, confidently and comfortably seated near the front to witness, at as close quarters as was possible, a sorry array from Auld Reekie's slums and underworld, charged with petty impropriation, with assault and battery, with manifold brawlings. How often must I have heard the clerk of court, in his capacity as legal assessor, charge some wretch in custody with having beaten, struck, kicked, or stabbed his neighbour *to the effusion of blood*! Those concluding words, uttered in curdling tones a score of times in this court-room of a Saturday morning, when wage-earners, paid the previous evening, went a-spree, were almost as dramatic as the pronouncement, *remitted to the sheriff*, when there came before the bailie a case too serious for trial and sentence by him. Under the Summary Juris-diction (Scotland) Act of 1908, if the assault be by stabbing, the case goes to the sheriff, automatically. "Remitted to the sheriff for trial" was a decision the more self-important of our bailies intimated with that gravity one associates with the black-cap.

But the time to see our Burgh Court in full sail was on a Monday morning, consequent upon the traditional insobriety of the Scottish Saturday Night, which, in the matter of orgy, often out-rivalled the drunken disorder at the Tron Kirk on Hogmanay. The Scots, as you know, believe in doing things well. Their penchant for thoroughness, in whatever sphere of existence they may find them-selves, is notorious. It follows, then, that the Old Year must be banished from the realm with the same abandon as that with which the New is ushered in. Many Scotsmen still think that they should 'celebrate', even to excess, in this way. In their view, 'A Guid New Year' can only be toasted traditionally, which means in the Best Scotch! With *Auld Lang Syne* on lips, and a generous dose of the native beverage in stomach and brain, they stagger and sway through the Old Town in noisy and fractious groups, often pressing upon complete strangers a dram from the bottle they carry, often steering an unsteady course, bumping into lamp-posts and pillar-boxes, to which they either bow and apologise profusely, or address remarks challenging the inanimate to fisticuffs.

Many a sore and even broken head lay in custody over the week-end in Auld Reekie's cells, provided thus with a measure of comfort, and ample time for sober reflection. Is it not distressing to think of the High Street, with its time-worn memorials in stone, testi-monials to an ancient splendour, being the breeding-place of so much proletarian squalor, upon which the new aristocracy of alcohol thrives so largely? See these environs, these hovels, on a Saturday night, and it will give you a pain at the heart for Auld Scotland. Why should so many degenerate and decay, lying in utter wretchedness and stupor on mouldering doorsteps, beneath fading coats-of-arms? I had seen drunkenness galore in the Highlands before the Colonel brought us south, since the Highlander has won for himself, with the bottle, a reputation as unsurpassed as it is unenviable. But in the Cowgate and the Canongate of Edinburgh, in the West Port and the Lawnmarket, I was now to see it in a concentrated form that staggered me at the outset of my Lowland pilgrimage.

However, I would not have you harbour the impression that everyone in Scotland drinks to excess, since that would be a monstrous libel. Nevertheless, we must acknowledge the unpleasant truth that a considerable section of our population, both rural and urban, is habitually addicted, and that we are, probably, the most drunken nation in the world.

Often on a Monday morning, then, I might have been seen slipping past burly and robustious police-officers to what had now become my wonted place on one of those hard public benches, under the bailie's eye, well in the centre of this accumulation of misery. What with black eyes, bashed faces, and a surfeit of bruises and bandages, it was a melancholy assembly, to be sure. And such an array of victims, some of them emboldened and brazen through repeated appearances, others abashed and timorous, on their first trial, the women-folk usually shawled and slatternly, more downcast than the men! Despite such hygienic precautions as ventilation allowed, the atmosphere of the court-room was often musty, fusty, and frowsty, charged with the smell of stale medicaments, and with those fetid odours one associates with dirt and poverty, with human degradation and misery, so much of which, I do avouch, was directly attributable to whisky, Scotland's most accursed product. Whisky, consumed *more Scottico*,[1] explains much of our trouble north of the Tweed. On Saturday nights the Scots are fervent worshippers of Bacchus, attending in vast droves those temples of his, occupying the most prominent and accessible sites in the poorer parts of every town and village. Wellnigh drowned in Lethean stupor, they come to their senses on the Sunday morning to find themselves immured.

While on the topic of insobriety, one recalls the classic reputation for orgies won by Dawney Douglas's, a tavern that stood of old in a dingy close off Edinburgh's High Street. Dawney's was a place of dark profundity; and, in reflecting on him and his time, one remembers the occasion when a wag, solicitous for his betterment, lent him one of Clarendon's large historical volumes. Each day, on visiting the tavern, he surreptitiously put Dawney's bookmark back to the same place. After he had been doing this for several

---

[1] *i.e.* 'neat'.

months, he enquired of Dawney how he was getting on with Clarendon. "Verra weel," Dawney replied; "but, man, dinna ye think it's gey muckle the same thing ower an' ower again?"

*   *   *   *   *   *   *

After drunkenness and offences arising therefrom, the commonest category concerned petty theft. Some old and drooping hag would come shauchling in by the side-door and make her way, unassisted, undirected by the court's uniformed officials, to the same spot, and face the bailie. She had been brought to these premises so often on one charge or another, during her long and wayward life, that she was more than familiar with its procedure. With a listless sag denoting indifference to whatever punishment awaited her, she usually pleaded guilty. There was no sense in her doing anything else. Her record was there, before the court, after her plea. She admitted the vast number of similar convictions. She was a habitual visitant.

"D'ye want tae say onything?" the bailie would ask her, swithering whether he should just sentence her, as aforetime, or invoke the services of the court missionary. Sometimes she wagged her head and remained silent: sometimes she embarked on explanations as prolix as they were implausible. "Guid gracious me!" the bailie might continue in the dialect they both understood. "Ye've telt us a' that afore—ay, a hunner times. Ha'e ye naethin' else tae say?"

She made her exit by the side-door through which she had entered. She was on her way back to the cell, wherefrom, in the course of the forenoon, she would be conveyed to prison by motorcar. I have witnessed old and broken people disappear through that selfsame door after more than their hundredth conviction; and through my mind has surged that sentiment expressed admirably by Montaigne, and frequently quoted by the Colonel from his armchair, when reading in the evening paper of some criminal's unsocial conduct: "There is no man so good, who, were he to submit his thoughts and actions to the laws, would not deserve hanging ten times in his life."

What interested me as much as anything in this Burgh Police Court was the benchful of apprentice journalists constituting 'the press'. There they sat, representing Auld Reekie's three daily newspapers, looking so very young and irresponsible, for all their efforts to appear adult and important, enthusiasm and a knowledge of shorthand their principal qualifications. They were starting their careers by attending this sordid chamber six forenoons a week, enjoined by their respective employers to seize upon any printable details of our city's criminals and their crimes. To the most imposing of these reporters a pimply messenger was attached. Every now and again, during the hearing of a case more protracted than usual, transcribed notes on the proceedings would be borne away by him to this news-editor or to that, keeping him informed on the most trivial details and developments. Such terrific urgency about so little! No wonder our values get ridiculously out of perspective, and we find so little time to examine those expressions of modern society that render some major calamity inevitable every fifteen or twenty years!

If I strained my ears to hear the charge, or those passages in the evidence which the witness hesitated to utter audibly in public, I strained them even more when the clerk of court stood on a chair engraved with civic emblems to whisper a word of direction in the bailie's ear, guiding him on legal technicalities, lest he should commit some monstrous blunder, such as that of passing sentence of fine or imprisonment in excess of the statutory scale. "Forty bob or fourteen days!" the bailie would announce, as if entirely off his own bat, adding in an admonitory way, and now quite irregularly, "An', mind ye, dinna let me see ye here again, for ye'll no' get aff as easy next time, mind ye!"[1]

Ah! how well one remembers the plush chair upon which the bailie sat, and the city's motto picked out in gilt lettering, as if in the nature of a scriptural mandate for these sordid proceedings. *Nisi Dominus, Frustra*: Except the Lord [keep the city, the watchman waketh but] in vain.

In 1914 some easement was granted the offender in the matter of time in which to raise the fine. "D'ye want time tae pay?" the clerk, equally fluent in the vernacular as in English, might ask in special cases. But, as often as not, the person convicted plunged his fist deep into his trousers pocket, extracted all his wealth in coin, counted out the fine in a measure as deliberate as it was metallic, handed it over to a police-officer standing by to receive it, and made his exit as emphatic as his footgear would allow.

In the dock by this time another delinquent had taken his place,

[1] Nowadays, when, despite such a warning, an offender comes back and gets a heavier sentence, the conviction can be quashed on the grounds of such previously expressed prejudice.

confronting the bench with woeful sag while the charge against her was being read.

"Plead guilty or not guilty?" the clerk would enquire.

"Not guilty!"

"Clear the court!" might now resound, in tones of executive efficiency, while the police uncovered much minor waywardness which was but the superficial symptom of all the worst of life's tragedies. Then followed an immediate and momentary bustle, as this peremptory instruction was being acted upon. Officials now proceeded to turn out the curious who, like myself, were dilatory in quitting. In the dock there now stood a demirep, either a very painted and haughty one, or an equally slovenly and humiliated one. Detected members of this sisterhood were usually extremely gay or extremely sordid. The charge was then read—"importuning for the purpose of prostitution", or perhaps keeping a house of ill-fame. One or two of our plain-clothes men had shadowed some trollop accosting seamen coming up Leith Street from dockland, or had visited certain suspected premises in the guise of clients. And there they were, ready to rattle off the oath in the witness-box, perhaps more callous then than now in their determination to secure a conviction. With requisite confidence, each stepped up into the box in turn. Having delivered himself of the oath, he now read, from his notebook, particulars admissible as evidence. I cannot say that, even as a dull-witted Watsonian,[1] I felt altogether happy about our legal ways of securing conviction, any more than I did about the accused marched in for the umpteenth time, and as often marched out again, freed if he could pay something by way of fine, committed if he could not. I was still very much in my nonage when I realised how our prisons remain full of poor people who cannot find the money that saves their wealthier brethren in crime from sharing with them this penal accommodation, which His Gracious Majesty provides so freely and abundantly for the penurious.

[1] Not necessarily a case of *post hoc, ergo propter hoc*, as my friend, the Secretary to the Merchant Company, would point out.

CHAPTER XI

THE TERRACE

A FEW years ago, publicity was given to the exploits of two Reading boys, fired with the ambition to go to Scotland on a hunting expedition, a country they pictured as untamed and barbarous. For this adventure they had saved a little money. Unbeknown to their parents, they set out for the Caledonia of the history-books. Early one morning a policeman found them wandering disconsolately in the residential area of Stirling, more than four hundred miles from home. They were armed with a couple of air-guns, and accompanied by a young Alsatian. When interrogated, they explained that they had come from Reading, and that they were "terribly disappointed with Scotland". The northern kingdom was not the least like what they had expected to find. They had hoped to discover a cave, in which to spend their nights, and from which they might have issued forth, in primitive style, on hunting sorties. One of the boys had in his possession a card bearing the place-name, Muir-of-Ord. When asked as to whether he had friends there, he replied that he had not, but that he had taken the card from a case containing a stuffed eagle in a London museum. They willingly accompanied the constable to the police-office at Stirling, where food was provided for them. The Reading authorities were communicated with immediately; and by the night train the lads left stern Caledonia for home.

I relate this incident by way of preface to this chapter, because many of our first neighbours in Auld Reekie, and not a few of our schoolmates, had a similar conception of the Highlands lying beyond Inverness, and reviewed the Colonel's progeny rather as wild aborigines who had found their way south by untravelled ways, for reasons quite unknown, if not actually sinister and subversive.

As you may already have gathered, we lived in a street distinguished by the promising title of Leamington Terrace. To those who knew it intimately, it was simply Leamy. Situated on the south side of the city, it runs uphill between Gilmore Place and Bruntsfield Place. Generally speaking, everything to the south-west of Princes Street is regarded as being on the south side, in contradistinction with these older parts of Auld Reekie, which occupy the seaward slopes to the north and north-east of it.

Leamy is composed of blocks of tenements at top and bottom, on alternate sides only. Between these, for the most part, are quantities of semi-detached villas. Facing the tenements at the top, one finds some larger self-contained houses, each consisting of four storeys and a basement, in which 'the nobs' lived in our time, though, even then, these dwellings were being transformed, one by one, into boarding-houses. Nowadays, of course, one never alludes to them in a term so plebeian. Owing largely to the redistribution of economic honours and hardships arising out of the last war, these establishments rose rapidly in the social scale, so that, today, they enjoy the more exclusive title of private and residential hotels. And no mistake about it, as their large, brass nameplates advertise! By similar token, only working-class people, or the very poor, are obliged, nowadays, to take in a lodger; whereas their economic, and therefore social, superiors deal only in that species more recently added to human society, and known by the euphemism, the paying-guest. The introduction of this conventional designation, even in Auld Reekie, has tempered the wind to many a shorn lambkin, who would have perished sooner than have had it breathed that he or she ever let an apartment to anyone as commonplace as a lodger!

For the most part, our Terrace was peopled with what one would have termed the petty bourgeoisie. Not in any snobbish superiority do I mention this, but in order to assist you in arriving at an estimate of such neighbours as I essay to describe in the next chapter. They were mainly of the prim-and-proper variety. On week-days they went about their several businesses, punctilious in thought as in action. On Sundays they had a way of looking rather glum, for they seemed unaware that laughter and joyousness on that day were not necessarily incompatible with a love of God. Terrified lest they might appear the least out of step, they maintained a provincial neophobia. Most of them regarded it as socially embarrassing to have any dealings with a family as eccentric as the Colonel's. In those days, it must be remembered, matters that would be of very minor importance to many of us now, were liable to set Edinburgh agog. It needed little to disturb the ears of the ultra-respectable districts of Murrayfield and Morningside; and even the homelier hearths of Newington experienced domestic upheavals with but small provocation. A first-class scandal could be inaugurated on the slenderest presumption. Very little was required to make our douce citizens look askance. The idea of a man wishing to marry his deceased wife's sister, for instance, they deemed infinitely more heinous than if he lived with her in overt naughtiness. Indeed, we knew a case of this. A perfectly honourable professional man, well-known in Auld Reekie, who had lost his wife and was anxious to have someone to look after his infant daughter, actually entered into matrimonial relationship with his deceased wife's sister. This gross act—this flagrant indecency—was the scandalmongers' topic for several months. They all but ruined the victim of their malice. Many of his lifelong friends now declined his friendship, and even refused to receive any member of his household. It was some considerable time before the legalising of this quite reasonable nuptial accommodation was reviewed in our churchy Capital with anything but abhorrence.

If reckless scandal sometimes swept through our city, so too did flying rumour. Who has forgotten the fanciful pronouncements connected with the chocolate factory at Portobello in 1914, based solely on the fact that the owner had a German name? Guns and ammunition and signalling apparatus and all manner of imaginary nonsense were declared to have been discovered on the flat roof and in the cellars! In fact, no one doubted for a moment that the roof had been made flat purposely, in preparation for the Kaiser's war! As the Portobello tramcar passed by the front of the building, many citizens, firmly believing all this, travelled specially to view the scene of such dastardly treachery! Substantial weight was added to this canard when, with the outbreak of war, and but a stone's-throw from the factory, the military authorities dug a line of trenches and beset it with sandbags and barbed-wire entanglements, just in case the Germans might attempt invasion by way of the Portobello beach, and join up with their spying countrymen in the chocolate factory!

And what of the alarm that seized Auld Reekie when, early one morning during the last war, someone discerned a pole on the summit of Allermuir, a few miles away? A German spy at work, everyone concluded! The pole had been placed there, without a doubt, as a landmark for the enemy fleet when it might seek to enter the fortified Firth of Forth! It afterwards transpired that a hill-climbing schoolboy, *in excelsis*, had erected it the previous evening.

*　　*　　*　　*　　*　　*　　*

Between Leamy and the adjacent streets there existed a certain rivalry. This found readiest expression in the abuse the youths hurled at one another when returning from school of an afternoon. Only when freed from the restraint of the classroom did our exuberance find such outlet. If, while wandering home from school, the physical nature of our environment precluded us from following the example of the schoolboy who, as the poet tells us, picked the primrose gay, and imitated the skylark's lay, we assuredly were at liberty to pick quarrels, and to exacerbate one another with vocal imitations of a kind less ethereal.

The middle section of the Terrace enjoyed a social aloofness, inhabited, as it was, by tradespeople and their aspiring families, most of whom observed the full gamut of those social differences so precious to climbers. The heads of many of these homes were members of session in Auld Reekie's more prosperous kirks; and not a few of them were, themselves, the more prosperous in consequence. Six mornings a week, they passed by our windows on their way to business, each of them complete, in all weathers, with umbrella, top hat or bowler, gloves dangling at the trail, spats as spotless as they were perennial, tie-pin with an expensive gem glittering thereon, and moustache twirled to a T.

What these business fellows thought of one another, there was little way of knowing. Since they were turned out to pattern, we believed that, at all events to outward appearance, they liked it to be known that they were members of the same fraternity, worshippers at the same shrine, close students of the philosophy of getting on in the world. What their respective children thought of each other was much more cognisable. The jeweller's were not necessarily on speaking terms with the upholsterer's or the paper-hanger's, though they lived next door to one another, and occupied houses as identical in lay-out and in assessment as any semi-detached villas could be.

But the differentiation that went even deeper might be expressed in terms of 'the old school tie'. Auld Reekie specialised more in school caps than in school ties, however. And, since most of the boys residing in Leamy went either to Watson's or to Heriot's, there was already ample ground for social distinction. It took a Herioter a long time to be 'received' by the Watsonians of the neighbourhood. It took a Boroughmuir or a James Gillespie's boy still longer. Even pupils at Edinburgh Academy or at the Institution (the *'Stution*, as we called it, because of the difficulty those small boys in red blazers and red caps had in pronouncing the name of their school) had to serve a probationary period, if they sought friendship with us. They might have been the most estimable lads. Yet, that availed them little. If they desired to consort with the Watson's clique, they had to undergo their 'trials', like a candidate preaching before a Presbyterian congregation seeking a minister. It took some of them years to qualify; and, even after admission to our fellowship, they often remained suspect!

What matters all this now? How much more we all resemble Jock Tamson's bairns, when we look back across the years! Watson's is by no means the only Auld Reekie school that has sent its products out into the larger world, carrying with them the traditions of a great people, and the memorials of an incomparable city. And how many of the boys from its many famous schools have enhanced Scotland's reputation for scholarship and integrity!

$$* \qquad * \qquad * \qquad * \qquad * \qquad * \qquad *$$

Leamington Terrace appeared steeper in the days of my youth than it is today. Yet, how could this have been so? The houses on either side, with their abbreviated front gardens, seem to have maintained their original alignment and elevation. But it *is* so, since the halfway dip in the road itself has been filled up to comply with our modern roadmaking standards, so that, today, the speeder downhill on a bicycle is no longer granted that additional impetus enjoyed in the years before the experts insisted on an even gradient. The surface, moreover, was rougher then. In our reckless endeavour to gain speed, what quarrel had *we* with the few 'chuckie-stanes' sent flying to right and to left by bounding tyre and whirring spoke? That dip I speak of made all the difference. When the snows came, and a couple of nights' frost bequeathed to them a glistening crispness, one could sledge from the top of Leamy to the bottom, without alighting, the dip supplying just that extra bit of acceleration necessary to carry one triumphantly, if not also a little dangerously, to the tram-lines running transversely along Gilmore Place.

For all this, we took a personal interest in our Terrace, scorning him who would throw down rubbish upon it, and marking the household that had omitted to take inside its bin or ash-pail within a reasonable time after the passing of the civic dust-cart. In our well-groomed locality, nothing was regarded as better evidence of 'throughitherness' than failure to retrieve one's emptied utensils from pavement or gutter by half-past eight; and we felt gratified that no one in Leamy, to *our* knowledge, had ever been summoned to compear at the burgh court for leaving an ash-bucket out after the statutory time. The rag-and-bone woman, who went a-stooping up the Terrace each morning before the dustman arrived, sometimes left a trail of litter after her rummaging, thus giving the neighbourhood a slummy appearance; but, by the time the man of the broom and hand-cart had gone by, all was trim and salubrious once more.

Why should I remember so clearly that old and attenuated rag-and-bone wifie? The best explanation I can give is that, on the few occasions I rose at the sparrow's chirp to join the early swimmers at Warrender, she was the only other human being abroad in our Terrace. She hirpled along, arms akimbo, rather like a piece of ancient china with two handles, that had stood too long on the drawingroom cabinet without a wash. A life of stooping to rake Auld Reekie's buckets had bent her low. At times a tattered lassie—possibly a grandchild—attended her with the wreck of a pram, into which was thrown the rubbish she salvaged. And what a mess the pair of them was responsible for, when, on gusty mornings, a littering wind, equally devoid of a civic sense, followed in their untidy footsteps!

The Terrace knew many another vagrant. There was, for instance, the old and begrimed man with tousled beard, who, from time to time, wheeled through it a hand-cart festooned with paper-windmills and gaily coloured balloons, and announced his arrival in our midst by a familiar blare on a squeaky and battered trumpet. In a huge sack he collected bottles and jam-jars given him by children, in exchange for the gewgaws with which he tempted them. No child in the Edinburgh of those days ever had to buy a balloon. The periodic tour of the balloon-man made it unnecessary.

CHAPTER XII

SOME LEAMY INHABITANTS

LET US now review some of Leamy's inhabitants at closer range.

Number One consisted of six large and spacious flats, one of which, on the first landing, the Colonel and his madcap family now tenanted at an annual rental of forty-five pounds. In other words, taking one's bearings when looking southwards, uphill, we were to be found in the bottom lefthand corner of the Terrace. The rent of this flat, compared with that of similar accommodation correspondingly situated in London, for which one would pay in the region of three hundred and fifty or four hundred a year, was ridiculously low. The rooms were roomy, not the mere cubicles into which many of us are obliged to squeeze so expensively nowadays. Good Scots masonry gave to the house, as indeed to the whole tenement of which it was but the fortieth part, a sense of solidity and durability.

Our front windows faced the west. They looked out upon the Websters' back-garden, or, at anyrate, on such of it as had not been usurped by Mr Webster's photographic studio. This garden was a miniature orchard, white and creamy and pink in Maytime. It often gave the Colonel poetic inspiration, since his study windows confronted this bit of garden. The Websters are gone long since; and their house and studio are now put to other uses. But the quick of eye may still discern, very faintly, the word, studio, under the projecting lintel of the front door.

For a few pounds more a year, we could have occupied one of the several semi-detached villas already mentioned. This would have raised us considerably in our neighbours' sight. But a few pounds then seemed to mean very much more than a few pounds now. So, we continued to reside in a tenement flat reached by a common (emphasis on *common*, please!) stair.

Immediately below us lived a grown-up family that let a couple of rooms, and continually had occasion to knock up to the Colonel's barbarous bairns, because of the infernal din they created from time to time. Of course, the Colonel's bairns, in open defiance, instantly reciprocated by knocking down! The folks below declared that, when we engaged in romping pursuits, their chandeliers danced from the ceilings, and often threatened to crash on the floors. Ornaments toppled off shelves and mantel-pieces; and even the plumbing and cooking appointments were put out of commission. When they knocked up and we knocked down, there was competition as to which knocked last. Jessie, our eldest sister, infuriated at such Lowland presumption, insisted that our household won! She was the most pertinacious of knockers, once these inter-neighbourly communications began.

Directly overhead resided the Archibalds, a quiet, refined, and rather aloof family comprising a father and mother, a son and a daughter. Willie, the son, and Frances, the daughter, were a little older than any of us. Reared in an atmosphere of discipline and self-restraint, they were allowed to play with us only so long as our Highland spirits did not involve them in pranks and capers calculated to bring the bobby to their doorstep, or irritate them to excess by our constant re-iteration of the music-hall quip, then so much in vogue—"*Archibald, certainly not!*" But, if this annoyed Frances and her brother, the latter derived more than adequate compensation from his constant recourse to an original admixture of French and Braid Scots—*Je na dinna ken pas!* This 'Quien sabe' of his was particularly trying when one knew he had the information desired.

Nevertheless, with the Archibald children, as with others of the neighbourhood, we played all manner of games, especially in the dark. For instance, we had lots of hide-and-seek with them, in and out of back-greens, and over the railings of other peoples' gardens, trampling down the innocent flower-beds. And, although, on occasions, we all set off together for the Meadows with cricket equipment, and enjoyed the free swings and the maypole a gener-ous corporation had provided for us in a corner of the Links, we usually lingered back, sulkily, in ones and twos, having quarrelled violently over some triviality, much after the manner of the human species, whether adult or infant. The swings by the corner of Glengyle Terrace, yonder, were a never-failing source of juvenile strife. They tended to emphasise the selfishness in most of us.

Games with the Archibalds after dark were possible only by special licence, as it were. With rigid discipline, they left us high and dry at what, today, we would term blackout time. Mr Archibald, you must understand, was a master at some school or other. And not merely a master. O dear no! He was a *head*-master. We therefore regarded him with awe, as he returned home in the late afternoon, carrying a commodious attaché-case that we believed contained examination papers for correction.

Twice weekly, on the nights my homework included two or three of those dementers known as quadratic equations, I was permitted to visit him. With some show of deference, I rang the bell, to be admitted by Mrs Archibald, who, herself, had been a member of the teaching profession before her marriage to this most admirable man. As she showed me in, she liked to mitigate my feeling of intrusion by assuring me that her husband was only too delighted. (As if such could really have been the case, having regard to what this quiet and well-behaved household had had to endure from the noisy Colonel and his offspring!!) Anyhow, she was always gracious and sympathetic when I called, and Mr Archibald helpful with my algebraic dilemmas.

Helpful, I repeat. Yes, if only to the extent that he resolved the equations in his copper-plate penmanship, on odd sheets of school-notepaper, from which I afterwards copied them into my exercise-book. They were always correct, of course; and, since at this time I was among the most brainless things at Watson's, it was common certainty that I had not done them myself—with the encouraging result that I was never awarded a single mark. Still, there was consolation in being the only pupil with *all* the prescribed problems properly solved, even when the brains behind them were somebody else's—a touch of reflected glory in being on terms with a headmaster who could assist one in obtaining such perfect correctitude as to bring no reward whatsoever. One could afford to be stoical in face of such disappointment.

I revere the memory of this genial and generous man. He was the most sympathetic headmaster who ever came *my* way; and it was with a sense of something strangely satisfying that, during a parliamentary candidature I had in Glasgow a few years ago, I should have received from his widow a letter assuring me that she and her daughter's household would all be voting for me. Voting, mark you, for the weird loon who used to come so timidly to her door, twenty and more years earlier, to have her husband help him with his lessons. "I never thought I would ever have anything to do with the Socialists," she wrote. "But, after hearing you the other night, I am beginning to wonder how we have all remained so smug in our Conservatism."

Mrs Archibald and I have continued in amicable correspondence ever since; and I seldom visit Glasgow without calling on Frances and her mother. "What do you remember of the strange ongoings in the house below you?" I asked them, when on a recent visit.

"We often wondered what you were all up to," Mrs Archibald replied, "especially so early in the morning. The Colonel frequently had you all assembled in the hall as early as 6.30, putting you through something that sounded like drilling. But Catriona so drowned his words of command by her screaming that sleepy-headed neighbours like us had difficulty in determining whether there was a first-class brawl in progress, or whether it was an organised muster of the clan, to keep it fit and disciplined. In any event, it was a deafening hullabaloo, especially at that hour of the morning!"

Frances and her brother, unable to stand the vociferous discord rising from the flat below, particularly when engaged at their lessons, rapped down at times, just as the folk below us were wont to rap up. But, if they rapped *down*, we immediately mounted chairs and other elevated pieces of furniture, in order to rap *up*. (The broom-handle proved very serviceable on such occasions.) Our house was so often the scene of weird rappings that the uninitiated might have suspected something occult. Their frequency increased when we sought to communicate with the Archibalds in this way. The pretext was that *we* could not do *our* homework, so long as Willie sat upstairs, making such a noise at the piano! But Willie played well; and, in truth, we found his playing more pleasurable than distracting. I wonder whether, on his tea-garden in Assam, he sometimes plays those melodies he practised before supper-time! His garden, by the way, is situated not far from the Burma border. In 1942 it was badly bombed by the Japanese, who killed forty of his employees, and seriously injured sixty. The terrified natives rushed into hiding in the jungle; and for several days thereafter poor Willie was engaged in coaxing and bribing them to come out and assist in the burying of their dead.

* * * * * * *

Above the Archibalds lived a family of brothers and sisters, middle-aged and unmarried. Most of them were members of the teaching profession; and I used to ask myself how I would have fared, had any of them been obliged to teach me. I doubt whether

they could have made a better job of me than did the masters at
Watson's, with all the acumen and resources of the Merchant
Company behind them.

This family would have nothing to do with the MacGregors.
They looked upon us as an infernal nuisance. They were impatient of our wild and primitive ways. It was doubly embarrassing, therefore, when we inadvertently banged into one of them
while dashing round a neighbouring corner, or in slithering down
the darkened banister. Although we sometimes encountered one
another several times daily, I have no recollection of a smile or of a
syllable uttered by a member of that cold household during the
decade we and they dwelt in such unavoidable proximity. The
Colonel they eschewed like the plague: his children they resolutely
ignored. As was the case with most of Leamy's residents, they
usually *heard* the Colonel before they *saw* him. He was either
roaring at one of us, or humming a Gaelic air to himself in
sublime contentment. He struck the happy medium but seldom.
Bland smiles or terrifying frowns were characteristic of him at
this time. The former gained the ascendancy when he was
wrapt in Celtic reverie: the latter displaced them the instant any
thought of Mabel supervened. This unneighbourly family, then,
steered clear of us all. In their view, we should never have been
uprooted, and transplanted among decent Lowland folk. We
were, to them, a pack of incorrigible Heilan deevils, accustomed to
surroundings which we ought never to have left. We, on our part,
considered them 'very Edinburgh'. We thought the womenfolk as
plain as their clothes were badly tailored.

My most vivid recollection of them dates from the night in 1916,
when the German Zeppelin raided Edinburgh. I happened to be
home on leave, and out visiting friends, when this eerie monster
droned its way into our northern sky to drop the first bombs that
ever fell on Scottish soil. On hurrying home, whom should I
encounter in the entry doorway but one of the sisters? There she
crouched in her nightie, her teeth chattering with cold and
apprehension, the cat under one arm, and the alarm clock
ticking aggressively under the other. All the starch had gone
from her.

* * * * * * *

Then there were the Howisons, two handsome sisters who lived
with their admirable mother but a few doors away, and who might

be seen from our windows when stepping out to business so precisely that we could check our timepieces with their passing. They were the first of our Auld Reekie neighbours to show interest in us; and the reason for this was not far to seek. Old Mrs Howison, who hailed from Rannoch, was a member of our clan. This explained why father liked his children to show her special courtesy. We had to bear in mind that she was a kinswoman. Before many weeks had gone by, we were regarding her as a sort of great-aunt; and she was reciprocating by treating us as though we were her grand-nephews and grand-nieces. This arrangement ensured for us much kindness and sympathy. Mrs Howison was certainly a neighbour whose filial interest in us we had reason to esteem. It brought us many an unexpected pleasure—yea, and expected ones too, since she kept a sweetie-bag well filled with such old-fashioned confectionery as peppermints and pan-drops. Like the Colonel, she was clan-proud, though not to the same fanatical degree. She thoroughly enjoyed having a squad of youngsters bearing her maiden name, living so close at hand, for whom she could show congenial concern, and to whom she could relate Rannoch stories of our clan's prowess, as we sat by her fire, eating fruit-cake and sipping lemonade.

Nothing gave her greater pleasure than pausing at her bow-window to watch us as we indulged in our wild capers on the street below. Only Highland bairns accustomed to an open life, she used to say when praising our agility, could scale the tall gate on the opposite side of the road, over which our ball went all too frequently. Behind that gate were some stables and a yard, which a local chimney-sweep shared with a creamery company. It often took us a considerable time to locate an errant ball among the piles of slates and ladders and limy buckets belonging to the sweep, who appropriately added slating to his sooty pursuit. But we found the athletic effort entailed in getting over the gate more than compensated for by a few feverish minutes' fun with the hose used by the creamery company's employees when washing their vans, and the fetlocks of their horses in muddy weather. Still, it was preferable to lose one's ball indefinitely among the sweep's paraphernalia than to have it *stot* on the glass roof of Mr Webster's photographic studio, but a few yards away. Miniature cricket, played to wickets chalked up on the adjacent wall, was responsible for most of the balls that broke poor Mr Webster's panes.

*   *   *   *   *   *   *

And now we come to No. 15, where lived the Robertsons. My most persistent memory of them relates to the occasion upon which Mrs Robertson presented (that, I think, is the correct euphemism) Mr Robertson, headmaster at Bruntsfield, with yet another child. She had come into possession of it, not through the agency of her saintly husband, my sisters had been led to believe, but by some channel far more unusual and elusive. (The crude facts of birth, you must understand, were never explained to us.) It couldn't have been Santa Claus *this* time, my sisters held, since the presentation took place in summer, when Santa, for all his accommodating ways, had never been known to visit anyone in Auld Reekie. But they were ready to accept that some other invisible entity may have been responsible—perhaps someone of the faery order, accredited with coming down the chimney with such squealing gifts for prayerful parents.

* * * * * * *

No. 28 was occupied by a family we children spoke of as the Whisky MacLennans, because the father had a pub somewhere in the profitable heart of our slum-land, and all too frequently consumed good draughts of his most potent spirits himself. Only once was I in the MacLennans' house; and it happened to be while Mr MacLennan, then advanced in years, lay upstairs, on his deathbed, in a front room, the blinds of which, in anticipation of his demise, had remained drawn for what appeared to have been an unreasonably long time. Is Mr MacLennan never going to quit this bed-ridden life? we asked ourselves in passing to find its apartments still so fearful of the daylight. My visit I remember clearly. I had been invited to enter, on tiptoes, by one of the sons, to see the model sailing-ship he had rigged. Stealthily, I was taken into the diningroom, where the exclusion of light by the dropped blinds prevented an adequate examination of it. But the duskiness of the scene did not prevent my noticing that on the sideboard the tantalus and the cut-glass decanters (all well filled, as became such receptacles in a publican's home) stood alone, in silence, like spectres of foreboding, untouched by the hand that had grasped them rather too freely, and that now reclined, in like silence, on a bed of death, immediately overhead. This weird picture always recurs whenever I see a tantalus, which, I believe, is the name our parents gave to the now obsolete spirit-case once found on the sideboard.

When, at last, Mr MacLennan did depart this life, the outward appearance of the house remained unaltered. Even after the funeral, the blinds stood drawn. Some time afterwards, however, the Campbells succeeded the Whisky MacLennans at No. 28; and I clearly recall the day Mrs Campbell arrived to pull up the blinds with a right, good, hearty thump, thus dispelling, in a few light-some seconds, the pall that had settled on this particular house. Those blinds, God knows, had functioned long enough as the conservers of gloom and depression!

Soon Iain and I got on terms with Mrs Campbell's sons—with Ian and with G. Beresford, the G standing for George. It was thought stylish to allow no more than the initial of the first Christian name, and to give, in full, a favourite middle name, together with the surname. As the Scots are inclined to be lavish in the matter of middle names, there were usually two or more to choose from. Where there existed no middle name, which was exceptional, one was readily assumed, and on the pretext that, as in the case of the peerage, it was a *family* name. G. Beresford Campbell was by no means the only youngster affecting this mode of designation, and signing himself thus. There were two youthful devotees at No. 40, where the father had set the example! The vogue became very fashionable among the 'select' of Auld Reekie about this time; and I see that many have since inserted the hyphen.

On *real* friendship with the Campbell boys, we MacGregors put a brake, lest they might betray us, as their namesakes had betrayed ours, in the days of that bold, auld-farrand carle, Rob Roy! As the offspring of Clan Alpin's Bard, we had been warned never to trust a Campbell too far! [1]

I recall one daring prank with the Campbell boys and some

[1] The extent to which the name of Campbell remains anathema among the Scots would surprise many. Vice-Chancellor Sir James Frederick Rees, of the University of Wales, tells me of an interesting case that occurred in the autumn of 1943. While lunching with Sir Robert Robertson, the government's ex-plosives chemist, he happened to relate a story told him by one Weir, an Edinburgh solicitor.

A business man from Glasgow, named MacDonald, was in Weir's office, and wanted to send a letter to someone. Weir suggested that his secretary might type it for him, and so he called her in. "Miss Campbell," he said, "will you type a letter for this gentleman?" MacDonald objected. "I have never been beholden to a Campbell in my life, and I will not be now!" he responded with some heat.

To my friend's surprise, the great scientist confessed that he would have adopted the same course. That is one of the amazing things about the Scot—his romantic-mad spot.

other 'Leamingtonians'. It was while the new Boroughmuir school was being built in Viewforth, quite close at hand—so close, in truth, that, during the course of its construction, we were much given to intruding upon its site *via* the back-greens a little farther up the Terrace. While the Boroughmuir towers were being erected, we thought it would be a grand idea to clamber, after dark, up the scaffolding at one of them. No sooner had we reached the precarious top than someone dislodged a plank. Down it travelled through the reverberating stanchions with a clanging that instantly brought forth the night-watchman, lantern in hand, and in a state of great perturbation. *"Come doon oot o' there, ye b——s!"* he yelled. *"Ah'll break yer bluidy necks if Ah get a haud o' ye!"*

These tones inspired in us the fear of death. We were in a dreadful quandary, as you can imagine. Descent, in conscience, was perilous enough in broad daylight, without any threat of apprehension at the base of the tower. How were we to extricate outselves, in the dark, and at the same time avoid being caught? Somehow or other, we eluded him. As we made for safe cover in the adjacent greens, he continued to shout after us rude and threatening remarks. We never dared set trespassing foot near Boroughmuir thereafter.

*   *   *   *   *   *   *

What more should I tell you about the Campbells other than that they were not long in flitting across Leamington Terrace to occupy No. 45, and that the Bonnie George Campbell (not to be confused with the chiel of like name, whose fate is recorded in the auld Scots sang, but the Bonnie George of baritone fame) and his wife were accomplished musicians? It was, indeed, a pleasure in youth to linger by the privet hedge separating front garden from pavement, so as to listen to the Bonnie George, while he and his wife ran over a few songs in tuneful amity, before quitting the house for one of those 'Nichts wi' Rabbie Burns', in which Scotland then specialised. He was greatly in demand at public dinners, as much for his handsome appearance as on account of his voice. And it was no secret in Auld Reekie that he had an appreciative eye for the ladies, and that quite a number of the ladies were flattered in consequence.

Anyhow, Leamy rang with ballad when, in the summertime, the Campbells' windows were thrown open to the dusky twilight,

and the Bonnie George gave full-throated vent to those inspiring
lines—

> March, march, Ettrick and Teviotdale!
> Why the de'il dinna ye march forward in order?
> March, march, Eskdale and Liddesdale!
> All the Blue Bonnets are bound for the Border.
> Many a banner spread
> Flutters above your head,
> Many a crest that is famous in story.
> Mount and make ready then,
> Sons of the mountain glen,
> Fight for the Queen and our old Scottish glory!

The Bonnie George had been connected with music all his days.
Born in Westmorland in 1873, he received his early musical
education as a choir-boy at Carlisle Cathedral. At the age of
thirteen he began his apprenticeship with the Edinburgh music-
selling firm of Townsend & Thomson, a business of which he
eventually became proprietor. As a youth he pursued his musical
interests, studying singing, pianoforte, and the organ. For many
years he continued in great request throughout Scotland as an
exponent both of oratorio and of the ballad; and we remember
the generous services he rendered in this capacity to those good
causes to which our Capital has always been given. We remember
him, too, for the energy and enthusiasm he contributed to the
activities of the Edinburgh Opera Company, the president of
which he remained throughout the sixteen years of its enterprising
career with the operatic Hedmont as producer—a career that
witnessed several notable productions, conspicuous among them
being the first performance of Sir Donald Tovey's opera, *The Bride
of Dionysus*. Alas! in 1939, at the age of sixty-six, bronchial
pneumonia carried off the Bonnie George Campbell.

I must just add a word or two about *Mrs* Campbell (Kate Gray,
as she was known professionally) for she did more than dispel
gloom by the resolute pulling up of those blinds I mentioned.
Indeed, she was most talented and, for at least a quarter of a
century, a vocalist almost without rival. She had been trained
by the wellknown Mrs Millar Craig of Edinburgh, and later by the
celebrated Sir George Henschel. While in London with the latter,
another celebrity in the person of E. C. Hedmont—Emanuel
Christian Hedmont—engaged her to sing throughout his operatic
season at Covent Garden, where she had parts in *Tannhäuser* and
in *Lohengrin*, and was one of the Valkyrie maidens. It was,
perhaps, as a singer of oratorio she was best known; but, since she

attained her prime when I was no more than five or six, only from hearsay do I write of her distinction in this regard.

Still, there is one little matter with which I associate her felicitously. It was while the Campbells lived at No. 28 that there occurred the incident of the *fleurs-de-lys*, related in the next chapter. An evening or two after this wilful damage had been committed, and I, in trembling, awaited the arrival of the Black Maria that never came, I happened to be passing by their gate when Mrs Campbell beckoned to me and invited me within. I complied, rather apprehensively, thinking I was in for a good scolding. Imagine how agreeably surprised I was when, on the contrary, she assured me, very privately, that I need not worry further about those *fleurs-de-lys*, as Mr Porter really had no intention of setting the police on our tracks! For the relief those few words brought me, I was never able to repay Mrs Campbell.

Apropos music, I should tell you that our Terrace was among Auld Reekie's most musical. While the Colonel's daughters might be strumming at one end of it, practising their scales for school, the less juvenile residents at the other were playing seriously. Then, halfway up, the rich baritone cadences of the Bonnie George Campbell might be heard, as he entertained his friends, or rehearsed for an impending concert. As an intermediary contribution, the family at No. 16 (how is it that one remembers these inhabitants and their dwellings so vividly?) consisting of a grey-haired and elderly mother and three grown-up daughters, formed a family quartette which lent colour and delight in an age when most of us liked to produce our own music.

*   *   *   *   *   *   *

With the Campbells lived their nephew and cousin, Arthur Young, the son of parents extremely musical and talented. We remember Arthur best when, shortly after the last war, he enjoyed the distinction of being one of the two kenspeckle fellows who then went a-wheeling through Auld Reekie on a motor-scooter, a means of conveyance but newly placed on the market. (His rival was a clergyman we used to watch as he sped through the city, in an era less urgent, at a pace putting our cable-cars to blush.) Arthur, while indulging his enterprise in this mode of mobility, wore a bowler, bright spats, fur gloves reaching well beyond the elbows, and a raincoat that flapped noisily, as do sails brought too close to the wind. He, indeed, created an eccentric spectacle when scooting between Leamy and his uncle's music-shop, in George Street, where, for a time, he was multifariously employed; and I will not deny his novel method of transport was the envy of many of us. At a later date, Arthur played the piano at a Princes Street cinema, where he was a big draw, and where his picturesque arrival in flowing opera-cloak and collapsible hat always created a sensation in the queue awaiting admission. Then, he sailed once or twice to South America, as a member of the ship's orchestra, and for a time thereafter played with Jack Hylton's band. Prior to the outbreak of the present war, he was exercising his musical talent with great acceptance in a Berlin club; and now, I am told, he is similarly engaged in the West End of London. So Arthur, you realise, is something of a celebrity. You can refer to him in the catalogue of "His Master's Voice". He is 'hot stuff' on 'hot rhythm'! Hear him at the piano-keys with *St Louis Blues,* or *Tiger Rag!!*

*   *   *   *   *   *   *

In No. 38 lived old, white-haired, and widowed Mrs Tullo, with one of her daughters. A pair of nosey-parkers they, assuredly, were! A fair encyclopædia of gossip! They found the sills of the drawingroom window too high to allow of their seeing, without the expenditure of some small effort, all that went on below. They, therefore, engaged a local joiner to make for them a window platform, in order that, from the ease and comfort of their chairs placed thereon, they might witness all that occurred, and scrutinise everyone who passed.

Mrs Tullo we remember principally because of the delight she derived from failing to return, and in preventing the losers from recovering, such balls as went over into her garden. Any tennis-ball, intruding upon this sacred reserve, she was adept at puncturing, thus rendering it useless. It would no longer *stot*.

Chief among the victims of her uncharitableness in this regard were the Hendersons, her neighbours, living but a doorstep away. Balls were continually going over from the Hendersons' back-garden into hers, since there were five Henderson sons, all of whom were much given to games, and two or three of whom were, eventually, famous rugger players. When, on one occasion, a quite expensive football belonging to this family went over, Dame Tullo snatched it up and retreated with it, leaving its owners to imagine that the customary fate was about to befall it. However, some weeks later, when the suspense had become too much for Alick Henderson, he rang the Tullos' doorbell, in dire trepidation, and asked for it. He was answered by the maid, who, with firmness, informed him that he could not possibly have it, since Mrs Tullo was at prayers. Whether that football was ultimately recovered, the chronicles of Leamy fail to disclose. But it was taken for granted by the youths of our neighbourhood that spherical objects, irrespective of size and cost, depositing themselves, unwittingly, in the Tullos' sanctum, were instantly ripped with a knife ever maintained in a state of readiness and efficiency for the purpose of invalidating such intruders.

Would you believe that our balls' occasional invasion of the Tullos' *front*-garden exercised them immensurably more than did our seasonal depredations among their apple-trees, in the *back*-garden? The latter offence they tolerated: the former they resented with all the vehemence they could assemble, because, as Mrs Tullo once, twice—ay, a hundred times!—declared, it derogated from the tone of their abode, a semi-detached villa of quite suburban status.

That stretch of the wall at the back lane, conterminous with the Tullos' back-garden, you cannot mistake, for, to this very day, as I discovered when prowling recently about these parts, it is the more thickly set with broken glass, immovably cemented, to keep us away from their apples. A long rod, to the end of which we attached a net, enabled us to partake of this forbidden fruit without having to contend with this sharp, vitreous array.

*　　　*　　　*　　　*　　　*　　　*　　　*

In No. 40 lived stately John Milne Henderson, C.A., together with his wife and the not inconsiderable issue of his loins, as the Bible says. He had five sons (the two eldest falling in the last war) and one daughter, the youngest of the family—the mischievous Margaret who, as a child of seven, habitually crawled into the hen-house, where her young brothers and their friends were smoking clandestinely, and threatened them with "Gi'e me a puff, or I'll tell!"

Mr Henderson was the last word in personal appearance, and yet no dandy. Had he been of smaller build, one might have pronounced him dapper. His clothes fitted him perfectly. They were well made, well put on, and well disported. They seemed to go with his decisiveness of tongue, his alertness of movement. His necktie conveyed the impression of mental, as well as of physical, fastidiousness. His top-hat, wiped meticulously upon overcoat sleeve while having a final glance at his good looks in the hall mirror, betokened his importance to the community. Gaiters lent a finishing touch to footsteps that carried him down Leamy with clockwork precision of a morning. His walk was as pointed as was his short, trim beard. Though already in his sixties, he was possessed of an enviable mobility.

We had the notion that, although the Hendersons occupied nothing grander than a semi-detached villa, this was not necessarily attributable to any impecuniosity. On the contrary, we believed that Banker Hendy had access to as much ready cash as any creature on this planet could possibly desire. All he had to do, we fancied, was to summon a subordinate official of the bank, and ask him to hand over a hundred or two, as required. There was no one to say him nay: he was *manager*—manager, in point of fact, of the North of Scotland Bank, a concern of which he made a startling success. His living in comparatively modest circumstances we ascribed to his observance of the Christian virtue of moderation in all things, more especially, perhaps, as behooving an elder of the kirk. John Milne Henderson was a prominent member of session at Free St George's, where the blind Dr Hollins was organist—St George's West Kirk, as it is now called. You should have seen this patriarch setting out with his family for the kirk, togged up in all their Sunday braws. Even yet, he carries in his erect and alert person a whiff of the old United Free Church, so namely for its stability and integrity, its good, sound logic. It is nearly a quarter of a century since the U.F., as we called it, amalgamated with the Auld, or Established, Kirk to form the present Church of Scotland, and in so doing forfeited its individuality, except for that earnest minority known as the United Free Church of Scotland, Continuing, which still maintains the old spirit of independence. Today, Banker Hendy, with more than fifty years' membership of session behind him, is the senior elder at St George's West—the greatest of all churches in the ecclesiastical history of Scotland, in my view—a church still famous for its preachers, and its trained army of elders and deacons.

*　　*　　*　　*　　*　　*　　*

"Whereabouts are you in your class?" was the embarrassing question Banker Hendy fired at every schoolboy in Leamy.

"Rather too near the bottom for my father's liking, Mr Henderson!" was the reply he received, without variation, from *me*.

"Tuts, tuts! I was top of every class except one; and then I was second. You ought to hurry home to your lessons!"

In our Leamy days we thought the Hendersons, as a family, were inclined to be a little cocky, a little too 'swanky'. Yet, when Jimmie, one of the older sons (a rugger internationalist, who fell untimely), developed the affectation of carrying his head a little on one side, we younger fry thought this an attractive pose, and tried to cultivate it too.

In our resolve to take some of the starch out of the Hendersons, we decided to make a beginning with the paterfamilias, himself. So, one afternoon, as we espied him returning home down Leamy, we hastily suspended a taut black thread between the lamp-post and the railing at No. 44, and at an altitude calculated to tip off his tile-hat as he passed. Sheltering behind the privet in an adjacent garden, we watched our unsuspecting victim. Off came the hat, according to plan; and it was with difficulty we restrained ourselves from giving sound to pent-up hilarity which, assuredly, would have disclosed our whereabouts, with consequences too fearful to contemplate.

*　　*　　*　　*　　*　　*　　*

"I'm on the borders of ninety!" John Milne told me the other day, when we confronted one another on Princes Street, and adjourned to Mackie's to chat over a cup of coffee. He is as vigorous, as weather-proof, at ninety as are most men at forty-five, and as full as ever of his surviving sons' doings.

The most conclusive proof we had, in the olden days, of his illimitable wealth was that Alick (the son who was a classmate of mine and, to my increasing annoyance, wore a kilt of MacGregor tartan) always came to school with a copper or two for sweeties—for 'the gundy', as we termed those sweetmeats that had a mass-production flavour about them. We had been resident in Auld Reekie but a few days when the Colonel encountered Alick, then a youngster of ten or thereby, and asked him whether his name was MacGregor. *You can imagine the reception given to the wretched little impostor's confession that his name was merely Henderson!*

Get Mr Henderson in narrative mood, and he will not be long in telling you how, in boyhood, he steered a plough in Aberdeenshire, behind a pair of oxen. But, by the time he was sixteen, he had deserted the feudal acres of Don-side for accountancy. It is one of his proudest boasts, nevertheless, that he is the oldest surviving member of the Highland & Agricultural Society. He is greatly addicted to committees. I am assured, and by those best informed on public matters in Auld Reekie, that, in the course of seventy or more years of feverish activity, he has never been known to appear at a meeting at which he did not speak, if only with the object of drawing formal notice to his presence. When I tell you that he has attended every one of the seventy annual general meetings of the Agricultural Society, aforementioned, you will agree that he is more than justified in emphasising his unchallenged record by a few words, even if at times they may appear, to the uncharitable, a little pointless.

Mr Henderson represents the Merchant Company on a committee which has not met for years. During each meeting of the Company at which are given the annual reports of its outside representatives on the activities of such committees, Mr Henderson, when called upon, always rises to say, "Master, no meeting: no report," and then sits down. The very essence of brevity!

In our Watsonian days, the Hendersons' home at No. 40 was famed for its eggs, since, in addition to the product of their own hens in the back-garden, they had a box, capably of containing thirty dozen, continually passing between Leamy and the farm of some Aberdeenshire relatives. Every few weeks the empty box was returned: every few weeks it reached Leamy again, chockfull. Eggs, more eggs, and yet more eggs! It was their bounce that they preserved one hundred and twenty dozen, for consumption throughout the winter. You see, there was a growing brood of six to feed. Yet, to us, their neighbours, it seemed ridiculous—nay, monstrous—that so colossal a number of eggs should be devoured by one family! "And not mere hens' eggs," as Mr Henderson impressed upon me lately, "but *big* eggs, each weighing not less than two-and-three-quarter ounces!"

The Hendersons still specialise in eggs; and, if you should meet John Milne on Princes Street, whither he travels thrice weekly to do the shopping, he is pretty certain to invite you to "come up to your tea, and we'll give you an egg to it, and may be a lump or two of sugar that escaped from Singapore before the Japs took possession". And you must go—out to Merchiston Park, where he now lives—for you will enjoy his hospitality, and find his wife so very charming, for all her years, for all her deafness. Yes, do go! Fifteen's the number! You will find them remindful of that fine type of parent Scotland has scarcely known since the closing years of the last war.

* * * * * * *

Then, there resided at No. 47 the immaculate Mr Lightbody, a wellknown tutor who, when enjoying respite from the task of cramming ambitious heads for those examinations in which Edinburgh has gained preëminence among this planet's cities, wheeled himself up and down our Terrace in a bath-chair. We used to be told by those who had reason to know (perhaps, the less diligent of Mr Lightbody's clients, who had felt the truth of it!) that, albeit he had no life in his legs, his arms were inordinately powerful. He certainly propelled himself in his chair up our steep thoroughfare with amazing velocity. We had been assured, moreover, that he could tutor in every language known in the world. In response to so reckless a claim made on his behoof, and so often repeated to us Highland bairns by way of demonstrating what a wonderful lot of folk we had come to dwell among, we, of the ancient Clan Gregor, insisted there was at least one exception we could name—Gaelic—of all the world's languages, the most difficult to acquire, as father was continually impressing upon us in terms engendering much self-satisfaction. From his own command of this archaic and dying tongue, he derived an imaginary superiority, if not actually a degree of regal nobility. The blood of Kenneth MacAlpin was strong in him! If Mr Lightbody, for teaching easier languages, received seven-and-six the hour (a rate we children thought extortionate!) what could our father not make, if he undertook to teach Gaelic?

* * * * * * *

Our Terrace was numerous in lads named Robert, all of whom were called Bertie This or Bertie That. Such as were not Watsonians were Herioters. The former, as you now know, constituted an exclusive and formidable set. The fact that the father of one of the Berties was Clerk of Works to that splendid institution, the Heriot Trust, made not a whit of difference. Bertie Anderson had to serve his apprenticeship like any other candidate, and finally pass the qualifying standard, before the Watson's clique recognised him.

Now, one of the Watson's Berties (ah! how well I remember No. 51, because of my importunate visits for help with my homework!) had a sister, Maysie, a brilliant pupil at George Square.[1] You will find Maysie's name writ in gilt there, for she was dux in 1913. Maysie saw to it that her brother's home-exercises were correct to the last detail. For quite a time, it remained a mystery how a boy, who acquitted himself but indifferently in the classroom, turned up with his written work done to perfection. Eventually, it was discovered that he was the younger brother of the clever lass at George Square. The mystery was solved; and I can still see the sheepish look on poor Bertie Deas when, questioned before the class as to the explanation for his faultless homework, he confessed that his sister occasionally helped him "just a wee bittie, sir". This brought peals of laughter from the rest of us, as he stood there in discomfort, his ability now unmasked. But I always remember his retort when the master asked him whether he had anything to say for himself. "Better to have them done properly by someone else, than not have them done at all—don't you think?" A most cogent observation, *I* thought. However, the master thought otherwise; and the perpetrator, consequently, was kept in.

Yet another recollection of him pertains to the way in which he 'played the daft laddie' in the classroom. While we sat hushed at some problem, and the master presided on his dais, attending to his own affairs (surreptitiously snatching some of the Merchant Company's time to write to his girl-friend, we suspected) the studious silence might be rent by a loud and comical comment, followed by the kind of half-witted giggle one associates with perambulated infants. When the master looked up for an explanation, to be greeted by a blank and daft-like smile from Bertie Deas, he never knew whether to treat the incident as an exhibition of downright insolence, or as something attributable to mental disorder. Any question now directed to the offender brought a volley of gibberish, succeeded by a burst of merriment more idiotic than ever. He once got a good leathering for his behaviour, and giggled gleefully when the chastisement was over. I can picture him now, standing accommodatingly on the classroom floor, still holding out his hand for more of the strap, and pretending to be apologetic to the master for not realising that he had received as much as the latter proposed giving him. We all knew, of course, that this strange conduct was intentional. If this jollity served to relieve *his* boredom, it certainly did mine; and I must

[1] George Watson's Ladies' College, sister school to my own.

confess to having egged him on in these unseemly performances when we happened to be seated in reasonable propinquity. He and I were now to become firm friends; and he remained my Achates during the remainder of my stay at school.

In course of time he qualified in medicine, went to sea for a spell, returned to Scotland, and purchased a practice in the mining district of Armadale, with a branch surgery at Bathgate. More than a decade ago, this good-natured fellow brought his life to a close with a draught of lysol. One spring morning, he was found dead in his Bathgate surgery. He left a wife and child, but no writing which might indicate why he had departed thus. But I gather he was afraid the bold John Barleycorn had got the upper hand.

      *   *   *   *   *   *   *

At No. 55 lived George Ferguson, with his widowed mother, a tall lady, stately and cultivated. Mrs Ferguson supplemented her none too affluent viduage by conducting, in her home, in coöperation with her sister, a dancing-class for young people. To this class the Colonel once thought of consigning me, as he believed dancing to be a necessary accomplishment, and felt that a few lessons might improve my deportment. In the end, however, he was not satisfied that these ladies could teach the Highland fling, the sword dance, and other picturesque expressions of Celtic culture. So I was not enrolled. In truth, he was a little afraid, as I afterwards learnt, that I might be taught the waltz and other girlish twirlings, such as he deemed almost any dance that did not extol the heather and the kilt. But I have cause to remember Mrs Ferguson in another regard. For some reason or other, she was the first lady in Auld Reekie to acknowledge me with a smile, a concession that bestowed upon me my initial experience in raising my cap to ladies. I practised on Mrs Ferguson until I had acquired the knack to a nicety.

Since it is better that we should give nosegays to the living, as the Japanese say (or is it the Chinese?) than strew wreaths upon their graves when they are dead, you must hear a little more about Mrs Ferguson's son, George—Fergie, as his affectionate associates have called him since his schoolhood at Watson's.

In his younger days, and for a reason he himself was never quite able to give, he joined a troop of scouts located away down in Trinity, at the seaward end of Auld Reekie. But one day the troop took wee Georgie on a very long walk, which so exhausted him that, on his return home, his mother had to put him to bed. Thus ended his connection with the Trinity scouts.

Latterly, he was one of the 'high heid yins'—one of the 'big noises'—of Warrender, our celebrated swimming-club. More than that, he was our trusty goalkeeper, when Warrender played water-polo with other teams. I imagine I see the doughty Fergie now, standing in goal at the shallow end, yelling deafening exhortations to his team, and then crouching like some savage beast, when it looked as though the ball might be speeding his way. The swiftest polo-ball, coming into contact with the redoubtable Fergie, met the kind of reception a careering motorist gets on charging into a wall; and Stonewall Fergie could dispose of the ball, on its return journey, with a velocity that sent a palpable draught over the surface of the pond, compelling the more timid to duck until it had passed on its withering way. Scottish water-polo never produced another 'goalie' quite like Fergie; and I sincerely trust that, as an S.S.C.—as a Solicitor before the Supreme Courts—he acquits himself as notably as he did in this arduous rôle. To ascertain this, however, one would have to pay him a professional visit at 40, Melville Street, Auld Reekie, where he was apprenticed before the last war, and where his one and only employer has had the good sense to take him into partnership. I ought to tell you that he is now a Justice of the Peace; and there is no gainsaying that, before the decade expires, our estimable Fergie will be a full-blown bailie of the city of Edinburgh, with the emblematic lamp standing outside his garden gate in Craiglea Drive!

No one has ever done more to promote an interest in swimming and water-polo than this indomitable, indefatigable fellow. This fact was recognised when, eventually, he staggered up the administrative ladder to the dizzy height of President of the Scottish Amateur Swimming Association. I should mention that he also organised the Scottish National Sports Federation, a body which looks after Scotland's interests in the British Empire Games, and that, a few years ago, he took a team of athletes—boxers, wrestlers, and swimmers—to London and to Canada. How many have been elevated to the peerage for services less commendable?

And what has he done in years more recent but re-constituted Auld Reekie's Special Foot Constabulary, an organisation of which he is commandant? Small wonder that, a couple of years ago, someone or other—His Majesty, we presume—was pleased to award him the O.B.E. for his estimable services. "Good old Fergie!" as we used to yell above the uproar when, during a hotly contested match with some crack team from the west of Scotland, he brought down the polo-ball making for the goal at terrific speed.

It was none other than Fergie who, in our more juvenile years, inaugurated the Leamy Amateur Dramatic Society, a select—a *very* select—company, consisting exclusively of Leamy talent, which rehearsed all manner of plays in his mother's dancing-room, but which, so far as I am aware, never got the length of giving a public performance during the whole of its somewhat erratic existence. Among the plays it studied with grim earnestness was *The Ghost of Jerry Bundler*; and we all thought that *this* time an exhibition was bound to be staged. But no! This we the more regretted, because the rumour that the ghost was attired in a certain black, silken under-garment lent by Mrs Ferguson, and never alluded to in polite society, was not without foundation.

And now Fergie writes me that he is married, and has carried exclusiveness to the extreme by deserting the locality of boyhood for Morningside. "But I pass the top of Leamy every morning and evening in the tram," he adds; "and I never miss an opportunity of walking down the old Terrace when in the neighbourhood, and of picturing the people and ploys of bygone years. . . . It may amuse you to hear that I am also a J.P. Why I have been honoured thus, I know not!" Well, *I* know. There's a dearth of disinterested men for administrative positions, even in Auld Reekie! (I do hope, dear Fergie, you haven't found the nosegay too heavily scented!)

Here we leave Leamy at No. 55, which is as far as the recollections of youth now carry me with any precision. But I vaguely recall an Alastair, yet another Watsonian, who lived with his parents a few doors higher up than the Fergusons', and who was some years my senior. His father was minister of the kirk, near at hand. Shall I ever forget the awe with which I reviewed Alastair Shannon after Mr Porter, in white apron and in reminiscent mood, at his licensed grocery shop one day, let me into the secret that this elusive lad had just published a wee volume of poetry?

CHAPTER XIII

NUMBER THIRTY

GOOD GRACIOUS Me! I have omitted to mention Number Thirty and its inmates; and that will never do! Such an oversight must be remedied instantly, since the head of the house, John Stormont Porter (haven't you heard tell of, and perhaps even tasted, the famous blend of Stormont whisky he sold at his licensed premises in Fountainbridge?) became one of the very particular friends of my youth. My first dealings with him, however, were none too propitious.

One afternoon while I, in company with a band of Leamy loons, congregated outside Number Thirty, trying to persuade the tantalising Willie Porter to abandon his homework and join us, a mood of mischief seized us all. Between Numbers 28 and 30 runs a grassy lane, deep-rutted with the wheels of vehicles conveying coals round to the backs of the houses served by it. A coal-man, when heavily laden, was never permitted to carry his sack in by the front door of the respectable domiciles comprising so considerable a proportion of the Leamy of youth. What would the neighbours have thought, had they witnessed anything so improper? And think of the coal-heaver's boot-marks on bricked doorstep, on rugs and polished waxcloth! In order to keep up the tone of our Terrace, then, he had to deliver his load circuitously, by way of the lane.

The lane is separated from the pavement by a high gate and railings, the upright bars of which terminate, either halfway up or at the top, in an ornamental pattern of *fleurs-de-lys*. In idle mood, one of our number, exasperated at Willie Porter's failure to appear, and suspecting that his big sister, Liz, was doing his French 'ekky' for him, placed between the bars of the gate the end of a large club he was carrying. With but little leverage, off came a *fleur-de-lys*. The apparent ease, with which this cast-iron projection snapped, was as surprising as it was fascinating, wherefore we now borrowed the club in turns, and assisted in denuding gate and adjacent railings of their only embellishment. *Fleur-de-lys* after *fleur-de-lys* crashed to the pavement as we, in senseless delight, pursued our destructive course. Then, up went a window in a neighbouring villa. Someone shouted threateningly to us, whereupon we skedaddled.

At school the following day, Willie was strangely uncommunicative. "What's the matter, Willie?" I asked him on the way home, as he walked sulkily by himself, his eyes fixed on the pavement in front of him.

"Fine you know!" he muttered in ominous tones. "And, if you don't, you'll know soon enough. Wait till Pop gets you!"

I now realised that not only had I offended him grievously by my share in the previous afternoon's wantonness, but that something more was to be heard about it. Furthermore, I knew Pop Porter to be a man of action, and of unbounded resource and energy. Once *he* set the machinery of the law agoing, God alone knew where it might stop!

That evening a bulky figure in dark blue approached our doorstep. He was none other than the fearsome Ginger, so styled because of his ginger moustache, and the ginger hair we knew he had under his helmet. Ginger walked at what we called 'a quarter-to-three'. His gait was so lumbering that we could not imagine his overtaking and apprehending anyone fleeing from justice, until one day we witnessed him in hot pursuit—so hot that, spite our own fleetness, we could not keep him in sight as he sprinted up Leamy, and vanished among the tall tenements of Bruntsfield.

Anyhow, here was Ginger on our threshold. The tug he gave the bell sent a shudder through me. Conscience-stricken, I rushed to answer the door, fearing the worst. This was not the *first* time he had had occasion to call on my account, you may remember.

"I've come to see the Colonel," he said with gruff voice, meanwhile flourishing a piece of paper that looked very important. There would have been no use my saying the Colonel was out, since he was so punctual in his routine that everyone who knew him, if no more than by sight, could tell precisely where he would be, or what he was likely to be doing, at any given hour of the day. The citizens of Auld Reekie might have set their timepieces by him, just as those of Königsberg did when they observed Immanuel Kant passing by this or that object, while walking in the grounds of the university.

I showed Ginger into the study, where father was having his

afternoon pipe. I closed the door behind me, lingering tremulously to listen. In slow and deliberate accents, the unwelcome visitor unfolded the affair of the *fleurs-de-lys*. The Colonel's voice was soon ringing through the house. I was summoned, and obeyed. I stood there, at attention, literally 'on the carpet', mute and pale and quivering. Ginger now began to rattle things hidden somewhere about his hips, and made a move as if, at any moment, he might again produce those terrifying symbols of his authority. The proceedings concluded in his leaving me with the firm impression that, in the matter of a few minutes, the police-van would be arriving. He had gone out to telephone for it, I believed. Throughout this recital of wrongdoing, father remained almost unperturbed, which made me suspect that something really sinister was afoot. That night I scarcely shut an eye, imagining that every wheel I heard belonged to the Black Maria that, at last, had come for me. All next day, I quaked at sound of vehicle.

In the course of a few days, I observed from our windows that workmen were engaged in replacing the broken bars. The worst had still to come, I feared. What would happen when Colonel MacGregor received the bill for his son's share in this outrage? But the dreaded bill never came. In a moment of magnanimity, Mr Porter had met the entire cost, an act of charity about which I learnt with inexpressible relief.

One day later, as he stepped out to business with that amiable alacrity his neighbours so much admired, he caught sight of me as I, in embarrassment, tried to avoid him. "Come here, ye Heilan deevil!" he cried. "If once I get my hands on ye, ye'll rue the day ye wore the kilt!"

In trembling, I approached him. To my amazement, he subjected me to no reproof, but rather invited me to realise how foolish I had been. It was true, he admitted, that my accomplices in this delinquency were older than I, and that, to some extent, they were more to blame for having set me so foolish an example, and egged me on to take my share in felling those perfectly innocent *fleurs-de-lys*. He had no difficulty in extracting from me an undertaking that I would never be so wicked and stupid again.

From that moment, Mr Porter and I became friends. And so, also, did his family and I. The very first parcel I received in Flanders came from his daughter, Liz—Liz of the deep voice, who was so very free with her pennies where her brothers' playmates were concerned. When I returned to this country on leave, it was Liz who wired me an invitation to spend a few days with her in South Wales, where she was then superintendent of a munitions factory. I accepted. Liz paid all expenses. My holiday began at Mumbles and finished at Llanelly, where I was nearly drowned in swimming out from the docks toward the open sea! Liz was in full sympathy with me in my adventure, however, since the entire Porter family had been crazy about aquatics. Both her brothers had gained distinction as swimmers and water-polo players; and even Pop Porter, though considerably older than any of us, cut a tidy line in the water. Those were the days when we calculated athletic merit to the fifth of a second. When Johnnie Porter, meanwhile perched high among the branches of the plane-tree in the back-garden, sent his much younger brother down to Dymock's dairy for a pennyworth of confectionery, he always added, as an inducement to speed (lest the laddie should linger on the way back, and perhaps help himself to a sweetie or two!), that he would time him. When the panting Willie returned with 'the gundy', Johnnie would hold his hand as though it embraced a stop-watch, and yell down to him a fictitious time of so many minutes, so many seconds, and always one-fifth of a second tacked on, to make it sound the more professional. I wonder whether Johnnie, now pursuing the pious paths of architecture in Canada, remembers this deception of his as clearly as I recall that he was by way of being a comedian and juggler! No one gained from the younger fry in Leamy as much admiration as we bestowed upon Johnnie Porter, when he juggled with those three tiny balls of cork he carried in his pocket.

Johnnie's aerial perch reminds me that tree-climbing was a favourite pursuit among those participating in the adventures provided in the Porters' garden. Who could forget the House in the Trees, constructed with all the skill in arboreal tectonics Leamy could command? This leafy habitat, though primitively lit with candles, was well appointed in the matter of victual, which, for the most part, consisted of biscuits and 'ginger-pop', from Pop Porter's shop.

*   *   *   *   *   *   *

"And do you remember," Liz asked me, "how you used to pester us in the mornings for help with your French 'ekky', when I was busy giving Willie his breakfast, and getting him off to school?"

Of course, I remembered. I had had excellent reason to, since, on a trenchant occasion, the Porter family tried to stop these perpetual visits of mine by supplying me with a crib known to have been wrong in every alternate word, wherefore the scene in the French classroom, later in the day, was truly pitiable. "How do you explain this unprecedented performance?" enquired the master. You can picture the plight I was in, when I sought to mitigate matters by saying that Willie Porter's sister had assured me the exercise was correct, and that everyone knew her to be good at French!

"And do you remember the letter we once posted back to you?" Liz continued. I remembered it perfectly. Her younger brother, who shared with the rest of the Porter family its flair for comedy, was in the habit of going to the variety show at the Empire Theatre twice weekly. From each performance he derived additional material for his own repertoire of wholesome nonsense, and often a string of meaningless sayings. One day he presented us with his rendering of a turn in which a nigger came rushing on to the stage to ask the question, *'Kara-ma-latchie?'* When the audience responded with loud laughter, he answered himself with *'Dee-baa-go!'* One got heartily sick of Willie's inane repetition of these odd phrases, since he resorted to them, together with appropriate gesticulations, whenever he was addressed. One morning, thinking I might help to cure him of the habit, I wrote *'Kara-ma-latchie?'* at the top of a postcard, and *'Dee-baa-go!'* at the bottom. On the way to school, I posted it to him at Number Thirty. That evening the postman, feeling a little more dyspeptic than usual, arrived with an unstamped envelope addressed to me, which he refused to hand over until he had received twopence by way of surcharge. Having a shrewd suspicion what the letter was about (since the envelope bore the same handwriting as that of the fatal French exercise I had copied so confidently) and with *l'affaire fleurs-de-lys* still fresh in my mind, I pled with one of the maids to lend me the required sum before the Colonel appeared on the scene. I opened the envelope to find that it contained the card I had posted so hilariously that morning. It had come back to roost, with four times the postage to pay on it! The outward journey had cost but a halfpenny stamp. His Majesty's Post-Office now brought it back to me for twopence! Liz wasn't going to let her little brother be the meek and acquiescent recipient of such evil communications! Not she! For months afterwards, I refused to speak to either of them, and would not deign to look in their direction. That was the one and only occasion on which I addressed so foolish a card to anyone. Quite early in life, Liz cured me of any such tendency. Yet, when I visit Willie at his home in Edinburgh, as I am wont to do about once a year, we usually exchange greetings in those time-honoured, if somewhat idiotic, terms:

'*Kara-ma-latchie?*' says I.

'*Dee-baa-go!*' says he.

*   *   *   *   *   *   *

For several years after I resumed civilian life in 1919, I visited Mr Porter at his shop in Fountainbridge on Thursday evenings, at closing-time, and had high-tea with him there. This truly Scottish repast we shared on a newspaper behind the counter, surrounded by wines and spirits of very conceivable kind, and all the palatable things one might have seen on a licensed grocer's shelves in those plenteous days. The Colonel even accompanied me on one such occasion. He wanted to tell Mr Porter about Burma and Indo-China, in which the latter had expressed some interest. On arrival, we found the shop door closed, since it was already a minute or two after closing-time. But I soon dealt the door one tremendous bang with the side of my clenched fist, as was the custom among those of us entitled to admittance after hours. My father thought I was committing a felony, until Mr Porter opened the door from within, to assure him that this was our private practice. The newspaper table-cloth the Colonel did not mind in the least. He was too engrossed in talking about himself and his travels to be finicky about such a trifle, and felt himself more than adequately provided for when our host insisted that he should have the use of the only napkin on the premises.

"What are you wanting for your tea, MacGregor?" Mr Porter would ask me punctually at seven o'clock, as he followed the last customer to the door, closed it, and bolted it. Although I already had moved toward vegetarianism, the tinned foods in his establishment still offered ample scope, when we had had enough of boiled eggs. There were those tins of peaches and pears, which went well with the sponge-cake to be had at the bakery nextdoor.

Mr Porter permitted me the full run of his warm, shining, grocery shop. If I wanted a few sweets, I merely had to plunge my hand into the bottle containing those I fancied: if I preferred a

chocolate biscuit or two, all I had to do was to extract the appropriate tin: if inclined for a handful of sultanas, I knew the drawer
behind the counter: when thirsty, I went to the tumbler and the
bottle of fizz in the wee office at the back of the shop. It was so
wee, this office, that no more than two quite slim persons could
stand upright in it at a time, and only one could be seated. Yet,
it contained the cupboard at which I slaked my thirst when
passing on a hot summer's day, and also a few reference books I
was in the habit of consulting from time to time.

*   *   *   *   *   *   *

I learnt much from Mr Porter during those years of high-teas
with him. He had acquired, largely by accident, a perfect chaos
of information, and had known men engaged in the weirdest of
pursuits. Among his odd acquaintances was a fellow who made
wooden seeds for raspberry jam. When I doubted the existence
of so dishonest an occupation, he reached for a pot of a particular
make, and asked me (pointing to the seeds through the glass)
when, in the name o' God, I had ever seen a rasp wi' seeds *that*
size! Ocular demonstration convinced me.

And what was there he did not tell me, the bigoted teetotaller,
about underproof and overproof, and the specific gravity of this
liquid and of that? I soon realised that what 'The Trade' did
not know about the world's ways was simply not worth knowing.
And, indeed, it was remarkable how this man, deriving much of
his income from the sale of liquor, respected my rigid temperance.
Never once did he allude to it, not even in a bantering way.

Then, his reminiscences of Auld Reekie were legion. Though
perhaps a little disjointed, they were always entertaining. He could
recount many an amusing anecdote concerning some of our
leading citizens and merchants. "The fact that I cannae say them
in public, without getting had up for slander, doesna mean they're
no' true, mind ye!" he often remarked. "Man, but I could tell
ye a fine yarn aboot the Lord Provost! I mind him when he was
jist a bit laddie at the schule, wi' a patch in his breeks . . . Ay,
my! but I could tell ye a rare yin!"

He used to relate, with great relish, the true story of an Edinburgh amateur string quartette, the members of which, seeking
helpful criticism, invited a prominent professional musician to
hear them play their special piece. The professional arrived
slightly inebriate, and listened without a murmur. On being

asked for his opinion, he pointed his pipe-stem at the 'cellist, and remarked "That b——— is the worst!"

If you had junk to dispose of, or wanted to procure some, you were wise to consult Mr Porter. He could direct you to a nicety in such matters. If you were anxious to obtain an old and rare book, you had but to mention it to him, when he could tell you where a copy had been seen fairly recently.

His topographical knowledge of Scotland was immense, despite the fact that business kept him closely tied to his counter. I envied him his fine set of the *Ordnance Gazetteer of Scotland,* and considered myself privileged to be allowed to consult it without my having to travel as far afield as the public library. "Dash along to yon secondhand shop in the West Port!" he once yelled at me, as I entered his premises, "and ask for the parcel of books I bespoke. Give the mannie that ten-shilling note. He doesna ken the value o' them!"

I duly dashed, collected the parcel, and handed it over to Mr Porter. "Open it!" he continued, meanwhile slicing ham for a customer standing by. I did so. There, before me, lay a complete set of the *Gazetteer,* in perfect condition. It had come from a house near Galashiels, where there had been a sale of books some days previously. "There's a set for yourself," he added, without any demonstration. "It's a better one than my own, as you see." I frequently refer to these volumes; and they have travelled far and often with me since that day; and I never touch them but with remembrance of the kindly hands that bequeathed them, and of the heap of fallen *fleurs-de-lys* by the lane at Number Thirty.

Mr Porter shared with his descendants a grand sense of humour. He was, moreover, the repository of all sorts of nonsensical things. Take, for example, the following specimen of what he termed American rhyme, which amused me mightily the first time he quoted it:

'Arise, my son, and shut the shutter!'
This I heard a mother utter:
'The shutter's shut!' the boy did mutter,
'I cannot shut it any shutter!'

I think I enjoyed him best of all when he fell to relating his experiences as a shepherd-laddie living with his grandparents, and roving the hills of Angus and the Mearns in pursuit of his calling. He knew ilka linn of the North and South Esks, having fished them in boyhood for "wee broon troot"; and he had a store of homely recollections of the little country towns of Brechin and Fettercairn, of Edzell, Forfar, and Kirriemuir. The last-mentioned naturally brought us to his reminiscences of J. M. Barrie. And you should have heard him describe his rencounter with a ghost, one snowy night in 1880, as he drove his flock over the romantic Bridge of Gannochy. His stories of early years, with their hardships, certainly smacked of adventure. Those long tramps when gathering the sheep, or when droving them along the dusty highways and byways of a pre-petrol Scotland, were a topic that never lost its savour. How he loved to tell of his solicitous granny, when the laddie that he was returned from the hills at nightfall, wet and tired and famishing! His testimony to her goodness soon bore me away in imagination to Aunt Dorothy, living a life so full of flavour and idiosyncrasy among the sterner hills of Ross, and she so complete in her own works and ways, so assured in her hyperborean felicity, that the world of ordinary mortals scarcely impinged upon her.

*   *   *   *   *   *   *

My allusion to that snowy night at the Gannochy Bridge brings me to snowstorms. With stories of these, as experienced in his boyhood, Mr Porter soon lured one away to the wintry hills. And I have often wondered since, whether the terrific snowstorm, of which his grandparents used to tell him, and to which he so frequently alluded, as though he, too, had lived through it, was the same heavy fall—the same on-ding—as that about which another dweller in those parts told her little son. "I have seen many weary on-dings of snow," wrote Barrie, in the biography of Margaret Ogilvie, his mother; "but the one I seem to recollect best occurred nearly twenty years before I was born. It was at the time of my mother's marriage to one who proved a most loving, as he was always a well-beloved, husband—a man I am very proud to be able to call my father. I know not for how many days the snow had been falling, but a day came when the people lost heart, and would make no more gullies through it, and by next morning to do so was impossible: they could not fling the snow high enough. Its back was against every door when Sunday came, and none ventured out save a valiant few, who buffeted their way into my mother's home to discuss her predicament, for, unless she was 'cried' in the church that day, she might not be married for another week, and how could she be 'cried' with the minister a field away, and the church buried to the waist? For hours they talked, and at last some men started for the church, which was several hundred yards distant. Three of them found a window and, forcing a passage through it, 'cried' the pair; and that is how it came about that my father and mother were married on the first of March."

I wot not but that this was the very on-ding of which John Porter, recalling it as from his grandparents' lips, was wont to speak no less authoritatively.

*　　*　　*　　*　　*　　*　　*

Mr Porter, one would have said, was a talkative person. He once told me that he shared with Franklin the belief that, since we must account for every idle word spoken, so we must for every idle silence. And there was a sense in which he had read widely. He claimed to have perused every book on Syria and Babylon published in the English language; and he had a penchant for anything appertaining to Ur of the Chaldees. But, now that I am better qualified to assess the advantages of broader knowledge and discernment, it seems to me that the paths to literature, along which he had travelled, were rather too heavily macadamised, if one might use the term. It rendered him somewhat mercurial in conversation. Yet, I have to thank him for a part in my own initiation, so far as the world of books is concerned. "As Gibbon says in *The Decline and Fall*" was one of his favourite openings, when in the mood for exact citation. "Mind what I was telling you the other day about Abraham and his journey out of Ur?" was another. "Do you recall yon fine passage in Motley's *Dutch Republic*?" was yet a third that recurs to me. His literary interest at this time lay in old and decayed empires; and I vividly recall the precious wee book on the Persian dynasty, so beautifully bound, which he insisted on lending me. "See you read it, now!" was his monition, as I squeezed it into an inside pocket for safety, "because I'll want to discuss it with you later."

This man's walk in life should have been closer to Periclean paths. Had circumstances of birth and economic opportunity been less of a handicap, he would probably have been a classical scholar, or, perhaps, a professor of ancient history. How often did he express the desire to escape from his life of routine behind a counter! No one was more fully aware than himself that his abilities lay in some such direction. "MacGregor," he used to say, "I'm just a square peg in a round hole, or, if you prefer it, a round peg in a square one. I'm like so many folk, whose destiny is arranged for them." Yet, he never complained. The lines, he considered, had fallen to him in places tolerably pleasant. He believed he had a goodly heritage; and he was now reconciled to such limitation as the mere accident of birth had placed on him.

When my first book appeared in 1925, Mr Porter was doited with delight. He could not have been prouder, had I been his own son. For weeks beforehand, he had been telling friends and customers about its advent. On the day of publication, he sent his message-boy off to Princes Street, posthaste, to purchase a couple of copies. One of these he took home with him: the other he placed on the counter, conspicuous amid a collection of bottles containing his best bonded and blended wares, where it might be seen by all who entered.

"That's a book just published by my young friend, MacGregor," I once overheard him remark to a commercial traveller, as I lay out of sight behind the huge cardboard advertisements screening the rear part of his shop from public gaze. "I'm sure you've often seen the laddie in here. He has his tea wi' me here every Thursday, on his way to choir-practice. You'd better get a copy soon, mind ye! Afore they're a' sold out! And, if ye like, I'll get the laddie to write his name in it, the first time he's in."

The laddie in concealment behind cardboard heard every word of this. When he arrived for his weekly high-tea, he was frequently presented with a copy of his own book, left by friend or customer who wished to have it autographed.

Mr Porter was greatly interested in philology, I ought to have mentioned earlier; and I felt proud of myself when, on entering his shop one day, he began: "Ay, MacGregor, the very lad we're talking about! I've just been telling this 'traveller' that you're conversant with every word in the dictionary—every word in *Chambers's*, anyway."

"What's yon word you said he wouldn't know?" he now asked a commercial traveller who prided himself on his being more learnéd than others of the fraternity.

"Sizzygy," he replied.

"Sizzy what?" responded Mr Porter, scornfully, and a little afraid lest I might let him down. "Write it!" he insisted, meanwhile supplying this know-all with paper and pencil.

"Sizzygy," wrote the latter.

"Go on, MacGregor, lad! Tell him!" urged our umpire, by way of inciting me to verbal valour.

"Syzygy—s-y-z-y-g-y," I repeated. "You mean the time of the new or full moon, don't you? But you've misspelt it, haven't you?"

"My word, now!" observed Mr Porter, turning on the 'commercial' with an air of reflected triumph, as he hurried to the wee office for the dictionary. "What did I tell ye? The laddie's right. An' ye cannae even spell it!"

*   *   *   *   *   *   *

In the course of my visits to Fountainbridge, I came into contact with many an odd specimen of humanity. Among them was a man of but slight build, then in his sixties. He came at regular intervals (*i.e.*, in celebration of pay-day) to purchase a gill of the best 'Stormont'. This dissipated fellow interested us, for he wrote good poetry. William Archer was his name. He never had had more in the way of education than what the old board-school had given him. Yet, he had a talent for poetry, and a vocabulary and phraseology remarkable in a man of his station. His red nose and bleary eyes left no doubt as to where his worst enemy lurked. Not infrequently, Mr Porter would delay the departure of the better educated of his customers, that he might recite to them a verse or two of Archer's. "Ah, MacGregor!" he would say in a whisper, if I happened to arrive as the poet was leaving with his gill—"Ah, MacGregor, d'ye mind yon last line o' his?—'*And the beech-woods still sang on*'. Man, but it's sad the way he's going. He's awa' there wi' his gill, as contented as can be."

I also remember an old soldier—a *very* old soldier, I should say—one of those who, according to the barrackroom ballad, never die. He used to reach this rendezvous at closing-time on a specified day. His name was MacGregor. This I knew before meeting him under Mr Porter's auspices, since it was his wont to draw himself to attention whenever the Colonel passed, and to acknowledge him in a style so regimental as to cause him to totter a little on his agéd pins. The king himself never got from this nonagenarian representative of the Black Watch a salute more royal than he gave father on the streets of Auld Reekie.

Once a week, then, this ancient pensioner, living in a common lodging-house somewhere in the vicinity of Fountainbridge or the West Port, came to Mr Porter's by arrangement—nay, *by appointment*—to receive such odds and ends as fell so generously from the grocer's counter. These he stuffed into the pockets of an old and frayed greatcoat, said to have been with him since Crimean days. Those pockets at all times bulged with bits of things wrapped in tattered newspaper. Mr Porter always sent MacGregor on his way, rejoicing, for his receiving scraps of ham and the like was but a prelude to his getting other things as well. "Here, MacGregor!" he would shout to my unwashed clansman, as he toddled toward the door. "Would that make a supper to you?"

"'Deed, but it wud!" the superannuated hero would respond, as our host thrust into his gnarled and grimy hand a tin of salmon.

Nearly half a century had slipped by since my grubby clansman had been pensioned off; and all were agreed that the day he left the Forty-Second Highlanders—'the Gallant Forty-Twa'—was the day he last sampled, to any appreciable extent, the cleansing properties of soap and water. This explained why Mr Porter included in MacGregor's Christmas-box a bar of the most potent soap on the premises. MacGregor took this gift in good part, and, for a week or so thereafter, looked a little less begrimed.

In a somewhat different category were those who, sharing with Mr Porter his interest in philately, and duly equipped with pocket magnifying-glass, tweezers, and like accessories denoting professional seriousness, visited him regularly at his shop, and embarked on much converse of a technical nature, while exchanging their duplicates, or trading with him the scarcer of their wares. Was it not to Mr Porter that Stirling Melville, seeking a little ready capital to assist him in the purchase of electrical equipment he wanted so badly, sold his stamp collection for the vast sum of twenty pounds ten? You should hear Stirling himself relate how this transaction redeemed a bankrupt schoolboy, and enabled him to live opulently for a year or more.

*   *   *   *   *   *   *

A few years ago, Mr Porter went over, at the age of seventy-seven. In the old premises in Fountainbridge, strangers now reign in his stead. Yet, when I visit Edinburgh and pass this way, I still see him there, in his doorway, as of yore, wiping his pince-nez with the corner of his apron, or perhaps trimming a frayed finger-nail, in daylight, with the slim scissors, the point of which usually protruded from a waistcoat pocket.

The sign of the City Wine Stores now flourishes over the shop-front, yonder, by the corner of Fountainbridge and Earl Grey Street. His successors, however, have retained the vermilion freshness that characterised this frontage in the heyday of their memorable predecessor.

Why is it that cold, cast-iron inanimation outlives us, and with but little deterioration that one can detect? Even the old paint on the *fleurs-de-lys*, scarcely faded, has survived most of those neighbours who were in tangible being when Mr Porter replaced the ones we had wrecked.

In remembering this genuine friend of my youth, this man who bore so little of the taint of worldliness—in remembering our years of high-teas together, our mutual quest for knowledge, and our simple delight at the finding—I feel there is something here that places upon Time the imprint of Eternity. Deep down in me, he enjoys a mystic athanasia. Could I be forgetful of all the bounteous benefits bestowed on me in early life by such loving folk, now beyond recall?

Coat of Arms of the North British Railway Company

The Old North British Up-Highland Express at Perth—the train that conveyed me the first stage of my long journey between Auld Reekie and Aunt Dorothy's, among the Highland hills

CHAPTER XIV

STIRLING MELVILLE

WITH HIS parents at No. 50 lived Stirling Melville of the bonnie, auburn locks. They were the happiest trio in all the world. Stirling's parents' marriage, in contradistinction with the Colonel's and Mabel's, was an unending honeymoon. Their only child, beloving his parents, was beloved of them. He, too, went to Watson's; and he and Iain, both of like age, and sedulous in their enthusiasm for foreign stamps, had some sporadic intercourse when exchanging their duplicates.

We of less studious disposition regarded Stirling Melville as the only truly brainy lad in the Terrace, excepting, of course, our own Iain. And he appeared as facile of hand as of mental abstraction. While the parents of this somewhat delicate and refined youngster filled the evening hours with music of their own making (his father played the 'cello to his mother's piano accompaniment) he would be working out his own little problems in his own little room, or seated pensively at the drawingroom window, conning some learnéd tome. There never existed a household more harmonious than the Melvilles'. It continued in striking contrast with the Colonel's, farther down the Terrace, where, as though a power, at once sinister, impious, and malevolent, had laid hold upon it, bickerings and flytings were the established order.

Stirling's father used to ply him playfully with the notion that the Melville Monument, in Auld Reekie, commemorated an ancestor of theirs. Whether the son actually believed this, or even lent as much as a whisper to it, we never knew; but we certainly had heard that the Leamy Melvilles put forward some vague claim to relationship with the historic figure represented by fourteen feet of statue at the top of the tall column in St Andrew's Square. One wintry school-day, however, a classmate greeted Stirling with the announcement, "Your uncle's got snow on his shoulders this morning!" This jibe Stirling reported to his father on his return from school that afternoon; and therewith ended Mr Melville's innocent claim to kinship with the family of Henry Dundas, Viscount Melville!

The Celtic monks who, of eld, laboured on the Book of Kells and the like, never produced work more exquisitely adorned than did Mr Melville, in the course of his professional lithography; and many an Auld Reekie home at the present day possesses specimens of his handicraft. There was no one in all Scotland defter than he in the matter of illuminated addresses. His office in Thistle Street was as much a place of surprise as it was of industry. It diffused that atmosphere of particularity, that standard of perfection, which has given to the more industrious of the Scots their reputation for accuracy and efficiency, combined with scholarship.

Stirling's maternal great-uncle, by the way, was none other than the Rev. Archibald Bisset, of Ratho. This typical old parish minister, greatly revered, was, of course, R. L. S.'s tutor. Bisset, in the personal reminiscences he gives us of his charge's university life at Edinburgh, describes him as a fragile youth with a very noticeable stoop of the shoulders, and a poorly developed chest, suggesting constitutional delicacy—an impression confirmed, as he says, by his long hair, which lent to his face an emaciated appearance. It was when a mutual friend introduced Stevenson to Bisset as "son and successor of Thomas Stevenson, the wellknown lighthouse engineer", that the former made the oft-quoted retort, "Son, certainly; but not successor, if *I* can help it!"

Stirling tells me (and it is surely a matter of pertinent interest) that, when Bisset died, and his library, among other effects, was being sold off, the few volumes inscribed "To my friend and tutor, from R. L. S." realised more than did the remaining thousand or two, the majority of which, doubtless, were large and antiquated theological works. This fragment of information Stirling, as a boy, had from his grandmother, the Rev. Archibald Bisset's sister.

*　　*　　*　　*　　*　　*　　*

It came as no surprise to us in Leamy when Stirling's flair for originality found expression in *The Leamingtonian*, a magazine he edited and produced at varying intervals. There never existed more than one copy of each number, of course; but the entire production was Stirling's own. He wrote it, illustrated it with his own hand, and, in his capacity as editor and proprietor, conducted it on business lines. Who of Leamy, where, in the main, it circulated, forgets the important public notices appearing

on the inside of the cover? A particularly memorable one ran thus:
"This Magazine is lent out on the understanding that it must
not be torn, or dirtied, or damages will have to be paid for.
The price per night is as quoted at the time of lending." This final and
somewhat arbitrary reservation enabled Stirling to alter the price
to subscribers, as and when he chose. It was printed prominently,
in these exact words, on the cover of all issues, and was never
seriously challenged, though the more plackless often wheedled
him into reducing his prices when they found them beyond their
very slender means. But it was usually a case of 'take-it-or-leave-
it'. Stirling had a monopoly in this, the work of his own brain
and hand; and he regulated his monopoly with what we were
apt to regard as anything but impartiality.

The contents of *The Leamingtonian* were as numerous as they
were varied. The nature-study notes—a standard feature—
ranged from an intimate treatise on earth-worms (I still see his
illustrative drawings of those squiggly things purporting to represent "tiny ropes of black soil that are called wormcasts")
to the damage done by monkeys and other animals to the telegraph
wires stretching across British East Africa. One is reminded that
"the hippopotamus is also a nuisance, because he uses the poles
for rubbing-posts, and sometimes knocks them over".

Never an issue of *The Leamingtonian* went to press at No. 50
that did not contain instructive data on inventions, and on how
to construct such things as electro-magnets and helicopters.
Jokes and conundrums (the answers to the latter being artfully
supplied in subsequent issues, by way of maintaining circulation)
were a specialty. Quotations from the poets always lent a touch
of uplift, as did those stories with a moral, without at least one of
which no number of *The Leamingtonian* ever found its way into
public hands. Of the latter, the following story, entitled 'As You
Please', was typical:

"In ancient times there lived a wonderfully wise man, of whom
it was said that he could answer correctly any question put to him.
There was one, however, who thought himself clever enough to
outwit the sage. This man took a poor, captive bird, and clasped
it so closely in his hand that only the head and tail were visible.
'Tell me,' said he, to the renowned guesser of riddles, 'is the bird
I hold in my hand alive or dead?' If the answer were 'dead',
thought this artful plotter, he would just open his hand and let the
bird fly: if the answer were 'alive', he would, with one small

squeeze, crush the poor bird to death. But the wise man proved himself equal to the occasion, and replied, 'It is as you please' !

"Each one of you holds, within his or her grasp, the fair bird of life. Which is it to be? A blessing or a bane? It is *as you please*."

* * * * * * *

If, however, I were asked in what connection No. 50 was best known to us all at the period about which I write, I think I would have to answer with the apple-tree growing in the Melvilles' fourth of the large back-garden. That tree, though of quite modest dimensions, often bore, in a season, as many as 90 lbs. of fruit, as the accurate Stirling reminds me. Now it is much decayed. A mere stump is to be seen where, but a decade ago, flourished its trunk. In its heyday, as you may well believe, it was subjected to many a ruthless raid. When a frontal attack upon it seemed impracticable, it was set upon from the rear. The boys from Viewforth, accustomed to contemplate its temptatious boughs from the back-windows of the tenements in which they lived, slipped in by the *cul-de-sac* known as Admiral Terrace, then came along the top of the lofty wall, to 'dreep' its twelve feet, or slither down some elder bushes, to garden level.

* * * * * * *

Today Stirling Melville is one of Auld Reekie's principal experts in the matter of corporation gas. So, if anything of a technical nature be worrying you about your gas-supply, *after office hours*, do not hesitate to telephone him, and put the blame on me !

When visiting him recently, he handed me a volume—*The British Empire Illustrated Dictionary*—which Mr Porter (the purchaser of his stamps, as already related) had given him many a year ago. Quoth the donor at the time of donation, "I always look at a dictionary to see whether it contains the words, *plankton* and *until*. This dictionary contains neither. So it's of no use to me. Take it with you, if you'd like it."

That dictionary, as I plainly remember, lay on the desk in the wee office. Mr Porter's contempt for it, as it gathered dust beside *Chambers's*, which stood, upright, but a few inches away, aye ready to hand, was shown by the wine-glass and tiny tumbler that reposed on it for years, and, as the circular stains on its morocco cover indicated, had often been replaced when their bases were none too dry.

The feel of this volume in my hands was of something I had known before, and had handled often. Its coloured plates, I rather imagine, had been its chief attraction for me, in my less discriminating days. In turning it over, for Auld Lang Syne, I found on the fly-leaf, pencilled in John Porter's clear calligraphy, like a warning to the intending user, "Awanting—*Plankton, Until*." With the rubber-stamp his friends knew so well, he had placed his imprint on the title-page, for he was much given to lending his books, and borrowers, then as now, were no less prone to retain them. Thus ran his imprint:

JOHN S. PORTER

TEA DEALER
AND SCOTTISH WHISKY
MERCHANT

57, FOUNTAINBRIDGE
EDINBURGH

By no means the least odd among the books available in that wee office was a French guide-book, published somewhere about 1870, and containing a thousand everyday phrases calculated to assist the English in learning French. One such phrase this tome enshrined I have never forgotten: "*Send help at once! Our postillion has been struck by lightning!* "

*   *   *   *   *   *   *

See, before you die, Stirling's mystery room in the basement of his present home at Inverleith Row, with its workshop, nextdoor, where he and his father constructed many a complicated device. The walls of the latter apartment are hung with myriads of tools, methodically arranged for ready use. Its floor is set with machinery —lathes and the like. The uninitiated dare not put finger to anything down there, lest it should go off! The nether regions of his home are, indeed, a terrifying place except, perhaps, to the electrically-minded. What experiments have father and son not carried out in that basement? The alchemists of old could not have mystified their contemporaries more completely than did Stirling, when I first descended to this abode of wonder. To him, of course, there does not appear to be anything the least unusual about all this. He finds everything simple and entirely rational.

Was there ever a fellow who knew so much about so much, and had less nonsense about him? No wizard—not even the Warlock Laird o' Moray—ever inaugurated stranger ongoings in his laboratory.

And what is there he does not know about the science of sound, which is his particular interest? He is, in fact, one of our foremost experimenters in sound, and an authority on the physics of music, though I warn you he is the sort of chiel who will roundly repudiate any such claim made on his behalf. But is there anything, from mermaids to mathematics, about which he does not know? You should hear how his pick-up arrangement reproduces his superb collection of gramophone records. Hear its treatment of Chabrier's *España*, for instance. The most skilled technicians with "His Master's Voice", or with the B.B.C. for that matter, never produced finer results than does Stirling's own brand of amplifier. His is the place to visit to appreciate the real possibilities of modern recording.

You should just see his experimental equipment, all of it his own manufacture. See, for example, the great baffle-board that swings on hinges, carrying a battery of loud-speakers, behind which there lies hidden all manner of mysterious mechanism vaguely visible amid a multitude of glowing bulbs when the board is temporarily swung open to permit of some adjustment.

The baffle-board! What do you think it once was, and whence came it? It was once a *black*-board at George Watson's. At the auction-sale of superfluous furniture, following the dismantling of the old school by the Meadows, when Watson's was transferred to Colinton Road, a dealer bought, at a shilling a-piece, those individual desk-&-seat arrangements, which we had known in Henry John Findlay's geography classroom. The black-boards went for a few pence. Stirling shortly afterwards purchased three of them for a shilling, from a dealer in Abbeyhill; and one of these now constitutes his baffle-board—so termed, he tells me, because its area is sufficient to prevent the sound waves, originating at the front of the diaphragm, from short-circuiting by flying round the back of the board. Ah! maybe, that very baffle-board once displayed those angles and triangles, those co-sines and tangents, that always baffled *me*.

Stirling's basement is a repository of scientific knowledge. The walls of its strange apartments are fitted with shelves crammed with scientific and technical books, used by father and son in their

respective pursuits. Drawers and cupboards are stacked with
delicate instruments, near which only the expert dare venture.

In a corner stands a chest-of-drawers, each drawer big in area,
but no more than an inch in depth. They are filled with an
assortment of sketches, plans, and designs, many of which were
prepared by the master-hand of Stirling's father. Would it interest
you to know that, for donkey's years, this piece of furniture stood
in Robinson's, the shop in Greenside, once known to every
Auld Reekie boy owning a toy-theatre? From this very chest-of-
drawers R. L. S. and his contemporaries were supplied with their
'penny plain and twopence coloured'.

CHAPTER XV

NEIGHBOURS

THE EDINBURGH of my youth was still a metropolis of dimensions sufficiently modest to permit of one's knowing the neighbours by name and repute, as well as by sight. In practice, this meant that everyone knew rather much about everyone else. The inhabitant, who had gained distinction, whether as profligate or as preacher, was given the fullest consideration, since Auld Reekie folk derived as much diversion in familiarising themselves with the sins of the former, as with the attributes and inspired utterances of the latter. The injunctions of the Paper Controller must necessarily place some limit upon what I might feel inclined to recall about such neighbours as lived in immediate proximity to Leamy. Let us look, however, at a few of those residing round the corner, in Gilmore Place. Every day, whether on the way to school or to church or to public entertainment, or when seeking contact with Princes Street and the city's more fashionable shops, we passed along this not unimportant thoroughfare, either on foot, or aboard the tramcar.

*   *   *   *   *   *   *

We had been resident in Auld Reekie but a week when the Colonel discovered Miss Annie MacAulay. Or was it Miss Annie who discovered the Colonel? The probability is that she, a Highlandwoman, made the first approach with a word or two in the Gaelic, as the Colonel swaggered past her shop-door in the kilt, so soon after our arrival from the North. She might have been on the pavement outside her shop at the time, reviewing her window-display of chocolates and tobacco, or pulling down the shade, lest the sun melted her delicacies, as often happened during those warmer summers. Having made father's acquaintance, she was not slow to extend the hand of beneficence to his children. She had no doubt Iain and I were his sons, the first day she spoke to us, MacGregor tartan denoting our origin. As this preface to friendship had to be sealed with Highland Hospitality, we were invited to enter the shop and be seated, while she plied us with

136

lemonade and biscuits, and presented each of us with a slab of cream chocolate, the better to impress upon us this first of many hundreds of subsequent visits. One half of her establishment contained every assortment of high-class confectionery. High-class, mark you! Printed notices stuck up here and there left no uncertainty on *that* score. The remaining half was divided equally between biscuits and aerated waters, on the one hand, and tobacco and cigarettes, on the other. Under the counter were stored all manner of commodities, ranging from halfpenny bundles of firewood to cartons of broken biscuits.

Miss MacAulay lived in the back premises. The bell that tinkled but feebly when the shop-door opened was sufficient to apprize her of customers. She spoke in slow, clear tones; and her accent was as unmistakably Hebridean as on the day she left her native Isle of Benbecula, thirty or forty years before, to try her fortune as tobacconist and confectioner in the Scottish Capital. What was there about Uist and Benbecula she had not told us children, during the years we lived but a couple of hundred yards from her? And how dramatic she could be when telling us of tragedies in the tides and quicksands of the Benbecula fords!

A day seldom passed that at least one member of our household did not enter her premises on one errand or another. Sometimes we might visit her thrice daily, according to the coppers we had in hand. She always gave the Colonel's bairns over-weight; and we liked to see and hear the scales going down with a hearty plump in our favour. There were even times when, having given us what we had come for, she refused to take our pennies. That, of a surety, was Highland Hospitality in excess.

Miss MacAulay's counter, I suppose, must have been the first, on the private side of which I had stood since Applecross days. And what a queer experience it was! It gave one the sense of a curious intimacy with those things in life that grown-ups did and felt; and it was, perhaps, for this reason that one was inclined to feel a little guilty of trespass. Although you had been invited behind the scenes, as it were, by Miss MacAulay herself (and who more entitled to invite one than the proprietrix?) you remained slightly conscious of your being where you had no right to be. But what a revelation it was! You now saw the shop through the shopkeeper's eyes, instead of through the customer's; and the difference in perspective was remarkable. How altered every-thing appeared! The very customers were changed when you looked at them from the private side of that counter! Hitherto, all counters had acted as an insurmountable barrier between the covetous schoolboy and those delectable things he eyed on the farther side of them. But here was I, in the midst of them, able to touch and to examine them closely. This initial privilege found palatable expression when I was actually encouraged to sample a few of the choice sweetmeats stacked around me. Was ever a lad more embarrassed, at the outset, by a suggestion so unexpected? But the embarrassment, I do confess, soon wore off, as my fingers began to take confidence, and feel their way among those well-stocked shelves. Not since infancy at Applecross, when old Mrs MacRae gave me 'the run of my teeth' behind *her* counter, had I partaken of anything quite so akin to paradise.

One of the curiosities about Caulay's shop (we soon found her full name rather long; and she encouraged us in the use of this abridgment) was the show-card prominently displayed, and bearing the legend, *Do not ask for credit. It is painful to refuse.* Ah! how little I then thought that one day, when more adult and sceptical, I should want to make some further enquiry into the nature and function of credit, and, in so doing, should forfeit any reverence I once may have had for our antiquated monetary system! Whenever I hear of credit, and those thousands of millions of pounds of non-existent money chancellors of the exchequer are in the bad habit of borrowing, to the utter undoing of mankind, my mind flies off to that quaint show-card in Caulay's shop.

As a youth, my greatest interest in Caulay resided in her frequent allusions to the Ardlamont Case—to the Ardlamont Mystery, as it is sometimes called. One Sunday afternoon she persuaded me to accompany her on her weekly stroll, so that she might point out the large, self-contained house in which Monson, the supposed murderer of young Cecil Hamborough, had lived. To the best of my recollection, it was situated somewhere between the Merchiston and Polwarth districts of our city, less than twenty minutes' walk from her shop. This incident had occurred roughly two decades previously. You would have thought it had happened the night before, had you heard Caulay expatiate on it! Indeed, while listening to her, as she and I stood on the pavement outside the house that Sunday afternoon, I might have been excused for thinking that Monson had encompassed the unfortunate Cecil's death that very day. So vivid was her telling that, in lingering near-by, as she continued to relate the entire story in detail, it would not have astonished me, had police officials been observed leaving the premises after a thorough search. The victim, of course, did not meet his end here at all but away by the lonely shores of Cowal, near Ardlamont Point.[1] Caulay, however, delivered herself so dramatically of her version, and in terms so gruesome, that I began to feel the murder had actually taken place within those walls, at which I now gazed with growing morbidity. My introduction to criminology, I do declare, dates from that afternoon's stroll with this imaginative Isleswoman.

Nothing gave Caulay more joy in her latter years than visits from people to whom, as children, she had sold her sugary wares. She dearly loved to have old friends calling upon her; and she was alert at placing the kent face. "My God! And is it yourself?" was her invariable greeting, if she had not seen you for some time. In so saying, she would raise her hands to the skies, as the minister does when pronouncing the benediction.

* * * * * * *

Up a stair in the old tenement, of which Caulay's premises formed a part, there lived, with his grey sister, a queer mannie named Shand. What he was to trade or profession, I now forget, if indeed I ever knew. He may have been a clerk or a bookkeeper. He resembled a fellow who, in boyhood, had started in an office at a few shillings a week, and had spent a lifetime perched on

---

[1] The trial of Cecil Hamborough's tutor, Alfred John Monson, in December, 1893, before Lord Justice-Clerk MacDonald and a jury, remains one of the most sensational, as well as one of the most complex and diverse, in Scottish annals. Hamborough, a boy of seventeen, was killed at Ardlamont, Argyllshire, by a shot from a sporting gun, while out shooting with Monson and a man named Scott, both of whom declared that he had accidentally shot himself with his own gun. Major Hamborough had entrusted his son to Monson at £300 a year. Monson was to coach him for the army. Not until he applied for payment of two life assurance policies, to the value of £20,000, which the unfortunate boy had taken out before his death, and had assigned to him, was suspicion aroused. Monson was arrested, and later charged at Edinburgh with the attempted murder and with the murder of young Hamborough. The motive alleged at the trial, which lasted ten days, was his interest in the considerable sum represented by Hamborough's life assurance, and also his interest in his ward's expectancy in the Hamborough estates. At the opening of the proceedings, the judge passed sentence of outlawry on Scott, whose real name was Edward Sweeney, and who had disappeared. The jury returned the peculiarly Scottish verdict of *Not Proven*. For an exhaustive account of the "Ardlamont Mystery", as it is called, consult *The Trial of A. J. Monson*, in the Notable British Trials Series, published at Edinburgh by William Hodge.

Each year, on the anniversary of Cecil's death, there appeared in the *Glasgow Herald* an In Memoriam notice: "Vengeance is mine; I will repay, saith the Lord." It may be inserted yet, for all I know.

a stool, gradually, but inevitably, assuming the appearance of a moulting parrot. Had he lived in London a century earlier, Dickens, for certain, would have immortalised him. In his spare time, and with an air of mystery, he peddled bits of jewellery and trinkets of one class or another. That large, leather jewel-case of his was thought to contain all manner of precious stones laid in precious metals. In the half-light of evening, one might see him in the vicinity, flitting by in stealth, his movements rendered a little more noticeable by reason of the whiteness of the bull-terrier bitch that dragged him along by her leash, and at a pace brisker than when he ventured abroad alone.

Our interest in this queer mortal began when he suddenly took to saluting the Colonel on the street. The Colonel, not unimpressed by this gratuitous deference, once stopped him and asked him to explain himself. It then transpired that he had been a soldier of sorts—a sergeant—"only in the Territorials", as father liked to remind us in sarcasm. For years this saluting continued; and old Shandy, as we called him, might be observed going out of his way to cross the road with his dog, when he saw the Colonel approach, that he might indulge his old-soldier fancy at closer range.

Shandy assured us, with no small gratification to himself, that he had some connection with the North, and that, a few years previously, he had been in the way of seeing Iain and me, in company with father, walking the streets of Inverness, all of us attired in the kilt. At times he himself paraded in the kilt, together with bowler hat, and an outsize Inverness cape dyed with crottles, and reaching down to his buckled brogues. The brand of cape gave weight to his declaration that it was in *Inverness* he used to see us. This sartorial array found little favour with the perfervid Colonel, who, in the first place, liked to maintain that the wretched Shandy was not entitled to wear the tartan (Who ever heard of the Shand clan or the Shand tartan? he would ask); and, in the second, that he hadn't what is known north of the Tweed as *the leg for the kilt*. Without being too uncharitable, I must confess he looked ridiculous in this get-up of his, especially when hurrying along with a tray of trinkets under one arm, all but hidden in the amplitude of his cape, and the dog's lead tugging at the other. As you will have gathered, nothing excited the Colonel's ire as readily as his encountering someone wearing a tartan to which he could establish no claim, or disporting the kilt without the requisite physique. He was firm in the conviction, of course, that no one in Auld Reekie wore this dress with greater distinction than himself. And there was more than an element of truth in this. For all his conceit in regard to such matters, he certainly had the build and carriage for this picturesque attire, as Edinburgh citizens still remind me. How could a puir cratur like Shandy adopt the swagger necessary to give this garment the swing to which it was entitled? he used to ask. Such pseudo-Highlanders only rendered our ancient dress ridiculous in Sassenach eyes.

In wet weather, when an old and very shiny mackintosh took the place of the Inverness cape, this odd neighbour of ours cut a sorry figure. Even his quite ample bowler hat did not protect his red and rather prominent neb from the raindrops that trickled down to hang in a large, luminous globe at the point of it, until gravity got the better of it, and it fell on his soaking front to make room for the gradual accumulation of another. In such conditions, he looked like a drookit hen.

* * * * * * *

If the Colonel were impatient with poor Shandy, there was another Highland family, living but a few doors away, which compensated him with kindness, and now and again found itself recipient of some special gem or trinket from his jewel-case, by way of token. To this family I myself became indebted, quite early in life, for my introduction to much good music, and, above all, to that lovely compilation, *Songs of the North*. The latter point may appear trivial to you, unless you claim acquaintance with our northern minstrelsy, and perhaps have experienced, at one time or another, a similar discovery in the world of music and poesy. Since that day, my life has been so full of song that it would ill-befit me not to mention my own humble beginnings among much talent, and in a home dominated by the traditions of Highland Hospitality. The happiest recollections and associations of my youth and early manhood are bound up either with water or with music. To this house I was in the way of being invited to my first musical evenings among musicians, nearly all of whom had attained professional status. And here, under gentle tuition, I learnt to sing a little, and then a lot, for the entertainment of others. My initial essay in this direction was with those lines by Christopher North,[1] set to an old Highland

---

[1] The pseudonym of John Wilson (1785–1854), who was Professor of Moral Philosophy at Edinburgh from 1820 until 1851, and whose fame rests mainly

melody arranged by Malcolm Lawson, a melody I so often had
heard on Mabel's lips in Highland childhood:

> *The stars are shining, cheerily, cheerily,*
> *Ho-ro, Mhairi dhu, turn ye to me!*
> *The seamew is moaning, drearily, drearily,*
> *Ho-ro, Mhairi dhu, turn ye to me!*
> *Cold is the storm-wind that ruffles his breast,*
> *But warm are the downy plumes lining his nest;*
>   *Cold blows the storm there,*
>   *Soft falls the snow there;*
> *Ho-ro, Mhairi dhu, turn ye to me!*
>
> *The waves are dancing, merrily, merrily,*
> *Ho-ro, Mhairi dhu, turn ye to me!*
> *The seabirds are wailing, wearily, wearily,*
> *Ho-ro, Mhairi dhu, turn ye to me!*
> *Hushed be thy moaning, lone bird of the sea!*
> *Thy home on the rocks is a shelter to thee:*
>   *Thy home is the angry wave,*
>   *Mine but the lonely grave;*
> *Ho-ro, Mhairi dhu, turn ye to me!*

Those verses are never far from my mind. Their Gaelic flavour
lingers with me, undiminished. The first phrase or two of this song
transports me instantly to that drawingroom at 38, Gilmore Place.
I feel the warm fire, and see the chintzes that matched those tiny
specimens of the most exquisite English china you ever saw.
This china crowded upon the mantelpiece and on the shelves
of several cabinets; and I do not exaggerate when I say that one
was terrified of sneezing in this room, for fear of bringing the more
delicately poised ornaments toppling about one's ears. You
might have been in a little museum of pretty things, all of which
had been inherited, or collected over a number of years. And,
somehow or other, among these dainty ornaments (how vividly
I see those little scent-bottles and delicate fans of a more graceful
age!) a host of ancestral photographs found a stance. Photographs
and ornaments had stood so long in this identical juxtaposition
that, by now, they diffused a mutual veneration. The vacant
chair could not have been more mindful of an absent friend than
was the removal, even temporarily, either of a photograph or of
an ornament. They had dwelt so long together in this harmonious
proximity that the displacement of one of them made the others
fretful. It was certainly thus with the two stuffed birds, ancient

---

on the *Noctes Ambrosianæ*, begun in *Blackwood's* in 1822 by several writers, but
continued by Wilson alone after 1825. This was a series of scenes purported
to have occurred in a tavern kept by one Ambrose, in Register Street, Edinburgh.
(See *Christopher North: John Wilson*, by Elsie Swann, published by Oliver &
Boyd in 1935.)

inhabitants of this place—the hawk perched on a twig, and the hoodie-crow standing on a block of imitation rock, eyeing each other with esteem from opposite sides of a wall mirror. Who would say that things so readily termed inanimate do not live?— do not reflect the hands that tend them, the minds that love them? The precious things in this room had been well cared for; and they knew it, and were unanimous in their appreciation.

And what does one recall more vividly of this drawingroom than its red window-blind, that excluded the dark of night, and proclaimed a note of warmth and welcome to the passer-by? I also visualise the piano about to be played, the corner of a violin-case protruding from underneath the sofa, as if suggesting that its inmate should be asked to contribute something to the evening. The very fragment of resin, reposing by the keyboard, became articulate at times, and called out to be brought into service. And I remember, likewise, the feel of those old-world tea-cups that were handed round in due course, and the rare plates laden with toothsome comestibles. Why has that admirable institution, the musical evening, been allowed to go out of fashion, taking with it so much harmony and civility? Do we really get from canned music the enjoyment we once derived from creating our own?

This Highland family was as superstitious as it was musical. It observed many an old custom, and gave credence to not a few of our old beliefs. At least one member of it read cups as cleverly as any spaewife. It celebrated Hogmanay in true Highland fashion, not in revelry and rioting at the Tron Kirk, but in the home; and each one of its members dreaded more than the other, lest their first-footer should arrive without bringing some material trifle with him. Even an apple, or a penny bar of chocolate, handed to whichever of them answered the door, was sufficient to allay anxiety. Of nothing were they so certain as that the New Year, upon which we had just embarked, would find them in want, if the first person to cross their threshold did so, empty-handed. Conversely, they believed that all manner of beneficence was sure to come their way throughout the ensuing year, if the first-footer happened to be a dark man who had brought them some small gift. They were genuinely alarmed if he came without anything at all, and would refuse to admit him. Had they done so, any misfortune befalling them during that year would have been attributed to ill-luck conveyed to them by their first visitor. He might have been the wrong complexion, for instance, or the wrong age. Or he might have come without some trinket or eatable, which meant that they were bound to face dearth before the year was out.

Once, in youth, I unwittingly first-footed them, empty-handed. Had I approached their doorstep, bearing them the Ten Plagues of Egypt, they could not have exhibited greater alarm. Never had a visitor been less welcome. Up went a window on the ground floor, and out went an arm. It was the arm of their Highland and very superstitious mother, then a woman well over sixty. She was holding out to me an orange, that I might have something to offer them as I entered. My ingress with that orange, they were convinced, vouchsafed to them peace and plenty throughout the year upon which we had embarked but a few minutes. It mattered not whether, thereafter, subsequent callers brought Hogmanay gifts. What *did* matter was that the New Year's *first* visitor should bring them some small thing.

Food and drink they pressed upon one, however incapable of intake might be the recipient—nay, the victim—of their traditional hospitality. It boded ill that anyone crossing their threshold should be reluctant to partake. It never occurred to them that this expression of kindness was little more than a "species of well-meant persecution", to quote the phrase Scott employs when alluding to the manner in which the natives of the Northern Kingdom insist that the stranger within their gates shall do more than comfortable justice to their board.

* * * * * * *

As might have been expected in the home of folk so prone to music, and who, themselves, did much reel and strathspey playing, one was liable to meet there talent ranging from that of the operatic vocalist to that of the pipe-major. The passer-by must have heard the skirl o' the pipes as often as he did the re-sounding arpeggios of *Maiden of Morven*, or the quiet cadenzas of the violin.

I sometimes met at this house one of the most picturesque of men—James Scott Skinner, "The Strathspey King". This celebrated exponent of the violin, with his enormous repertoire of reels and strathspeys, was always an attraction at any function where he performed. In the Scotland of my youth, no Burns Festival worthy of the designation failed to include, among its artistes, this quaint septuagenarian. Clad habitually in Highland garb, his dignified bearing soon caught the eye, as he strode our

Margaret Stewart as Mattie
(" *Stay! Ye may bring the bottle wi' ye, Mattie!* ")

THE MILLENNIUM BROTHERHOOD. *From left to right*: (1) *West African Seediboy*, (2) *Somali Warrior*, (3) *Arab Sheik*, (4) *Hindoo Dakeem*, (5) *Highland Cateran* (*the Colonel disguised as an Arab Chief*), (6) *Somali Swimming-boy or 'Have-a-dive,'* (7) *Tinpot-hooded Parsee*, (8) *Bearded Mussulman*, (9) *Ringletted Jew*, (10) *Pigtailed Chinaman* (*see page 210.*)

highways. About his platform habiliments he was fastidious to the merest minutiae. Skean-dhu and powder-horn were placed with meticulous care; and the very laces of his deer-skin brogues displayed a finish. His deportment was, in itself, a work of art. It fascinated his audience no less than did his playing.

Edinburgh saw much of Scott Skinner during the years of which I write, since his innumerable engagements in the Lowlands obliged him to leave Angus (he had lived at Kirriemuir, and also at Carnoustie) for Darling's Hotel, that homely hostelry in Waterloo Place, so wellknown to the Scotland of his generation. In 1917, while residing at Darling's, he was presented with his portrait—a striking likeness—now hanging in the Dundee Art Gallery. In 1922 he left Darling's for Aberdeen, where he spent the remaining five years of his life.

More than a century has elapsed since Scott Skinner first breathed the air of this planet, in quite humble circumstances, at Banchory, by the Dee. For the first twenty years of his life, he was just plain Jamie Skinner. In early youth, and under the guidance of his godfather, "Professor" William Scott, he had taken a course in Scots dances. Dancing ran in his family, which explains why William Skinner, his father, was known throughout Dee-side as "Dancie". At a competition in Ireland, when nineteen years of age, Scott Skinner wrested from John MacNeill, a famous Edinburgh dancer, the first prize for the sword-dance, a feat which encouraged him to advertise his qualifications as a dancing-master, as well as a solo-violinist. He taught Highland dancing, as I myself have heard him declare, "on Greek models", whatever that may have meant; and nothing gave greater enjoyment than the step or two of a reel he introduced at an unexpected moment, while playing in some vast auditorium, such as the Usher Hall. We used to watch his feet intently during his violin performances, lest we should miss this happy trick of his. It was just enough to remind one of his pristine renown as dancer and dancing-master; and nothing was calculated to warm up our rigid, frigid Edinburgh audiences in less time than Scott Skinner's gleam of eye, and the lightsome reel-step with which his "callisthenic feet" favoured us all too seldom. Never did brogues trip more lightly, more sprightfully, than on these occasions. Twice he toured America with his violin, playing reels and strathspeys, the like of which the New World had never heard before, and has probably never heard since.

L

When any little thing went wrong with a performance, he always blamed the accompanist. "You'll never know what solace the perfect accompanist brings me," he often remarked. "Fireworks all over the piano disturb the stream when one is fishing." Prime favourite among his many accompanists was George Short, of whom you may read in the next chapter. "After George, nobody!" was a frequent comment of his. George, by the way, harmonised the *Cairngorm* series, which constitutes but a fraction of Scott Skinner's published works. Of original airs, his output was prodigious: they number more than six hundred.

For many years the revenue from his concert fees must have been considerable; and there was always money coming in from the sale of his musical compositions. Yet, latterly, he accepted a civil pension. This leads us to the conclusion that, where the siller was concerned, he had been over-generous and none too provident.

It was one of his boasts that he had no compunction about appearing on the boards in London "after *any* violinist in the world, living or dead". But, as age crept on, he began to find the world harsher than, in the heyday of his splendour, he had imagined. "My playing has opened many eyes," he wrote, toward the end; "but it will close mine. . . . I'll compose no more. Better that I should compose myself."[1]

He was, of a surety, a very great artist; and I feel proud that I should have known him, and met him at a house we both loved to visit. There he would entertain us with his own lovely compositions.[2] In my ear, as I pen these words, there sings *The Cradle Song* he played on his muted violin:

Andante tranquillo.

[1] An intimate article on this unusual personage appears in the *Scots Magazine* for October, 1943.
[2] They are all published by Bayley & Ferguson, Glasgow.

Intellectually, Scott Skinner was keen and original. No one ever expressed himself more cogently. Albeit of a kindly disposition toward his friends, his mordant repartee devastated anyone courting his displeasure. "I knocked him down with intellectual shafts," was a favourite phrase of his, after a wordy engagement. How often did he silence an opponent by firing at him nothing but volleys of classical quotations! You cannot imagine how full he was of racy words, of quaint thoughts. This ardent lover of Strathspey and its music was certainly cast in the antique mould. He belonged, in reality, to the period when gentlemen wore periwigs and ruffles, flowered lappets, and gold-embroidered waistcoats. He was, unquestionably, the last of that race of picturesque personalities, for which our city had been so renowned.

The gods were envious that we mortals should continue in our monopoly of his estimable and entertaining society. So, in the year, 1927, they took him to themselves. He was then eighty-four.

*   *   *   *   *   *   *

In a number of contiguous villas at one end of Gilmore Place lived half a dozen medical practitioners, all of whom, to outward appearances at anyrate, were on the most amicable of terms with one another, while inwardly competing for the illnesses of their fellow-citizens. (Medicine was not so economically assured then as it is today.) A line of large, brass plates declared their names and qualifications, as approved by the Medical Council. I well recall the day when a distressed mother, in full public gaze, and with an unwanted following of all the 'cheekybreeks' of the neighbourhood, led her little, blindfold son past our windows to the house of one or other of these doctors. The boy, while playing at soldiers, had put a certain unnameable utensil over his head, by way of a helmet. He couldn't get it off. It sat comfortably on his shoulders. One heard his muffled cries, as they escaped from underneath. Of course, had the utensil been made of china, matters might have been simplified. A sharp bang would have rent it, and released the laddie. Many indentations, as also the loss of much enamel, showed that, before subjecting parent and child to the painful ordeal of appearing in public, serious efforts had been made to remove the ungainly head-piece. However, it looked as though these had but fixed it the more firmly.

It may have been to Dr MacLaren's this distracted mother took her sobbing son. As the situation demanded the skill of a worker in metal, rather than that of a general practitioner, it would have been better, had she taken him to Dr MacLaren's father's celebrated key-shop, in Bread Street, yonder. Mr MacLaren, in the matter of lock-picking, could have given points to Scotch Jamie, the most artful and notorious of our national burglars. There was nothing Mr MacLaren could not do with metal. His reputation as a locksmith had travelled far over the Lothians, so that the removal of the offending helmet (probably the first 'tin hat' ever displayed publicly in conventional Auld Reekie!) would not have taken him more than a minute or two. Anyhow, a little later the boy emerged, emancipated, wreathed in anything but the proverbial smiles—smothered, on the contrary, in sobs and embarrassments, and not to be consoled even by a visit to the sweetie-shop, near-by.

Mention of Dr MacLaren reminds me that, although we never solicited his professional services, nor yet those of any other member of his fraternity (having had the skilful and knowledgeable Colonel at hand to cure or to pooh-pooh our ailments), we children viewed Dr MacLaren with reverential awe, after father had told us that, for centuries, the MacGregors and the MacLarens had lived side by side, in commendable amity, by the shores of Loch Voil, at Balquhidder.

But, if the services of Dr MacLaren were never sought, our household was sometimes obliged to requisition his family's knack with locks and keys. I recall an occasion when father had to send for Mr MacLaren, because he could not unlock his despatch-box. In a jiffy, magician fingers had it lying open before us. Such child's-play to him! The defaced lock still serves to remind the Colonel's descendants of adventures with that box.

* * * * * * *

Near the other extremity of Gilmore Place there then lived, with his parents, a fellow now known to a vast concourse of people interested in stage and cinema. I allude to Alastair Sim, who, today, looks on the screen or on the stage exactly as he did when he and I were young. As a pupil at James Gillespie's, Alastair exhibited a precocious love for mimicry, and a liking for whatever was gruesome or grotesque. All his life he has revelled in dressing up in the oddest of costumes. Pageants and the like fascinated him. Edinburgh never staged a Masque of Learning, in which he did not appear prominently. At school he was by no means brilliant in orthodox ways. Yet, he was always entertaining and lovable. And there was nothing he enjoyed so much as giving a helping hand with those amateur theatricals in which our Capital, for a period anyhow, specialised.

The eccentric Alastair, with his bland smile, his forehead and temples prematurely bald, his full-moon of a face, and his eyes like living saucers of willow pattern, never wore a hat. This but emphasised the weirdness of his appearance. But, withal, it was an appearance calculated to secure for him any part in life he chose to play. Neighbours pronounced him harum-scarum. Yet, it is precisely what they regarded as harum-scarum that has got him where he is today. Those clever eyes of his, those gestures and mannerisms (rather like the forms of expression the Colonel strove hard to knock out of *me*) have been his fortune. He certainly adopted the profession for which nature had endowed him generously. You have only to see him as Captain Hook in *Peter Pan* to be assured of this.

Years ago, Alastair Sim and I were in the habit of meeting at the house of a mutual friend, whose doorstep we passed several times a week when on our respective errands. Alastair was then absorbed in elocution: I was no more than launched, precariously, as an author. Our friend liked to invite us to tea together, hoping that we might get to know each other better, and appreciate one another's good points as readily as, heretofore, we had noticed one another's shortcomings. The reverse, however, seemed to have been the result—at the outset, anyway. You know how the anxiety of a friend, that two people he or she likes should also like each other, often has exactly the opposite effect! On these occasions, therefore, our hostess presided with such affability as might ensure our good behaviour. Now and again she became a little apprehensive, lest one of her Alastairs should be rude to the other. Disaster was always averted, however, by artful recourse to the tea-pot and to those cakes she provided so plenteously. Whenever there was the faintest sign of our disagreeing, she proceeded to pour more and more tea on waters that looked as though, at any moment, they might have been sorely troubled. After many such tea-parties under her benign auspices, Alastair and I became reasonably tolerant of one another.

Alastair Sim and myself—two Edinburgh lads, both of whom

were looked upon as being decidedly queer—arrived in London about the same time to try our respective fortunes. *He* came south for the stage: *I* came for the pen. (Or was it for love? Which do you think, Louise?) Anyhow, he appears to have gone farther in his sphere than I have in mine.

One Sunday morning, not long after we had settled in London, we found ourselves seated opposite one another in an underground carriage approaching Hampstead, and otherwise empty. Neither of us could be bothered letting on he had ever seen the other before. There we sat, each pretending to be reading his newspaper too diligently to notice the other, but in turn having a surreptitious keek over the top of the paper to see whether the other still looked as eccentric! At Hampstead we both alighted, abreast, walked abreast to the deep lift, stood abreast by the exit gate, marched out into the daylight abreast, and then lost sight of one another. I have always felt heartily ashamed of myself for uncharity on this occasion; and perhaps Alastair Sim has also, for all I know.

*   *   *   *   *   *   *

Let us now proceed round the corner—up by what we called the Back Street—to a spot I see with remarkable clearness in my mind's eye. Here we displayed our pyrotechnics once a year, on the Queen's Birthday;[1] and it was our boast that the bonfire kindled on this spot by the lads of Gilmore Place and Leamy was the most glorious of all the city's, on that night of conflagrations. The fires of Merchiston and Morningside, of Gorgie and Murray-field, were already reduced to a heap of withering embers, when ours was still at the zenith of its splendour. Within the ambit of fifty yards or so of this spot (I'm standing on it at this very moment, in imagination, and see upon the cobblestones, at my feet, the permanent stain left by our bonfires) are situated a church, a laundry, a dance-hall, a huge education authority school, a blind-alley of a terrace, a front garden tended by a fruiterer-&-florist, lots of lamps to which the Limping Lamplighter put a lowe at dusk, and ill-set cobblestones that suddenly gave way to a stretch of paved road, upon which young folks played with balls, peeries, peevers, and marbles, or performed antics with bicycles. I also see the adjacent villa, tenanted by the Misses Niven—Jane, who was tall and lean, and gave tuition in pianoforte, for all her stone-deafness; Maggie, who was as vague as she was tall;

---

[1] May 24th.

and Aggie, the wee one. When Aggie went out, she liked the garden-gate to swing shut while she pulled on her gloves and looked up and down the street, in neighbourly curiosity, to see who else might be abroad. She never reached the pavement, unaided. The kindly gate always had to push her out the last step or two.

* * * * * * *

And I must just mention the corner-cottage, in which lived the Jacks. And, oh! so many of them were accommodated in that tiny place, which looked the tinier because of the lofty school that overshadows it. I seem to recollect at least ten members of that happy household. Little Mrs Jack, so very white-haired, so faerie, dwelt there with her numerous children, in circumstances none too affluent, rather like the old woman who lived in the shoe. I remember her in the patch of front garden, beside the lilac-tree, or by the rose-bush that bloomed all summer and autumn— little Mrs Jack standing by the lilac that drooped with scented heaviness in the springtime, or by those pink roses, such as one might see on Dresden china. A more exquisite picture never entered your vision. The roses' pink lent to her complexion a tincture the better set off by her white hair, as she stood in the doorway, enframed by their clusters. Indeed, the flush—nay, the blush—diffusing her cheeks might have been the πορφύρεον φῶς ἐρώτος, the 'purple light of love', to which Pindar alludes. It was as the faint tinting of the heavens, prelusive to the dove's twilight, as the Jews of antiquity called the dawn. No beauty-parlour pigments here. Her colouring was entirely natural.

The whitest of curtains graced Mrs Jack's casements; and the whitest gravel to be had in Auld Reekie defined the pathways intersecting this mere scrap of garden. When all were abed, an old board of faded green, acting as a wind-break at this draughty corner, often creaked eerily in the night-wind, as though in league with some screeching chimney-cowl, and with other fear-some things that go bumpety-bump in the dark.

And such a variety adorned that garden, tended so lovingly by Mrs Jack! I remember the wallflowers under the window-sill, the clump of ferns in a corner, the pansies bordering the paths, and the foxgloves that hid themselves from the winds, until they could resist no longer the urge to outgrow the protection afforded them by the faded board.

All is altered now. The lilac is gone; and so is Mrs Jack. The board is gone; and so, too, is the railing against which it leaned. Part of the latter may now be in some man's wounds, in compliance with the war measure directing its removal.

Whether the pink roses still bloom there, I cannot say. But they all linger in the memory of perfumed days—days that were peaceful and pleasant for poor Mrs Jack, until the death of Jimmy, favourite among her children. Jimmy fell at Passchendaele while serving with the Dandy Ninth—the 9th Royal Scots—in the holocaustic September of 1917. Though the benevolent hands of his brothers and sisters did much to winnow away the chaff of sorrow, Mrs Jack never quite got over Jimmy's going. His parents now share with him whatever celestial haven there may be for any of us.

Was it not Jimmy who took delight in sketching my little sister, Catriona Mairi MacGregor, when she wandered hither to the paved street, the better to play at ball? Catriona spent many an hour by the Jacks' corner, adopting graceful attitudes for Jimmy's sketch-book. "What an attractive child!" I once overheard Mrs Jack say, as I arrived to bring Catriona home in time for family-worship, one summer's eve.

It was, to be sure, a tiny house that afforded living-room for so numerous a clan. Yet, its very smallness diffused an atmosphere of warmth and affection, an air of wellbeing and harmony, a sense of snugness round the fire at sundown, or of cosiness in bed when the blast of winter raged without. Often might the passer-by observe its inhabitants assembled in the fire-glow of the sitting-room at twilight, reading Stevenson to one another. The smaller children would rush to the shadowy window when the Crippled Piper played by the gate, expectant of Mrs Jack's customary copper, or when Leerie, the Limping Lamplighter, came posting up the Back Street to light the lamp at their corner.

> *My tea is nearly ready, and the sun has left the sky;*
> *It's time to take the window to see Leerie going by.*

Little wonder those youngsters thought R. L. S.'s lines referred to *their* Lamplighter!

> *For we are very lucky with a lamp before the door,*
> *And Leerie stops to light it as he lights so many more;*
> *And O! before you hurry by with ladder and with light,*
> *O, Leerie, see a little child, and nod to him tonight!*

And then the wee-est members of this loving family would begin
to file out—

> *And face with an undaunted tread*
> *The long, black passage up to bed.*

Were there ever children who travelled so hopefully in the
Realm of Storybook, in the Pleasant Land of Counterpane,
in the Slumbery Land of Nod? Was there ever a cottage in which
The Child's Garden of Verses was read more eagerly?

> *Now my little heart goes a-beating like a drum*
> *   With the breath of the Bogie in my hair;*
> *And all round the candle the crooked shadows come,*
> *   And go marching along up the stair.*

> *The shadow of the balusters, the shadow of the lamp,*
> *   The shadow of the child that goes to bed—*
> *All the wicked shadows coming, tramp, tramp, tramp,*
> *   With the black night overhead.*

It is long since the Crippled Piper came to this corner. And
what was the tune he played, invariably, but *The Green Hills of
Tyrone*? We never heard him even attempt another. And
Limping Leerie, the Lamplighter of those redolent years—
Ah! years redolent of lilac refreshed by the touch of vernal shower,
of pink rose in the glint of summer rain—is very, very old now,
if he be alive. In any case, his services wouldn't be wanted, these
blackout days.

As for Mrs Jack's brood, it is fully-fledged now, much of it
scattered, most of it married. Christina writes me occasionally
from a famous bookshop in Glasgow, where she is engaged in
what she describes as "just the nicest form of employment in the
world"—arranging books, talking about them, selling them,
loving them. Isn't it delightful to reflect that now and again
one's own volumes fall into such appreciative hands?

*   *   *   *   *   *   *

As I say, I do not know whether the rose-bush of former years is
still there; and I doubt whether, even if it were, the roses could be
quite the same. But the lilac, I know, has vanished, with the
tender grace of a day that is dead.

CHAPTER XVI

GEORGE, JOSEPH, AND ROBERT

BUT WE must retrace our steps along Gilmore Place a little, because I want to tell you something about Mrs Short and her son, George, who lived there, and also about one or two interesting musical recollections and impressions of youth. At the moment I cannot remember the Shorts' number: yet, I could go, unerringly, to the house in which they once lived, for it lay but round the corner from us. It was an odd number, I know. At a guess, I would say it was 59. One day, perhaps, the house may bear a plaque commemorating George's whilom residence there. Every morning, as I passed it on the way to school, a little old lady, rather like a gnome (and possibly not unlike the little old lady of the song), might be seen, busily engaged either in sweeping the doorstep, or in polishing the outsize brass plate advertising to the world her son's proficiency in pianoforte. This, of course, was in the days before it became fashionable for teachers of music and kindred accomplishments to congregate in studios such as Methven, Simpson & Co. have since provided in Princes Street, where the din of one practising pupil or potential vocalist out-dins the efforts of the other. And, oh! such an inferno of jangling and caterwauling to anyone using the stairs instead of the lift!

Jessie soon christened Mrs Short's son Georgie Porgie; and this, ever after, remained the name by which he was known to our strange household. To external appearance, at all events, he resembled, more closely than anyone we had seen hitherto, his prototype of nursery fame. In our juvenile eyes, he was as 'porgie' as he was Georgie; and he seemed more than ordinarily *au fait* with matters of pudding and pie. But we never heard whether he was in the habit of kissing the girls and of making them cry. In this rôle I cannot imagine him, though, for all I know to the contrary, he may have done his share of kissing.

To revert to a more serious topic, however, what I *can* testify to is that George is the supreme artist. As concert accompanist, particularly where Celtic music is concerned, he is quite unexcelled. And who would be so bold as to suggest that anyone has arranged those Scots and Gaelic airs of ours more acceptably? This, also, is a province in which no contemporary has rivalled him; and it is open to question whether even any predecessor has. See him move across the platform of the Usher Hall in Auld Reekie, in his curious lunging way, toward the piano! See him take those big strides of his, three or four steps at a time, up the gangway to the grand organ, his coat-tails swinging in rhythm as he grasps the banister for assistance in his ascent! That climb of his always spells business; and I well remember how, as a preliminary to our Gaelic concerts in this same hall, he gave, on that organ, half-an-hour's symposium of Highland melodies, which the intelligent appreciated as much as any of the items more prominently advertised. And, indeed, what pride, when one or two of the Colonel's own airs were included!

George's coming in sight on any platform immediately arrests attention and focusses interest. His presence inspires confidence. One is at ease in the assurance that, whatever high-jinks the vocalist may get up to, George is there to fill in gaps and cover up mistakes. I have known him to change the key twice or thrice throughout a single rendition, when accompanying a singer who could not keep in pitch; and so artfully did he execute these transpositions that only the musical members of the audience could detect them. He has saved the reputation of many a vocalist.

Few people associated with Celtic matters in the present generation have done as much as George for Highland music. When he might have been gainfully employed in his professional teaching, he was training individuals and choirs, arranging part-songs and duets for them, and rehearsing unceasingly. What would Auld Reekie's Gaelic Choir have achieved but for the years of active interest taken in its affairs by this accomplished and good-natured musician? No one has ever given, gratuitously, to any cause more time and talent.

At varying intervals during the past quarter of a century, he has accompanied most of the distinguished artistes, foreign as well as British, who have appeared in Scotland. And we all felt very proud of our Georgie when, in 1921, Joseph Hislop, already a celebrity, came home to his native Edinburgh to sing for the first time amang his Ain Folk, for it was George who accompanied him, and afterwards went on tour with him. During the nineteen-twenties, Joseph frequently returned to show his love for Auld Reekie, and for Burns. Now he is head of the Royal Opera

School at Stockholm, where he has been since 1937. In consequence of the invasion of Norway, he has remained cut off from his friends in this country, though his sister tells me that he occasionally communicates with her by airgraph. His leisure time he spends in painting in oils, you may be interested to hear.

Who could forget those Burns Festivals at which Joseph and George, friends since they were at school, performed together in such consonance?

> *Of a' the airts the wind can blaw,*
> *I dearly like the West,*
> *For there the bonnie lassie lives,*
> *The lassie I lo'e best:*
> *There wild woods grow, and rivers row,*
> *And mony a hill between;*
> *But night and day my fancy's flight*
> *Is ever wi' my Jean.*
>
> *I see her in the dewy flowers,*
> *I see her sweet and fair:*
> *I hear her in the tunefu' birds,*
> *I hear her charm the air,*
> *There's not a bonnie flower that springs*
> *By fountain, shaw, or green,*
> *There's not a bonnie bird that sings,*
> *But minds me o' my Jean.*

There seems to be a mis-impression in this country, and quite unjustifiably, so far as I am competent to assess, that Joss (for as such he is known to his family and friends) has distinguished himself in little but Scots Song. Could anything be more remotely accurate? Have we failed to realise that he has taken the leading part, all over the musical globe, in almost every famous opera we have? There never sang in *La Bohème* a Rudolfo quite like Joss. Certainly, no other Rudolfo ever walked the Covent Garden stage with such outstanding inevitableness. Puccini, himself, told Joss he was his ideal Rudolfo.

"How's your son, Mrs Hislop?" neighbours used to ask his mother.

"My son! But I've *three* sons!" she would reply, knowing full well the enquirer was alluding to the singer, yet anxious to show that she harboured no favouritism where her children were concerned.

The Hislop family attended Lady Yester's Church, where every member of it was baptised. They all participated in the Sunday-school picnic each year; and Stephen, now doctor at East Linton, remembers how he used to get a touch of ear-ache with blowing peas through his pea-shooter at rival picnics entraining simultaneously at the Waverley. Ah, yes! and *I* remember a sunny forenoon spent most agreeably in tearoom-crawling along Princes Street with his sister, May, having a cup of tea here and a cup of coffee there, while exchanging reminiscences of Joss and his triumphs; and I truly glow when she assures me that, in manner and in speech, as well as in appearance, I remind her family so forcibly of its celebrated member.

* * * * * * *

This reminds one of George Short's musical association with yet another notable singer—the late Robert Burnett—the Scottish Baritone, as he was styled in latter years. Robert, born at Lasswade in 1874, died in Edinburgh in 1943, leaving the city of his adoption, as indeed all Scotland, much the poorer. Was there ever a finer exponent of Scots Folk Song? The consensus of opinion is that there never was, and that we may have to wait a long time ere we see his like again. Endowed with a fine voice, and artistic qualities as unique as they were original, he gave us performances, with George at the piano, that reside among the most memorable musical recollections of my life. George became his accompanist as a very young man; and I was somewhere between boyhood and youth when a neighbour took me to a Burns recital of theirs. From that occasion dates my interest in Scots Ballad and Folk Song.

Until Burnett came on the scene, it had been held that our national songs depended primarily upon a superior voice, and that the scope was limited to those suitable to a particular voice. Burnett, with George's assistance, demolished this fancy. He approached Scots Folk Song in an entirely different way. He considered the voice as of secondary importance to the illustrative treatment, so that, with his imaginative genius, he was able to deliver our folk-song in an arresting and entertaining manner, and always through the medium of artistic voice-production. In this field he was a precursor. His influence survives him well. In his singing, in his teaching, as well as in the encouragement he gave to musicians to arrange these songs in an up-to-date fashion, he liked to feel that he was making some contribution to Scottish culture. And there is no denying that, in his performances at our Burns Festivals, he set a standard to which many singers have aspired, but which few have achieved. (The Colonel, I might interpolate, thought nothing of him as a singer. This ill-judgment was easily explained, however. Burnett and he had had a semi-public tiff, because the former did not receive with enthusiasm the suggestion of the latter that *The MacGregors' Gathering* should be added to his repertoire ! !)

How well I remember those Scots song recitals which, from time to time, Robert and George gave from the Borders to the Shetlands! Usually an outstanding feature of them was Burnett's rendering of *The Wee Wee German Lairdie*, one of the most spirited and virile of our Jacobite ballads—

> *Wha the de'il hae we gotten for a king*
> *But a wee, wee German lairdie!*
> *Whan we gaed ower tae bring him hame,*
> *He was delvin' in his kail-yairdie:*[1]
> *He was sheughin'*[2] *kail*[3] *an' layin' leeks,*
> *Wi'oot the hose an' but*[4] *the breeks,*
> *An' up wi' his beggar duds*[5] *he cleeks,*[6]
> *This wee, wee German lairdie!*

Many a fellow, who previously had considered it bad taste to countenance Scots song, was converted at these recitals, for Robert Burnett had, in a rare degree, the faculty for adapting himself, instantly and dramatically, to such changes as proper interpretation demanded.

No one could ever forget his treatment of *The Sands o' Dee*. It was overwhelming—as overwhelming as the waves themselves. One almost heard the Cheshire tides come surging up, wellnigh engulfing singer and audience. "If you want to hear perfection," a wellknown critic once remarked, "hear Burnett sing that song, with Short at the piano!"

> ' *O Mary, go and call the cattle home,*
> *And call the cattle home,*
> *And call the cattle home,*
> *Across the sands o' Dee':*
> *The western wind was wild and dank with foam,*
> *And all alone went she.*
>
> .   .   .   .   .   .
>
> *They rowed her in across the rolling foam,*
> *The cruel, crawling foam,*
> *The cruel, hungry foam,*
> *To her grave beside the sea:*
> *But still the boatmen hear her call the cattle home*
> *Across the sands o' Dee.*

*   *   *   *   *   *   *

[1] Kitchen-garden, cabbage-patch; [2] planting; [3] cabbage; [4] without;
[5] clothes, rags; [6] catches.

Robert Burnett's voice is still with us, and may remain so, if we stop smashing culture and civilization to bits reasonably soon. If you write to the Parlophone Company, they may be able to let you hear *Duncan Gray*, that song he rendered with supreme abandon. No man born of woman ever made a better job of it. Here the two Roberts—Burns, who wrote the words, and Burnett, who interpreted them—are at their best:

> Duncan fleech'd,[1] and Duncan pray'd;
>   Ha, ha, the wooin' o't:
> Meg was deaf as Ailsa Craig;
>   Ha, ha, the wooin' o't:
> Duncan sigh'd baith oot and in,
> Grat his een baith bleer't and blin',[2]
> Spak o' loupin[3] ower the linn!
>   Ha, ha, the wooin' o't.
>
>   .   .   .   .
>
> Duncan was a lad o' grace;
>   Ha, ha, the wooin' o't:
> Maggie's was a piteous case;
>   Ha, ha, the wooin' o't:
> Duncan couldna be her death,
> Swelling pity smoor'd[4] his wrath;
> Now they're crouse and canty[5] baith:
>   Ha, ha, the wooin' o't!

Burnett was kenspeckle in Auld Reekie for many a day. If you had known him, as we all did, and could now sit back and listen to a gramophone record of his, you would experience the impact of those lines by yet another Edinburgh laddie—

> Bright is the ring of words
>   When the right man rings them:
> Fair is the fall of songs
>   When the singer sings them.
> Still they are carolled and said—
>   On wings they are carried—
> After the singer is dead,
>   And the maker buried.

* * * * * * *

During the Colonel's latter years, George Short and he saw a great deal of one another. Let George tell you, in his own words, how it all came about, and how it ended:

"I remember well the first day I spoke to Colonel MacGregor. It was in my studio in Princes Street. The impression made on me by this first meeting is still vivid. I can recall how the elevator-gate crashed back as if an important and impatient personage were

---

[1] Supplicated, flattered; [2] cried till his eyes were bleared; [3] leaping; [4] smothered; [5] blithe and cheerful.

getting out, and how the corridor shook as thundering footsteps proceeded. But I stood up with a jerk when these sounds were succeeded by the vigorous rataplan of a walking-stick on my door. I hastened to open the door, and was not a little taken aback to see the figure of Colonel MacGregor come striding into the studio. Without any preamble, he shouted in a barrackroom manner:

" 'Are you Short?'

" 'I am, Colonel MacGregor!' I hastened to reply.

" 'Ah, you know me, my boy!' he added.

"I replied that Colonel MacGregor was well known to most people in the Scottish Capital. This remark pleased him, I think.

" 'Well, then, Short, I'm told you can note down my songs, if I sing them to you! Is that so?'

"Realising the personality before me, and the possibility of difficulties, I was hesitant and somewhat diffident. I replied, however, that at least I could try.

" 'Well, then, see what you can make of *this* one!'

"Thereupon he proceeded to bawl what seemed to be among the most primitive and unrelated human noises I had heard. When he had finished—nothing daunted—I asked him if he would mind repeating what he had expressed.

" 'Very well! I waant [sic] you to be very careful about this one, as it may be sung after my death!'

"I thought this a curious statement, but later I was to learn of a high aim he had in mind. On his repeating the tune, I was able to hear more clearly the association of the notes, without being confused by the manner in which they were emitted. Indeed, I think I had been gradually getting into line with his mind, and better able to appreciate his outlook. I then proceeded to play on the piano what I thought to be the notes he had sung, but, at the finish of this, I nearly jumped off the seat when he came down with a whack of his oak stick on the middle notes of the piano, shouting 'You've got one wrong, *thaare*!' I thought this was the end of my piano notes, but they still sounded, little the worse.

"I have often related this incident with enjoyment. At this date, I can recall no more than a snatch of the tune. It was original and well built. Colonel MacGregor called it *The Lewismen's March*. Thereafter he and I met on many occasions, over a long period, to do this kind of translating of his tunes. He explained to me that, while in the East, where it was the custom of officers to spend their leisure in drinking and card-playing, he resolved to devote *his* leisure to writing Gaelic songs, and to contributing something to keep the Gaelic language alive.

"On each occasion we met, I noticed how keen and industrious he had been with the MS. sheets of a book of Gaelic songs he intended publishing. These seemed to increase on every visit. I imagine he had written about two hundred by the time we ceased working together. Concerning the publication of his collection, he also told me he had been thwarted in his intention. . . . However, he continued to come along, and always, when leaving, he amused me with the remark that he was going now to see the pretty girls on Princes Street.

"After this, we didn't see so much of each other, as the music part of his work was completed. But frequently, when I met him in town, he said he was still working at his collection, though his eyesight had begun to trouble him. Too close application to his writing, he told me, had caused this; and later he told me that total blindness was a matter of time. As a surgeon, he knew this. I remember, too, how sorry I felt to see him almost blind, stepping vigorously in town with a white stick in his hand. When I made myself known to him, he generally greeted me facetiously with 'Ah, Short! You bad boy! You made me stick too closely to my songs!'

"Later I learnt of his death. I often have wondered what became of his collection of Gaelic songs. But I never heard.[1]

"Pride of race was the inspiration of his writing, and often he used to exclaim, with great dignity, that the MacGregors were descended from Kenneth MacAlpin, first King of Scots. This certainly added to the sense of awe I used to entertain in his presence. But withal he was a kindly and generous gentleman. I never knew anyone so original, so full of characteristique."

I make no apology for having given you this letter *in extenso* because, in my view, it is so excellent. No bit of writing ever portrayed a man's father more faithfully. Those years of collaboration must have been irksome at times for George. And, alas! for John MacGregor, Bard of the Clan Alpin, they ended in tragedy. What did he now begin to do but to copy out all these tunes, in staff notation, not a note of which he could read as a musician

---

[1] It would be gratifying if, after reading this passage, the person, who borrowed that MS. a dozen years ago, would now be generous enough to return it. My publishers would be happy to accept receipt of it on my behalf.

would. Day after day, week after week, as I afterwards learnt, he sat at them, diligently—nay, obsessed. He was afraid lest, in his old age, the original MS., as prepared by George, might be lost; and it was important for posterity, he held, that a second copy should be made available.

I returned one autumn from a couple of months' sojourn with kinsfolk in the Hebrides to find that my father, now in his seventy-seventh year, had made a complete duplicate, all on his own, and that, in the process, he had gone nearly blind. The most casual glance at this unnecessarily redundant document shows that he had got about halfway, when eye trouble began. Toward the end it becomes illegible. He was never able to read a word of print again. The strain had damaged something irreparably. At the age of seventy-eight, however, he took up Braille. This he mastered in no time, owing to his familiarity with the Scriptures. The New Testament, both in Gaelic and in English, he knew by heart, so that, by the time he had struggled through the first few books, he was moderately proficient in Braille. But his life, he felt, was now finished. Its last and greatest solace—literature, and the facilities for reading what and when he liked—had gone. Dire calamity had befallen him. His obsession for the Gaelic and for Gaelic music had proved his undoing. He was doomed, he said; and in this parlous state he lingered for five or six years, until 1932, when, at the age of eighty-four, he ceased to be seen by men's eyes.

CHAPTER XVII

CRAIGLOCKHART

THERE SEEMED little likelihood in my youth that, in the
course of a decade, Auld Reekie was to stretch her municipal
fingers so far to the westward as to render Craiglockhart obsolete
as a tramway terminus, in favour of Colinton, a mile or two
farther afield. In those days we regarded the intervening space
as rural in the truest sense. Indeed, the first cows I had seen
since quitting the Highlands were grazing between Craiglockhart and Colinton, in a meadow of gowans—of mountain-daisies,
if you prefer the English appellation—and poppies. And such
gowans, such poppies! In the background, among trees, rose the
red-sandstone spire of Craiglockhart kirk, withal a setting, as I
remember it, worthy of the brush of a Constable.

Solid, stolid, well-found homesteads now crowd in upon one
another on the site of that meadow. When I visit a friend now
occupying one of them—Ah! what Watsonian of the last generation or two does not revere the name of the science-master,
Johnnie Horne, whose Christian name is not Johnnie at all, and
who was always glad of a pretext for wandering from his subject
to matters of natural history? I still see the case of stuffed mam-
mals and birds that was standing in his classroom when I left
the old Watson's[1] to go to the war!—When, as I say, I call on this
friend, now living in retirement out there, I like to reflect that he is
entertaining me on a spot I associate with the first Lothian cows
and wild flowers I knew. Who would deny that cows and gowans
go well together? Ever since that early visit to Craiglockhart,
they have accompanied one another in my repository of associations, and with remarkable vividness. Surely they bear a similarity
of eye, a freshness, and yet a touch of amiable docility! And the
white petals and yellow centres of the one are not unlike the milk
and cream of the other. Even poppies are in keeping with this
setting, since they flourished here, between Craiglockhart and

[1] The building was demolished in 1933 to make room for the extension of
the Edinburgh Royal Infirmary, while the school was transferred to new and
commodious premises in Colinton Road.

163

Redford, as nowhere else on the outskirts of Auld Reekie. I have but to contemplate calling on Johnnie Horne (by which name he must be known by someone or other in almost every corner of the world, although his name is James) when there immediately comes to mind a picture of those cows and gowans and poppies of bygone years. You may think the mental process that brings me to milk and cream quite crazy, of course. But there it is, nevertheless, as much a part of me as are the colours I visualise whenever I hear mention of Iona, or Jura.

Once a year, and usually in summer or autumn, I go to see this old Watson's master, the only member of a numerous teaching staff who really befriended me in the true sense, and for a reason he has since disclosed, and which would probably sound pious and self-pitying, were I to divulge it here.[1] This annual visit of mine to Craiglockhart Park (for that is now the name of at least part of the meadow where browsed those cows, and gowans and poppies flourished) is always one of the most satisfying of the things I accomplish whenever I re-visit the scenes of youth.

*   *   *   *   *   *   *

Science, in all its wondrous manifestations, has been this dearly belovèd mortal's chief interest in life. It would be superfluous to enumerate the societies and committees in Scotland—geological, zoological, botanical, ornithological—which his knowledge and earnestness have not enriched. He was never so happy as when explaining to some enthusiast the habits of bird, of beast, or of flower, or the origin of rock or fossil. For years, as his pupils knew full well, he had been intimately associated with Auld Reekie's

[1] As we prepare for press, he writes me a long letter containing the following passage: "*I* never found you dull or uninterested in your science work; and your manipulation of the science-room instruments was the equal of anyone. Now and again you seemed to imagine that you could improve on the task in hand; but, with the exercise of a little patience, I found in your case this arose from some cause outwith ordinary school-work. Along with a bright and alert manner in class, you were prone to ask questions that often involved elaborate replies. Occasionally, curious and fantastic notions, indicating a vivid imagination, had to be set right by practical demonstration, and you proved yourself quick in appreciating the results. I cannot remember that I had ever to repress your eagerness to know how things worked, although I had to restrain your impulsive mode of displaying your dislike for certain people and actions. But your response to a kindly word of advice or commendation was immediate and hearty. Altogether you were a likeable pupil. Cattle-rieving had gone out of fashion by the time you came to Watson's, so that you had no chance to imitate your ancestor, Rob Roy, although, from the glint of your eye on occasions, and your curious taste for roving, and for poking into strange places, I felt often that you would have liked to wear Rob's brogues."

Geological Society, which explained the readiness with which they could divert him from less agreeable matters, such as geometry. He was among the first to recognise that science was too much the handmaiden of the "hard, dry Muses of the cube and square". So, in 1905, he founded the Field Club, the president of which he has been ever since. What do we Watsonians remember about him more clearly than his devotion to natural history, and the corresponding earnestness with which he sponsored the Field Club? The work of this laudable institution took the form of lectures during the winter and early spring terms, and of excursions and meetings throughout the summer session. Saturdays were reserved for outdoor activities in the field, principally in the Lothians and in Fife; and it is a whispered tradition that not once in three decades was the founder absent from its outings— evidence, surely, of his health and vitality, as much as of his versatility and enthusiasm. Of course, we are agreed there never was such a walker in all the Lothians as Johnnie Horne. His prowess in this respect, when Scotland was still fairly free from the degenerating influence of petrol, and her roads were rough and circuitous, is a by-word in Auld Reekie to this day. He had shown more than a modicum of interest in athletics, besides. If you once get him on to *this* topic, he will detain you as wilily as the Ancient Mariner did the wedding-guest. Records set up by runners at Powderhall in its less sordid days—before it, literally, 'went to the dogs'—are all stored away in his well ordered cranium; and, as someone wrote of him when he retired from Watson's in 1933, after forty years' most estimable service with the Merchant Company, he was no mean practitioner in the fistic science when Donovan, of olden renown, taught Edinburgh youths the tricks of the trade.

The Field Club certainly satisfied expectations. It enabled many a Watson's lad to learn about natural history under ideal conditions, and at a time when the sciences were still crowded out of the senior school curriculum. What could have been more instructive than the annual excursion to the banks of the Almond, at Cramond, usually in the month of June, to study water plants, or the outing to Aberlady Bay to see the nests of the eider-ducks? I regret, now, that I showed so little interest in those Saturday exploits, for they were much more in my line than indoor purgatory among schoolbooks. But, by this time, I fancy, I was beginning to find adequate recreation at the swimming-baths, where I plunged and ploutered for at least a couple of hours every day. I do remember my accompanying the Club on one occasion to Craigmillar Castle, however. This exploration concluded in our taking advantage of the permission granted us to walk through the grounds of the Inch, which, as you may know, is the name of the Gilmour estate adjoining Craigmillar. Such a concession, in those semi-feudal times, was greatly respected. Even yet, in Scotland, the policies attached to 'the big hoose' are regarded with as much veneration as is a church; and the law of trespass (which, contrary to the popular belief, does not exist, *as such*, north of the Tweed) restrains many a potential intruder. But there was no suggestion of trespass when, with due decorum, a band of Watson's boys entered the policies of the Inch under Johnnie Horne's leadership. Of course, it has been said that no master, who was not a bachelor, would have devoted to us so many of his weekends.

I likewise recall my subsequent disappointment at not having visited Inchcolm under the Field Club's auspices, since firsthand accounts given by one's contemporaries the following Monday morning were, indeed, alluring. Not only had they explored the remains of the Augustinian Abbey on this ancient Isle of the Forth, but they had examined the gun-mountings belonging to the time of the threatened Napoleonic invasion, when Inchcolm served as an artillery station. They may also have seen evidence of much earlier fortifications—possibly those erected by the Duke of Somerset, after the Battle of Pinkie, when he seized the Isle as a strategical position controlling "utterly the whole use of the Firth itself, with all the havens upon it". But none of these historical matters would have engaged me as much as the sail from Aberdour. I missed approximately three miles of seafaring by my failure to turn up on this occasion.

* * * * * * *

Watsonians the world over must owe to Johnnie Horne's inspiration—to his divine afflatus, one might justifiably say—their first stirrings of interest in the manifold beauties and wonders of the outdoor world. We are unanimously of the view that such knowledge of bird-life, as he did not possess, was not worth our seeking to acquire. And it just occurs to me that there were times when Johnnie himself looked very bird-like. He often resembled a prosperous barn-yard fowl, especially when, in his swallow-tail

166

days, he stood with his back to the classroom fire, his chest thrown out a little, his hands resting comfortably on his warmed haunches. This was a favourite attitude of his; and anything more like an outsize member of the feathered world you never beheld!

For the honour of having inaugurated the Field Club, I never dreamed our hero had a rival. Yet, men are wont to get all kinds of queer ideas into their heads, even the sanest of them. In London the other day, when exchanging reminiscences of the Club and its activities with another Watsonian, he informed me, calmly and confidently, from his editorial chair, that he had "a sort of notion" *he* had founded it. And this, mark you! from a person no less erudite, no less accurate, than one employed in an important capacity with William Collins, Publishers! I took this claim in the necessary saline solution; and I have chuckled over it ever since. I have no doubt, of course, that my friend was a foundation member, as well as one of the most active. (Do disabuse your mind of this fancy, dear Freddy! I might as justifiably enter your office one morning to tell you *I* had a sort of notion that I was heir to the throne. What would you say to that? We are all inclined to get a little fanciful after we have lived in London for a while, for we soon recognise the credulity of our southern associates. But don't you think we should reserve such flights for them, or for the Marines, if they still be in existence?)

*   *   *   *   *   *   *

Among the less popular subjects Johnnie taught was mathematics. "Please, sir, is this a fossil?" an impish juvenile might ask at the beginning of an irksome maths. period, holding up a stone taken from the playground. This ruse instantly sent Johnnie off at a tangent. It required little subtlety with matters of natural history to deflect him. He might be on the point of conducting us over the *Pons Asinorum,* when some pupil would intervene in this wise. Down would go the textbook: up would go the hand to adjust his pince-nez, so that he might examine the object more closely. Many a stone from the playground, many a weed from the adjacent Meadows, had necessitated the manipulation of those eye-glasses of his. By the time he had chalked on the blackboard what the stone might have looked like, had it been a fossil, a good twenty minutes of an otherwise boring forty-five had gone by agreeably.

When, by means of the blackboard, he had carried us through

some intricate problem of Euclid, and had got "Q.E.D." well and truly appended at the foot of the solution, and a grand paraph set down with lightning vigour to underline this signature to triumph, we often felt constrained to give him a resounding cheer for his having disposed of our worries so expeditiously, and with a touch so masterly. In the process of his deductions, there was never a suspicion of ostentation until, at last, those three assuring letters were added. They were the hallmark of proof; and the tempo always quickened as they went down on the board, to be punctuated by three sharp dabs with the chalk, which marked the full-stop after each. What were they but contractions for those three Latin words that gave me more relief than any others I ever beheld on blackboard? *Quod erat demonstrandum*: 'which was requiring to be demonstrated'. Never was a gerundive more welcome!

*   *   *   *   *   *   *

In my memory of happy visits to Craiglockhart Park, one in particular is delineated. It took place on an aureate afternoon in autumn. In the trim garden at the back of the house, encompassed about by festoons of rambler roses, sat Mr Horne and myself, deep and lazily in deck-chairs, sipping copiously of the teapot in Tempean contentment, and recollecting the passage of the years, as the shadow, upon the lawn, of the garden umbrella, but an arm's-length away, marked with unalterable precision the sun's diurnal footsteps. Never was there a garden party more enjoyably protracted. As one's mind receded from this place of warmth and quietude, so did the eye. In looking backward through the years, the eye carried one, unconsciously, down to the east, where lay the city in a haze, but a spire or two discernible, and the fleeting outline of Craiglockhart's twin heights, of the Castle, of Corstorphine Hill, and of the East and West Lomonds, away in Fife. My host remarked that, so clear had visibility been earlier in the day, that his eye had lighted for a moment on Aberlady Bay. (Ah! Aberlady Bay! That brings me once again to those eider-ducks. But we must not go chasing after them, if ever this chapter is to be brought to a close.)

A more exquisite pastorale, in more exquisite company, you could not conceive. Some small part of the credit for this must be given to the teapot. Who wrote that tea will always remain the favourite beverage of the intellectual? I agree cordially with him, whoever he may have been. Tea-drinking is not necessarily the spineless and effeminate indulgence many would have us believe. What manner of fellow is he who does not unbend in the homely presence of the tea-tray? Who be he that would deny its inducement to amiability, to conversation, and, as Longfellow remarked, to tranquillity of soul? We talk in our *wine*cups, one is assured; but I question whether we deliver ourselves of such good sense as when in our *tea*cups! Be this as it may, tea on the lawn at Craiglockhart Park, with roses rambling about one, is no less conducive to sojourn than was the lotus first tasted by Dr Johnson at historic Dunvegan. (It is in pensive reflection on the lives of such men as Johnnie Horne that one, who at times may feel a little frayed by the barbarities of the age, returns, if but temporarily, to a faith in the ultimate destiny of mankind.)

Conversation, this afternoon, was moistened by more than tea, since the garden-hose lay in sun-warmed loops upon the lawn, and I had been itching to get my hands on it. Water has fascinated me all my life. It is, for me, an unfailing anodyne, a panacea when mentally or physically troubled. Contact with it produces my best thoughts and my best ideas. It bestows upon me something of the happiness De Quincey found in opium. Indeed, it is my φάρμακον νηπένθες. I have never let slip an opportunity of playing with it since infant days at Applecross, where my earliest experiments in hydraulics consisted of pouring it by canister through the exposed roots of those beech-trees by the wayside. Give me a hose and a reasonable pressure of water, should you seek to provide me with the means of amusing myself when I visit you.

At Mr Horne's, then, I could not resist the lure of the garden-hose—the joy of regulating the volume and ambit of the spray, the soft smirr falling in infinitesimal beads on hands and cheeks and hair, filling the atmosphere with a misty moisture shot through with the hues of autumnal sunlight. Can you suggest anything more pleasurable, even to a fellow a bit over forty? An invitation, anywhere, is instantly rendered the more acceptable, I assure you, if it include the prospect of an hour's idling with the garden-hose. I know of few things more restful and gratifying than watering by such means. It was strange to contemplate that here, at Craiglockhart, I should have been amusing myself to the utmost, in such estimable company, by refreshing the soil that had once supported those memorable cows and wild flowers.

CHAPTER XVIII

TRAINS AND KINDRED MATTERS

OF ALL the works of men's hands I like to look upon, excepting perhaps ships, steam locomotives take pride of place. Trains have always fascinated me. The first I ever beheld in infancy at Kyle of Lochalsh is as vivid a recollection as any in life. Great puffs of white smoke rising in bulging clouds from the harbour-side one still, sunny morning, amid seagulls wheeling and screaming as small craft unloaded the night's herring catch, but a few yards away.

Then there were those trains travelling through High Wind, between the sunny South and snowy North—efficient in their way, but primitive in many respects when compared with the L.M.S. successors on the Highland Line. Yet, there was much to know about them, and no one at hand more competent than Aunt Dorothy to explain just how they worked, what this was for, and that, and how the locomotives performed their task. Having told me so much in the quiet of our moorland home at the Hill of the Peats, it was with something of the spirit of adventure that I examined, under her guidance, one of the engines daily drawing our northern mail-train to the seaports of Caithness. What this wonderful woman did not know about high-pressure and low-pressure cylinders, cylinder compounds, about piston-rods, cross-heads, crank-pins, driving-axles, about the dead-centre and expansive working, about first-hand and second-hand steam, and the intricate adjustment of valves, was scarcely worth knowing. When listening to her, one felt she understood all this better than did the engine-driver himself. She lacked his practical experience, of course. Yet, there was little doubt she could have explained to him the why and the wherefore of much he took for granted. This strange and eccentric woman, eminently feminine in ways, used to astound people with her knowledge of matters so masculine. In memory's ear I can hear her now, dilating on locomotives and their work, doing her utmost to interest me in anything, in the hope of bestirring my mind, then so alarmingly dormant. On the subject of engines and trains, however, she required little effort.

And I wonder whether the thermal efficiency—the percentage of heat in the fuel burned, which the engine actually converts into useful work—is any higher to-day than it was when she surprised me with the information that it was no more than 6%! My Scottish sense of thrift was shocked when I learnt that the remaining 94% was wasted, most of it being puffed out through the engine's chimney! Even in our most efficient locomotives, thermal efficiency, I believe, seldom reaches 10%.

"In the *Conservatoire des Arts et Metiers* in Paris, there's a funny thing on three wheels, believed to be the very first vehicle that ever moved under its own steam. It was invented by a Frenchman named Nicolas Cugnot, as long ago as 1763. It ran along the road, without any rails, at two miles an hour, carrying no more than four people. Just fancy that, my laddie! The four people could have walked in much less time. Well, Nicolas's parents were very poor; and this hampered Nicolas, for he couldn't buy good tools. And he hadn't a grand workshop, such as would have helped him with his invention. Well, one day Nicolas's steam vehicle was publicly exhibited in Paris; and a lot of clever engineers came to see it. They laughed at it, of course; and they laughed at poor Nicolas too. And then one day the silly thing turned turtle; and the escaping steam scalded some of the spectators; and poor Nicolas was thrown into prison for all his trouble."

This story of Aunt Dorothy's I remember, word for word. "And so that was the beginning of steam locomotion," she would conclude.

"Auntie, do tell me the story of poor Nicolas and his steam-engine again!" I would plead at intervals, when she was in storytelling mood.

A day or two later, the romantic story of steam was continued with reference to the contributions of James Watt, William Murdoch, Richard Trevithick, and George Stephenson. And I do not forget her telling how, about 1811, Blenkinsop introduced his rack-and-pinion locomotive, to be succeeded within a couple of years by Hedley's *Puffing Billy*. When looking for something quite different in the Science and Art Museum at South Kensington the other day, I accidentally found myself confronted with *Puffing Billy*, that primitive contraption once used so proudly on the tramway connecting Wylam Colliery with the Tyne. Instantly my mind carried me to the far hills of Ross, and the Goat-wife's deserted home on the hillside. I could see her there, as of yore, seated by the kitchen table, with paper and pencil, carefully sketching for my edification a railway-line with a rack at the side of it, into which fitted the toothed wheel of Blenkinsop's locomotive; and I remembered with undying gratitude what I owe to that remarkable woman, who handled me so tenderly in my difficult years, and implanted in me much that has gone into the fullness of my days. For all my backwardness, and my utter incompetence when it came to figures and angles, it now looked as though Aunt Dorothy had, at last, hit upon something with which it was possible to hold my attention. "You will see some fine engines in Auld Reekie when you go there, especially about the Waverley Station," she would add, by way of further encouragement.

Soon I took to sharing with others of my age the boyish propensity for drawing engines, signals, and railway lines heading inevitably for dark tunnels, all of them the very crudest of representations, notwithstanding the frills and details I sought to add from time to time. Apart from a piece of paper and pencil, a ruler and a coin or two were my tools. The ruler gave the framework something of a rectangular appearance: with the coins one drew things that looked like wheels. The drive-wheels were penny-size. The others, with the exception of those on the bogie, the circumference of which was determined by a three-penny-bit, were drawn round a halfpenny. These three coins fixed the ratios of all the wheels any locomotive of mine ever required. With the aid of the ruler, in went the spokes, any number of them. The *tout ensemble*, gaily coloured with crayons, looked quite well. However, I was never so satisfied as to delude myself into imagining such odd and disproportionate productions conveyed the idea of their resembling anything endowed with the power of locomotion.

For quite a long time, as I suppose it must have been, I appeared content with these puerile efforts, trying them out on everything capable of taking the imprint of my wayward pencil. Even the end-papers of my school-books carried them. When bored with the lesson (an occurrence not uncommon, as my quarterly reports consistently showed) I would turn furtively to an inside cover, or to the back page of an exercise-book, to add a spoke, or perhaps a squiggle or two by way of denoting smoke issuing from the funnel. Then one day, with my discovery that engines were classified under two main headings, locomotive and stationary, there came an element of variety into my idleness. These two big words, or rather what they signified, now fought for mastery in my tiny, eleven-year-old brain. The stationary won; and, in consequence, I now took to drawing them with increasing verve. Crooked railway lines, crude signals, and slanting tunnels made way for fly-wheels, belts, and pulleys. I found these stationary efforts easier, probably because they did not demand the skill necessary to impart the sense that they represented objects capable of moving themselves about from place to place. The type of movement for which they were designed seemed to call for less delineation. Realising, however, that I could never hope to make a good drawing of anything of this nature without first knowing a little more of how it worked, I eventually abandoned these childish practices in favour of examining rolling-stock at quarters as close as the authorities would allow. So, at this stage, the Waverley Station of Auld Reekie began to loom large in my life; and I developed a veritable craving to possess the model of a North British engine in the glass case facing the approach to platform five, and set in motion by the penny dropped in the slot, to swell the funds of the railwaymen's orphanage. That was the first working model of anything Iain or I had ever seen. It lured us; and, even when our pennies were exhausted, we might stand by, indefinitely, waiting for someone else to set it a-going. For old times' sake, I still drop a coin into that slot, and watch, rather sentimentally perhaps, the little crank-shafts and wheels performing the service allotted to them.

The creaking of wheels and the rumble of driving-shafts, as the big engines of the North British Railway moved under the Waverley Bridge, readily introduced me to more intimate acquaintance with them. They were olive-green in colour, those engines, you may remember, and were built at Cowlairs. For no reason other than the family's partiality for everything connected with the word, Waverley, I liked to imagine a preference for them, as against the blue locomotives the Caledonian Railway Company constructed for itself at St. Rollox. Each bore the company's coat-of-arms, an emblem so familiar to us in subsequent years that we came to revere it. Indeed, we looked upon it as though it were our own private insignia. And I cannot describe to you the thrill I experienced when, on a recent visit to the L.N.E.R.'s present headquarters near Hitchin, my eyes alighted on a reproduction of that coat-of-arms, which we used to see on all sorts of things besides engines, in and about the Waverley, a generation or so ago. Consequently, I left Hitchin with the photograph facing page 128, and a warm glow at the heart of me, for sentiment repleted. The ashes of the Colonel, mouldering these last twelve years by the dust of Rob Roy, may gather themselves together to rebuke me for the confession that, in boyhood and youth, the emblem of the Old N.B. meant as much to me as did that of the MacGregors!

There were other aspects of the North British Railway that engaged our attention; and we were proud to remind those, who expressed a preference for the Caledonian, that, after all, the N.B. instituted the first sleeping-car (or bed-carriage, as it was then called) in Britain. The actual vehicle was brought into service in 1873, on the Glasgow–King's Cross route. Its underframe and body were of teak. Its panelling was unpainted, but highly polished, and inlaid with panels of silver-walnut mounted in ebony and gold. All upholstery was in red velvet; and all metal fittings silver-plated. Venetian shutters came down over the drop-lights. In the lavatory there was a drinking filter. The tank lay outside, on the roof, "nicely placed to become frozen in winter", as a writer on railways remarked when this first British sleeper was thrown open to public inspection. The lighting was by vegetable-oil lamps, inserted in holes in the roof. Withal, it was very primitive when we compare it with the sleeping accommodation now racing so swiftly and smoothly, so commodiously, between London and the Scottish cities, every night of the year.

*   *   *   *   *   *   *

Mention of Cowlairs recalls my first railway journey from Auld Reekie to Glasgow, accompanied by father and Iain, before the days of corridor trains on this line. While the former, temporarily the soul of amiability (as he always was when on his way to some Celtic function in Glasgow), browsed upon Gaelic reveries, Iain and I rushed excitedly from window to window, as the train approached Cowlairs and the Queen Street tunnel, anxious to see in what respects we might compare the city, toward which we were travelling, with that we had left some fifty minutes earlier. On reaching Cowlairs, father began to tell us how, in his college days at Glasgow, and indeed even during the present century, the steep decline from this wellknown railway workshop and depôt necessitated the placing of two brake-vans in front of each descending train. These vans were fitted with powerful brakes, manipulated by experienced brakesmen, as gravity bore the train to its terminus at Queen Street; and, since the locomotives of those times were not able, unaided, to draw trains up the gradient as far as Cowlairs, except perhaps with difficulty and delay, they were assisted by a cable worked on the endless rope principle. There stood at Cowlairs a stationary winding engine, which operated this cable for over sixty years. However, a couple of years after it was installed, two heavy six-coupled locomotives, hopefully christened *Hercules* and *Samson*, were introduced as an alternative. They functioned none too successfully for four years, whereafter they were withdrawn, and the former cable haulage restored. The cables varied in length from 4,560 yards to 4,750. They had a diameter of 5 to $5\frac{3}{4}$ inches, and weighed just under twenty-three tons. They seldom lasted more than fifteen months. In 1909 the Westinghouse brake was substituted for the brake-vans, while more powerful locomotives, helped by banking engines, displaced those that, hitherto, had had to rely on cable traction.

As you may well imagine, father did not approve of all this interest in engines and engineering, although occasionally he himself contributed to it. His reaction to Aunt Dorothy's suggestion that, with my practical bent (I'm very practical, you may be surprised to learn) I might become apprenticed in good, Scottish fashion to a Scottish firm of repute, met with frown and scorn. In his view, no one in engineering, lacking a sound grounding in mathematics, as in my unhappy case, could be anything more in life than an engine-driver. That a son of his should aspire to a career as unbefitting was little better than if he had deliberately elected to be the wretched bank-clerk, whose pitiable predicament was perpetually dangled before one. "Great God in Heaven!" I hear my father say. "He wants to be an engine-driver!"

Nevertheless, my interest prompted a determination to find out things about the ways and workings of railways, and especially about the North British route between the Waverley and Queen Street. In 1942, by the way, this line, known originally as the Edinburgh & Glasgow Railway, celebrated its centenary. It was projected in 1835, authorised in 1838, and opened for passenger traffic in February, 1842, which means that it is one of the oldest components of what is now the L.N.E.R. It took three years to complete the forty-six miles of track between the Haymarket and Queen Street. The cost was in the region of a million and a quarter. At the outset, it carried four trains, daily, in each direction, all of them conveying first- and second-class passengers, two of them carrying third-class in addition. The single fares for the whole distance were eight, six, and four shillings, respectively. In these days of compulsory powers, it is at least of passing import that the opposition of the Forth & Clyde Canal Company obliged the railway promoters to abandon the idea of a high-level station at Glasgow. That long, steep tunnel between Cowlairs and Queen Street was necessary, therefore, to take the line into Glasgow *below* the canal.

As children we knew an old man who, when a schoolboy, was fortunate enough to have had a father who managed to secure two tickets enabling them both to travel, with about a thousand others, aboard the first train to reach Edinburgh from Glasgow. He used to tell us how three trains, each comprising ten first-class coaches, were hauled, separately, up the incline to the level at Cowlairs, where they were all coupled together. Three locomotives then pulled them into Edinburgh. The journey, which included a twenty minutes' stop at Falkirk to replenish the engines' tanks, took three and three-quarter hours—a speed of approximately five minutes to the mile, or twelve miles per hour. That same afternoon, a ceremonial train of nearly thirty carriages left the Haymarket for Glasgow, and reached the summit of the Cowlairs incline in just over two and a half hours, after two stops for water, one at Linlithgow, the other at Falkirk. This was a much better performance. It meant an average speed of twenty miles per hour. The return journey to Edinburgh late that evening was considerably delayed, however, owing to a breakdown in the haulage system at Cowlairs. The hemp rope, which preceded the wire cable, had been cut. Sabotage was suspected. After a deal of puffing and blowing and slipping, locomotives did get the train up to Cowlairs, and into Edinburgh just after midnight.

Nowadays, when most people travel on Sundays as on any weekday, it is perhaps amusing to reflect that the morning and evening train, running in each direction on that day, created an outburst of national indignation in Scotland. In the bitter controversy that ensued, the directors, who were members of the Sabbath Observance Society, eventually won, with the result that there was no Sunday service on this route for several years.

In 1865 this Edinburgh & Glasgow Railway, with its smart,

green engines of polished brass, was acquired by the North British, which not only adopted its coat-of-arms, but transferred its locomotive works from St Margaret's, at Piershill (Edinburgh) to Cowlairs, where they have remained. At the top of the incline there stood, until 1911, one of the last relics of the original railway, namely, the Cowlairs signal-box, the oldest in Scotland. For many years before it was demolished, it served as a store.

On New Year's Day, 1923—an important date in British railway history—the Old North British became incorporated in the London & North-Eastern.

* * * * * * *

It was not until 1847, five years after a regular service had been established between Queen Street, at Glasgow, and the Haymarket, at Edinburgh, that the extension, eastwards, toward the Waverley Station was opened. The Waverley—Bless it! What Aunt Dorothy had not taught me about steam locomotives, I certainly managed to pick up there, during my youth in Auld Reekie. I could have written a treatise on the advantages and disadvantages of our standard gauge, for instance, or on the notation of various types of locomotives.

Just as the London & North-Eastern Railway names all its big express engines after famous race-horses, and the Southern selects names from the legends of King Arthur and the Knights of the Round Table, so did the North British, with its headquarters at the Waverley Station, or at Waterloo Place, quite close at hand, choose, for similar engines, names from the *Waverley Novels*. This practice of naming engines is exclusively British, I believe; and I must say it created a pleasant diversion when wandering about the Waverley, or when travelling over the lines then belonging to the North British. What gave me greater joy than to entrain in the small hours for Aunt Dorothy's, and be drawn at least as far as Perth by an engine with a Clan Gregor association? —an engine called *Rob Roy*, or maybe *Bailie Nicol Jarvie*, or the *Dougal Cratur*? That always contributed a touch of romance at the outset of my long journey to the Hill of the Peats. Many a Scot now furth of Scotia remembers, perhaps with a heartache, those first lovely engines we knew in boyhood at Edinburgh. So different were they from those I had known in childhood—green ones radiating from Inverness, and named after the more famous of our lochs and straths, bens and glens, and other physical

N
177

characteristics of the Highlands. The Grampian and Cairngorm peaks furnished many a Highland Railway locomotive with its name. I have remembered all these years the titles of those that bore me to and from High Wind, and not a few of the incidents one witnessed *en route*. The mechanical lubricator with its innumerable feeds, now so easily actuated from inside the cabin, was still unknown to our northern trains, so that we had the thrill, especially at night-time, of putting our heads out of the carriage window to watch the driver leave his cabin and walk round the front of the engine as the train sped onward. In one hand he bore a lantern, and sometimes a flaming naphtha flare, and an oil-can with a long, tapering nozzle. With the other he clung perilously to the hand-rail. A dangerous practice it was, particularly in winter, with the train tearing through the Grampian snows at fifty miles or more per hour, against the blast!

But there was an atmosphere of by-laws and restrictions about the Waverley, to which I had not been accustomed in the Highlands. Whereas the drivers of our Highland trains, during shunting operations, occasionally invited me to the footplate, and allowed me to do a little driving, no one connected with our much beloved N.B.R. ever suggested anything so delightfully informal, though I spent many an hour gazing at its giant engines, trying to apply, theoretically, what Aunt Dorothy had taught me.

Even yet I dawdle on the Waverley Bridge, or at the bend of the Mound, to watch the coming and the going of the L.N.E.R. trains that have absorbed, and so largely displaced, our North British rolling-stock. How many hours did Iain and I spend on the battlements of the Castle, counting the trains as they went puffing along the fringe of Princes Street Gardens? I can smell at this moment the train-smoke that, rising in black clouds where the Haymarket tunnel terminates by St Cuthbert's kirkyard, hangs about for a few familiar seconds. The greater efficiency of the modern engine may be a saving on the coal-bill; but the valley, in which once lay the Nor' Loch, has been deprived of much of its homely reekiness since I was an Auld Reekie schoolboy.

This love of trains lingers with me constantly; and I never cease to marvel at the manner in which locomotive designers in this country, so restricted by the narrowness of the standard gauge (4 feet: 8½ inches) into which their constructions must fit, in order to prevent them from fouling platforms, and other erections overhead or by the side of the track, have produced our modern

British engine, with its enormous capacity for weight-lifting and speed. Especially in the matter of cylinders has our comparatively narrow gauge been a limitation. The biggest cylinder a British locomotive can carry, without danger of fouling, is one of twenty-two inches in internal diameter, such as may be seen on the Southern Railway 4-6-4 tank engines. Designers have been seriously handicapped, likewise, in the placing of large and powerful cylinders between the frames.

* * * * * * *

Even after I was quite grown up, I paid frequent visits to the Waverley to see the trains leave for, and arrive from, King's Cross. I never failed to glow when, of an evening, the *Flying Scotsman* steamed in from the south, having left King's Cross at 10 a.m. that morning. The discovery that a train so named had been plying daily between London and Auld Reekie ever since 1862 astounded me. It was marvellous enough to contemplate then, some thirty years or so ago. It is even more marvellous today, taking into account the strain two major wars have placed upon our railways in the interval. The *Flying Scotsman's* record is probably unparalleled in railway history.

I once made friends at the Waverley with the chief traffic superintendent, who used to pilot me through the ticket-barriers, that he might be ever telling me a little more about the Gould coupling, the Westinghouse and vacuum brakes, and other devices of modern railway travel. One of the most homely sounds to be heard about the Waverley at that time was the incessant chug-chug of the Westinghouse air-pump, fixed externally to the side of the engine. The Westinghouse attached to the lighter type of engine, such as is used on local and suburban trains, functioned with great energy, as if designed to infect with like quality the steps of tardy passengers. Throughout the long day, there was seldom more than a few minutes' interval during which this chug-chug could not be heard by the platforms from which departed those innumerable trains for Abbeyhill and Piershill, for Portobello and Musselburgh.

And I remember so well when, as the result of experiments in reducing coach-weight and train-length, the first coaches fitted with Gresley articulated bogies reached us from the Great Northern Railway's works at Doncaster.

The name of my superintendent acquaintance I do not think I

ever heard. Yet, I got to know him quite well. He was a kenspeckle figure about the Waverley. Like the rest of his fraternity, he wore plain clothes and a bowler. You know how popular the bowler has always been among the higher grades of railway employees, more especially with those who disport a drooping moustache to match, as it were! Top-hat and morning-coat, a bit of gold braid on the lapels, and a red rosebud in button-hole denoted the highest rank to which a North British Railway official could aspire in those days. Spruce fellows they looked too, particularly when superintending the departure of the London trains. If their distinctive clothing did not display quite such thick braid as did their rivals' at the 'Caley' Station, the freshness of those rosebuds certainly compensated. We liked to assume that there was a standing order for so many rosebuds each day, supplied by some florist at the flower and fruit distribution in the Waverley Market, early each morning.

The family's affection for the Waverley, and for the Old North British, which had brought us safely from the Highlands to the Lowlands, was even extended to the North British Hotel, at the east end of Princes Street. This was mainly because our father knew the head porter, who was usually to be found in appropriate uniform about the main entrance hall. He was a MacLeod from Skye; and he and the Colonel often parleyed in the Gaelic. Our curiosity about Mr MacLeod was intensified by the schoolboy rumour that the railway company paid him no wages, no salary, but that, on the contrary, *he* paid the company one thousand good pounds a year to be allowed to serve it in the capacity of hall-porter-in-chief, being able, through the magnitude of the tips he received, especially from tourists passing through his hands when visiting the Scott Country or the Trossachs, to pay off the thousand required of him, and have two or three thousand over for himself.

Now, I must just say a word or two about the Caledonian Railway and the 'Caley' station, since they also had their appeal. When tired of examining the trains at one end of Princes Street, there was less than a mile to walk to those at the other. And what Edinburgh laddie of my generation does not recall the blue engines steaming out of the 'Caley' toward Euston or Glasgow, almost any hour of the day? They fascinated us too, especially after older citizens had whetted our interest with accounts of how, in their younger days, the Caledonian Railway Company and the North British competed with one another in the matter of punctuality and speed. For many years, racing between Edinburgh and Glasgow, on their respective routes, was a feature of Scottish railway development as enthralling as it was sometimes alarming. Yet, serious accidents were surprisingly few. And it is an interesting reflection that, by the middle of last century, trains were travelling daily and nightly from Edinburgh and Glasgow to London in ten hours. This almost seems incredible, when we consider that, under present war-time conditions, the journey between Euston and Glasgow Central, or from King's Cross to Waverley, often takes twelve.

In ways, moreover, the carriages at the 'Caley' appeared more luxuriously upholstered than those at the Waverley. Accustomed in childhood to 'travel hard' on those Highland trains transporting Jessie and me to and from school each day, when the furnishings even of the first-class compartments were still much inferior to what one now finds in our suburban third-class at, say, Liverpool Street, the generous cushions supplied by the Caledonian often tempted me to steal a few minutes' furtive sprawl upon them, in make-believe of setting out, in royal comfort, on a long journey.

The 'Caley' station, however, has always been too full of insurmountable ticket-barriers to make it as inviting as the Waverley. Besides which, being a terminal station, it receives no through trains. At the Waverley, on the other hand, one could inspect those monstrous trains passing through by the East Coast route between King's Cross and Aberdeen, or between King's Cross and Glasgow. Truly, this was an exhilarating privilege for anyone with an eye for line and an ear for rhythm!

*　　*　　*　　*　　*　　*　　*

Another feature of Lowland railway travel calls for notice in passing, namely, *Murray's Diary*.

Who could live and move and have his wellbeing in Auld Reekie, or in Glasgow for that matter, without the corresponding edition of this compendium in his waistcoat pocket, into which it fits so conveniently? When equipped with both editions, one was in possession of all the travel information about Scotland necessary in the days when our bus services were but sketchy. *Murray's Diary* constitutes a veritable travel-bureau in itself. To-day it costs threepence: in my school-days it cost but a penny, and was obtainable at any bookstall or stationer's, a day or two before the beginning of each month to which it referred. What a bargain it was for a penny, especially the Glasgow edition, which remained half as thick again as our Edinburgh one, and contained, in addition to railway time-tables, information relating to the Firth of Clyde steamer services! It also supplied one with mileages, and with population statistics of most of the places mentioned, together with facts about hotel accommodation, early closing, and so on. Then, for each day of the month, there was a dated blank page for notes, headed with astronomical data—sunrise and sunset, moonrise and moonset, and the position of the tides on that particular day. All this was to be found in condensed form between familiar covers of a purple hue. Whenever I arrive in Scotland, whether by rail or by road, I find this *Diary* so indispensable that I make a point of purchasing both an Edinburgh and a Glasgow one.

This typically Scottish production had its origin in a broadsheet timetable first issued quarterly as long ago as 1842, and entitled *Neilson & Murray's Condensed Railway Time Tables*. It purported to show the summer train arrangements to and from Glasgow. The only lines on which trains were running at that time were the Edinburgh and Glasgow, *via* Castlecary; the Glasgow and Ayr, *via* Kilmarnock; the Glasgow, Paisley, and Greenock; and the Glasgow and Coatbridge, *via* Garnkirk. This precursor of all *Murray's* supplied only the departure times from the different terminal stations. The fares and number of trains shown totalled 190. The broadsheet, like its descendants, was sprinkled with asterisks and daggers and other distracting symbols, such as appear to have been indispensable to these compilations from their earliest beginnings. The fares between Edinburgh and Glasgow in the original *Diary* were shown as 6/- and 4/-, whereas the third-class fare from Glasgow to Greenock, or to Dunoon or Rothesay, was only sixpence—evidence of the intense rivalry a hundred years ago between the railway and the Clyde steam-packets. Tradition in Glasgow has it that this sixpenny fare also entitled the passenger to a bottle of beer aboard the steamer, when crossing the Firth of Clyde to Rothesay!!

Murray's has always been the national time-table of Scotland. From its inception it has maintained characteristics quite of its own. The trains in the first issue were shown in paragraph form, instead of being tabulated and alphabetically arranged, as they are now. In *Murray's Edinburgh Diary* and *Murray's Glasgow Diary*, Scotland's two principal cities have a combined time-table and diary unequalled in Britain, and possibly in the world. The monthly circulation of the Glasgow edition has risen from roughly 3,000, as it was in 1873, to about 140,000. Glasgow is, unquestionably, the greatest diary-using city in the world. It is estimated that four out of every five male, adult Glaswegians carry in the vest-pocket the current issue. The printing ink of a new edition is scarcely dry before one hears the familiar cry of "Murray's Diary", as newsvendors and others, alike in Edinburgh and Glasgow, hurry through our populous thoroughfares with fresh supplies of them. Before the paper shortage attributable to the war, this handy and indispensable companion, set by hand in 5-point type by an army of experts, contained 192 pages.

It is no exaggeration to say that *Murray's* is as symbolical of Glasgow as is the Tron Steeple or the Broomielaw, or the coloured tramcars; and I feel the same about the Edinburgh edition so far as Auld Reekie is concerned. This is well recognised. It explains why, in Auld Reekie as in Glasgow, a current copy is always placed in the foundations of a new building, along with coins in circulation at the time, and a current newspaper or two. In Glasgow and her more immediate environs, perhaps to a greater degree than in Auld Reekie and the Lothians, *Murray's Diary* is a badge of citizenship. Yet, who, knowing our Scottish Capital, is unfamiliar with the sight of someone pausing to jot down something in those blank, innermost memo. pages, or knitting his brow as he examines minutely, with the aid of the forefinger-nail, the significance of a particular dagger or asterisk? The smallness of the print, of course, is often a source of annoyance to elderly people; and even the younger users find it irksome when in a hurry. But how could one produce so much in so little —this classic example of *multum in parvo*—except by the adoption of such type? I am told, however, that Scottish opticians regard *Murray's Diaries* as one of their greatest benefactors! It's an ill wind, ye see, that blaws naebody guid!

Officially, the Glasgow and Edinburgh editions are now known as *Murray's ABC Time-table for Glasgow & the West of Scotland* and *Murray's ABC Time-table for Edinburgh & the East of Scotland*. This change was made when diaries became liable to purchase-tax. Nevertheless, no Scot ever refers to them but as *Murray's Diaries*. Recent custom and excise regulations, moreover, have required the elimination of the memo. pages we knew; but these are being restored to us with the return of saner times.

It is doubtful whether one could send to an exiled Scot anything more reminiscent of homeland than a *Murray's Diary*. Its contents-page readily reveals the vast scope of its information, all deftly included, without a fraction of unnecessary bulkiness. Herein you will find all you need to know about air services, steam and ferry services, bank and public holidays, shopkeepers' half-holidays, postal information, registrars, charges on cheques and drafts on bankers, suburban transport, particulars of places providing public entertainment, and of the movements of sun and moon, the dates on which fall the Terms in Scotland, tide-tables, burgh populations, and mileages. Add to this the hotel tariffs and other advertisements relative to most of the large cities and towns in Great Britain, and also the coupon-insurance, and what more could even the Scot expect for threepence? With regard to the last mentioned, the widow and children of a friend of mine, who lost his life in the Queen Street collision some years ago, received from the insurance company the sum named on the coupon signed by the victim, that very morning, in the *Murray's Diary* found on his body.

> *Mysterious Booklet, in whose ample page*
>   *Confusion reigns, whose second word*
>   *Corrects the first, and contradicts the third;*
> *Whose stars and double daggers still engage*
> *The traveller's eye to bootless pilgrimage*
>   *From reference to cross-reference so absurd*
>   *As to require Boyle Roche's famous bird*
> *Fitly to study all its verbiage.*
>
> *When will you cease to lead us in a maze*
>   *Of doubtful grammar and ambiguous sense,*
> *And wrap our pathway in a gloomy haze*
>   *Of musty columns, even made more dense*
> *By swarms of asterisks and little "a's",*
>   *Sprinkled around with gay inconsequence?*

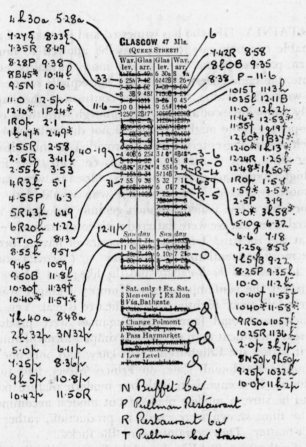

One of the three sections into which a page of *Murray's Diary* is cut, so that the compositor may make on the type the alterations penned in by the editor.

CHAPTER XIX

AMUSEMENTS OF YOUTH

"CERTAINLY, HE who has witnessed and partaken of pleasures attainable on such easy terms, may be allowed to murmur at modern parties, where, with much more formality and more expense, the same cheerful results are not equally secured."

So wrote Sir Walter Scott when contrasting the happy and homely amusements of an earlier Edinburgh with those of the era then opening. One might express, in not dissimilar words, what one felt about the entertainments provided in this selfsame city during one's own youth, when compared with those for which such high charges are made nowadays. Pleasures were rarer then, and more restricted in variety. But who would deny that we obtained for a few pence as much genuine enjoyment as when, at stated intervals, we were flattered with comparatively expensive seats at the theatre? I harbour memories of having been taken to the more conventional pantomimes—to *Cinderella* and *Mother Goose*, to *Jack and the Beanstalk* and the like; and I have not forgotten that the contemporaneous Humpty Dumpty was having his great fall, twice nightly, at the Theatre Royal. Yet, I cannot say these occasional family extravagances were productive of more real enjoyment than were many simpler forms of amusement. True it is that the Edinburgh I first knew had only one picture-house. The Kardomah Café, on Princes Street, had just made way for it. In comparison with our modern picture palaces, it was, to be sure, a modest place of but modest accommodation; and the films shown were crude in production, rather than in subject-matter. They certainly were 'the flicks'.

But our theatres—the King's and the Lyceum, the Royal and the Empire—were then in the height of their glory. Musical comedy had attained its acme of splendour; and variety programmes with Florrie Forde, Little Tich, Harry Weldon, and Harry Tate (who was still selling that tiresome motor-car of his!) attracted full houses. The Opera usually came to the Lyceum; and I recollect my once being mildly entertained there by what appeared to be an immense lady. Heavily draped, and scintillating in sequins that might have been fish scales, she reclined on a small sofa while singing her swan-song, looking exactly like a whale left high and dry on a rock by the shorelands at Gullane or North Berwick. You must not think me too disrespectful when I tell you that her name was Madame Tetrazzini!

The theatre we MacGregors patronised most frequently was the King's, chiefly because it lay nearer home than any of the others. We passed it at least twice daily, when on our way to and from Watson's. How often, of a Monday morning, with a few seconds to spare, did Iain and I linger by the scenery entrance in that rather mean thoroughfare called Tarvit Street, where a pantechnicon usually stood, backed, across the pavement, obliging us to duck or deviate! This lofty postern was always open then, to allow of the change of scenery occasioned by the weekly change of show; and we paused on the pavement there, to gaze up in wonder at the intricate rope and lighting arrangements among 'the flies'.

Children were admitted to the King's at half-price. This meant that we could make our way to the front bench of 'the gods' for twopence, provided we were prepared to stand outside the appropriate door at least an hour before it was opened, and then tear up those long flights of stairs, three steps at a stride, for fear of being passed by bigger and more lithe youths, who had arrived after us, and bade fair to gain the best places. Those hard, rough, wooden seats, on which, as a matter of civic routine, a regular clientèle expended fourpence at least once a week, ruined many a pair of breeks. They were extraordinarily uncomfortable, especially when, in addition to their asperities, one had to thole the restless footwear of the rabble seated immediately behind.

Not dissimilar were the conditions obtaining at the Theatre Royal, in Broughton Street. Iain and I frequently found ourselves at the head of the queue by the gallery entrance in that steep and unevenly cobbled side-street called Little King Street, so that, whenever the doors were flung open and we had paid the requisite sum for admission, we might dash aloft to have the first choice of front seats on that hard, posterior-polished bench our generation in Auld Reekie knew so well.

*   *   *   *   *   *   *

Once a year, toward the end of June, at the opening of the season that followed the spring-cleaning of Auld Reekie's theatres, father, as though by royal decree, mustered the entire household when John Clyde and his company came to the King's with a melodramatised version of Sir Walter Scott's *Rob Roy*, adapted from Isack Pocock's *Rob Roy MacGregor* (or *Auld Lang Syne*) an operatic drama, in three acts, first printed in London in 1818. Our supra-loyal parent regarded our patronage as a duty incumbent upon him, firstly, as a descendant of the notorious freebooter; secondly, in deference to 'the Old Name'; thirdly, as Bard of the Clan Gregor. Of course, we had been nourished on other heroics as well. William Wallace was very real to us, and even Robert the Bruce. *Even* Robert the Bruce, I say, because father discouraged our extolling him so much as to make us forgetful of his share in the downfall and ultimate execution of Scotland's *real* national hero. We were charged to bear in mind that Stewart of Menteith was not alone in bringing the brave Sir William Wallace captive to the Tower. We, therefore, had to resist the tendency to give Bannockburn publicity at the expense of Stirling Brig!

Our annual attendance at the King's to see *Rob Roy* was in the nature of a pilgrimage. Father could not have taken us, with a greater sense of duty and reverence, to Rob's birthplace, or to his place of burial. Consequently, we gave to the performance our undivided attention. In course of time, we knew this play so well that we could detect an altered word, or the slightest change of inflection, between one season's rendering and another. Either my brother or I, without a second's hesitation, could have given any of the performers his or her cue, had we been called upon to do so. Likewise with the musical passages, which had a good dash of Burns in them, or a flavour distinctly Jacobite. The following day we acted in the home the parts of Francis Osbaldistone and Diana Vernon, singing those familiar duets of theirs. Iain, being the younger and more lady-like, took the part of Diana. The duets they sang, in their protracted parting, we loved particularly. There were those somewhat sentimental lines set to an allegro version of the air associated with *Roy's Wife o' Aldivalloch*, and, of course, *My Luve is like a red, red Rose*, sung at the close of this first scene.

> My Luve is like a red, red rose
> That's newly sprung in June:
> My Luve is like a melody,
> That's sweetly played in tune.
>
> As fair art thou, my bonnie lass,
> So deep in luve am I;
> And I will luve thee still, my dear,
> Till a' the seas gang dry.

Till a' the seas gang dry, my dear,
And the rocks melt wi' the sun;
And I will luve thee still, my dear,
While the sands o' life shall run.

And fare thee weel, my only Luve!
And fare thee weel awhile!
And I will come again, my Luve,
Though 'twere ten thousand mile.

Never before had I seen anything quite so charming as Diana
Vernon. I found it hard to believe that she belonged to my own
century, rather than to the eighteenth. This was a reality too
unpleasant to contemplate. It intruded itself with poignancy
when, at the conclusion of the performance, I found myself outside, on the earth-binding pavement, once more, making for home
amid jostling crowds and horse-cabs and vociferous newsboys.
For many a day thereafter, and to the detriment of my homework,
I would be lilting the songs and ballads I had heard, among
them those lines by the Ettrick Shepherd, sung by the wistful
Diana.

Cam ye by Athol, lad wi' the philabeg,
Doon by the Tummel, or banks o' the Garry?
Saw ye oor lads, wi' their bonnets and white cockades,
Leaving their mountains tae follow Prince Charlie?
Follow thee! follow thee! wha wadna follow thee?
Lang hast thou lo'ed and trusted us fairly:
Chairlie! Chairlie! wha wadna follow thee,
King o' the Heilan hairts, Bonnie Prince Chairlie?

But the piece of music we enjoyed as much as any was the four-
part glee sung as the curtain rose to discover the exterior of a village
ale-house at the foot of the Cheviots, with its hostess in attendance
on a group of tuneful travellers about to fare forth at sundown.
Surely you, of Auld Reekie, remember it!

Soon the sun will gae to rest, Let's a - wa' the - gi - ther;
Com - pa - ny is aye the best, Cross - in' owre the hea - ther.

Soon the sun will gae to rest, Let's a-wa' the-gi-ther;

Com-pa-ny is aye the best, Cross-in' owre the hea-ther.

       *   *   *   *   *   *   *

E. C. Hedmont, the celebrated operatic tenor, who now took the part of Francis Osbaldistone (the part previously taken by Ben Davies, and also by Durward Lely) I invested with a quality not inferior to that I had invented for Diana. When I saw him about the King's in daylight, or coming out of the tenement in Brougham Street, so near at hand, where he returned to the same lodgings year after year, I could not dissipate the fancy that he was of an earlier era, and cherished the hope that one day I might be bold enough to touch the hem of his garment, as it were. Imagine my ecstasy when, at last, while out walking with father, we actually shook hands with this personage of another century! As he emerged from a shop in Home Street, where he was wont to get his groceries, father and he looked at one another as though they had met before. They probably had. Was it likely that, during all those years, Colonel MacGregor had failed to present himself at the stage-door to call on his friend, John Clyde, to give him a kindly wrinkle as to how the better he might act the part of our cattle-rieving ancestor? During one such importunity, doubtless, he had made the acquaintance of Emanuel Christian Hedmont. And now here was I, not just reduced to an inconspicuous touch of the great tenor's garment, but publicly shaking hands with him! I returned home from this exhilarating experience, resolved to emulate him even more conscientiously in the songs we had heard him sing. As for that handshake, it recalled the Dougal Cratur's observation when Rob Roy shook hands with him, placing upon him some especial obligation: *"She'll never wash that hand no more! No, never no more!"* How could I bear to have the precious influence of Francis Osbaldistone's handshake worn off by allowing my palm to come into contact with ordinary things? In childish fancy for some hours thereafter, I held my hand aloof, free from all earthly contamination.

* * * * * * *

Needless to say, the family wept for Rob, as he stood there, in the centre of the stage, a prisoner, his arms fastened to an old flint-lock, and now confronted by Rashleigh. I confess that we had great difficulty in restraining ourselves from greeting the dark and villainous Rashleigh with a big boo whenever he came on the scene, for he resided in our young MacGregor minds as the personification of treachery. We sobbed even more copiously with sheer relief at Rob's breaking free to scatter his armed captors. You must understand that to bind this man was tantamount to an affront to, if not actually an assault upon, ourselves. All the wrongs of the centuries seemed avenged in Rob Roy's spectacular triumphs.

I think the scene we loved best of all was that depicting the Bailie Nicol Jarvie's midnight visit to poor Mr Owen, imprisoned in Glasgow's Tolbooth—"shut up", as he described it, "in a nasty Scotch jail! A _H_olbooth, I think they call it! Oh dear!"—because he had disclosed to Messrs. MacVittie & MacFin, merchants in the Gallowgate, the untoward affairs of Osbaldistone & Co., Crane Alley, London, where he was head clerk and junior partner, and they, as creditors, had had recourse to a summary process of arrest and imprisonment. The choral setting of this scene was as tuneful as anything we had ever heard; and we peered into all the shadowy corners of the stage, watching intently for the arrival of Rob Roy himself. Did ever gaoler make clavigerous noises more appropriate to his chains of office than the Dougal Cratur, when admitting to the Tolbooth the Bailie, and Mattie, his buxom servant-maid and lantern-bearer? Ah! Mattie! I remember her vividly. "Ye'll offer nae incivility tae Mattie. She's an honest man's daughter, and a near cousin o' the Laird o' Limmerfield's."

One little joke in this production we relished particularly, although, in the prim Edinburgh of youth, it was considered so improper that few of the audience dared exhibit any hilarity over it. Says the Bailie Nicol Jarvie, in remorseful tones, meanwhile wiping his fevered brow with a large kerchief as though just emerged with thankfulness from great tribulation, "Let Rob

Roy sleep wi' his ancestors, an' me wi'-wi'-wi'-wi' his widow!"
That was the last word in naughty humour then. One almost
expected the curtain to be rung down on these faltering accents.

* * * * * * *

The entire Rob Roy production is the property of the King's
Theatre, at Edinburgh. All the scenes and costumes pertaining
to it were made there, by the Howard & Wyndham wardrobe,
from drawings specially prepared from historical documents.
They are still stored away at the King's, ready for the day when,
if ever, we may revive this essentially Scottish play. But it is very
doubtful now whether it could be produced again in the form
in which we knew it, and for a variety of reasons. With the picture-
house combines, and with the modern craze for crooning, tap-
dancing, and music-hall back-chat, I fear the *Rob Roy*, which Auld
Reekie folks knew so well, is a thing of the past. Yet, it remains
with them as one of their most cherished memories.

Some years ago, when it was still believed that this play could
hold its own against competing forms of public entertainment, the
costumes were remade at the King's, under the supervision of the
wardrobe-mistress, Miss Janet Rankin, the lady who now fulfils
that function for the entire Howard & Wyndham circuit. (My
word! Couldn't Janet tell you things, grave and gay, about stage-
life, if only you prevailed upon her to expand on her many years'
experience at the King's!) And it was strangely agreeable to
have her tell me, as she accompanied me round the lofty 'flies' one
day recently, that Margaret Stewart, whom I have known for at
least two-thirds of my life—Margaret *F*. Stewart, I ought to say,
since F. signifies Fraser, and Margaret's very proud of it—that
Margaret F. Stewart, as I was about to say, was the best Mattie
we ever knew during the years *Rob Roy* remained the most beloved
of our annual entertainments. Did ever a lass stand so well on any
stage? And she so chic, so debonair. Was there ever a Mattie
who, by temperament, by Scottish upbringing, was better suited
to the pert passages that fell to her part, or to the pawkier of our
auld Scots sangs?[1] Could you be bothered reading through that
passage where she acquitted herself so memorably?

[1] One of Edinburgh's best known epigrams had its origin in Margaret's
declaring that she attributes her success to her possessing "the fine, free manner
o' the West, coupled wi' the grace and refinement o' the East".

Act I, Scene IV.—*A Room in the Bailie Nicol Jarvie's House, in Glasgow.*

(*Enter* Bailie *and* Saunders Wylie.)

BAILIE: Ma conscience! I tell ye, Saunders, ye're daft—ye're mad! Osbaldistone and Co. in danger! It's no' possible!

WYLIE: It's very true, Bailie; an' I thocht it but right tae let you, ma auld maister, ken o't.

BAILIE: Troth, Saunders, ye've stunned me wi' the evil communication. Osbaldistone and Co. fail? Stop! Ma conscience! Mattie! Mattie! (*Calling off.*)

WYLIE: Maister Owen, the heid clerk an' junior pairtner, has been in oor hoose wi' the news, an' beggin' for time tae tak' up the bills.

BAILIE: Owen! I remember—he's a man o' figures, a man o' calculation; an' if *he* talks o' ruin, by ma saul, it's no' far aff! But what for did he no' ca' upon Nicol Jarvie? I'm a merchant an' a magistrate as weel as MacVittie. But he thinks nae mair o' me, I reckon, than o' an auld Scotch pedlar. Mattie! Mattie! Mattie!

(*Enter* Mattie.)

Tell the clerk tae bring the ledger.

MATTIE: The clerk! Lord, Bailie! he's safe in his bed these twa 'oors.

BAILIE: A-bed, the lazy blackguard! Then fetch it yoursel', Mattie.

MATTIE: I'se dae yer bidding, Bailie. (*Exit* Mattie.)

BAILIE: Ma conscience! I havena had sican a shock since ma worthy faither, the Deacon (peace be wi' him) left me tae fecht ma way alane in this wicked warld. But what says MacVittie? Will he grant the time?

WYLIE: No' a day, Mr Jarvie—no' an 'oor. Things look sae bad, I fear ma employers mean tae resort tae the severest measures. I heard them talk o' arrestin' Maister Owen. So, you'd best look tae yoursel'.

(*Enter* Mattie *with the ledger.*)

BAILIE: Look tae masel! Let me look at the ledger first. (*Putting on his spectacles, and opening ledger eagerly.*) L-M-N-O-O-O-Oh!-Oh!-Os-Osbal—as I'm a Bailie, the balance maun be enormous; but I havena the heirt tae run it up noo. (*Returning the ledger to* Mattie.) How muckle is MacVittie in wi' him, Saunders?

O   193

WYLIE: I canna justly say, Bailie; but some hunners.

BAILIE: Hunners! Only hunners! Damn their supple snouts! An' would they oppress a fa'en man for the sake o' hunners, thae that hae made thoosans by him? Your maisters, Saunders Wylie, hae ta'en mony a gude fat job frae atween ma teeth; but I'll snap them this turn! I'll snap them this turn!

WYLIE: I wish ye could, Bailie. I wish ye could. Ah! I made a sair change the day I left ye, tae serve twa sic infernal——

BAILIE: Whisht! Saunders, whisht! While ye eat their bread, dinna abuse the damn'd scoondrels ahint their backs.

WYLIE: Ye've a kind heirt, Mr Jarvie, an' an honest ane tae.

BAILIE: Ma conscience! so had ma worthy faither, the Deacon, Saunders—rest an' bless him!

WYLIE: Wad ye be pleased tae consult on this business wi' oor pairtners, sir?

BAILIE: No! I'll see them baith damn'd first! Ma conscience! That is, a man wha meddles wi' pitch is sure tae be defiled. I'd raither hauld a parley wi' Auld Clootie! Na, na! Nicol Jarvie has a way o' his ain tae manage this matter. Gang yer ways, Mattie, wi' that huge memorial o' misfortunes, an' bring me ma walking-gear an' the lantern.

MATTIE: (*somewhat surprised*) Yer walking-gear, Bailie?

(*Exit* Mattie.)

BAILIE: Aye, ma walking-gear. Gawd bless me? What's the lassie starin' at? As for ye, Saunders, speed ye hame again, an' no' a word that ye hae seen me. (*Here the Bailie takes out the snuff-box from his pocket, and Wylie holds out his hand in anticipation, but is disappointed.*)

WYLIE: No' a word, Bailie! No' a word!

(*Exit* Wylie.)

BAILIE: Osbaldistone and Co., stop! Ma conscience! I'd sooner hae dreamed o' the dounfa' o' the Bank o' Lunnon! Why, it's eneugh tae gar the very hairs o' ma wig rise up, an' stand on end! But the distress canna be permanent. At ony rate, I'se prove masel' a freend, and, if the hoose regain its credit, I shall recover ma loss; and, if no', why, I hae done as I wad be done by, like ma worthy faither, the Deacon, gude man—blessings on his memory, say I, that taught me gude-will toward ma fellow-creatures!

(*Enter* Mattie, *decked out for walking, bearing the Bailie's cloak, hat, lantern, &c.*)

MATTIE: I've brought the gear, sir. But, save us! whaur wad ye be ganging tae, at sic a time o' night? (*She helps him on with his things.*)

BAILIE: Ye'll soon ken that, Mattie, for ye maun e'en tramp alang wi' me. I wadna like tae be breakin' ma shins in the dark jist noo, for, truth tae speak, I had never mair occasion tae stand firm on ma legs, baith at hame an' abroad. Now, gi'e us the beaver, lassie.

MATTIE: Weel! Tae think o' puttin' on claes when ye should be takin' thame aff, an' scamperin' abroad, when ye should be ganging tae yer bed!

BAILIE: Time an' tide wait for nae man, Mattie.

MATTIE: But whaur are ye ganging tae, Bailie?

BAILIE: Tae mony places that I'd as lief bide awa' frae.

MATTIE: Now wrap this 'kerchief aboot yer thrapple. (*She ties a handkerchief round his neck.*)

BAILIE: Dinna chock me, lassie! Ye're a kind-heirted lassie, Mattie.

MATTIE: There, leave a wee bit room for yer mou'.
(*Exit Mattie, and returns with a bottle and glass.*)

BAILIE: (*aside*) Ma mou'! I wonder what the lassie's gaun tae dae wi' ma mou'. (*Stroking his chin.*)

MATTIE: Ye maun needs hae a drap o' the cordial yer faither, the Deacon, was sae fond o'. He aye likéd tae sip the cordial.

BAILIE: Rest and bless him! Sae he did! An' sae dae I, Mattie. (*He drinks.*) Ye're a gude-tempered soul, Mattie, an' a bonnie lassie tae. Ye're come o' gude kith an' kin, Mattie—the Laird o' Limmerfield's cousin, only seeven times removed. (*Mattie is taking away the bottle.*) Stay! Ye may bring the bottle wi' ye, Mattie; an' tuck yoursel' under ma airm. There's nae disgrace in a Bailie walking airm in airm wi' ane o' gentle bluid. Sae, come yer ways, Mattie! Come yer ways! Osbaldistone and Co.—Stop! Ma conscience!

(*Exeunt*)

* * * * * * *

These occasional visits to Auld Reekie's theatres fostered in me, at the age of fourteen or thereabouts, the covetous desire to acquire the toy theatre my neighbour, Andrew Walker, had fashioned with his own deft hands. (Yes, the same saintly Andrew as had given me that demonstration of how the besieged in Craigmillar Castle dealt with the besiegers—the very Andrew who had gained 100% in dynamics, and ever after retained my unbounded respect!) This theatre, made to his own specifications, was complete with trap-door for mystery scenes, and all manner of ingenious devices for scene-shifting and for making the puppets perform. What with its miniature lighting arrangements, its faery footlights, its curtain that ran up automatically, but often refused to come down at the crucial moment, it was indeed a wonderful piece of work. And I must mention the French musical-box that functioned orchestrally, in those pre-radio days. Copying the more conventional representations, we had snow-scenes of cotton-wool. The snow was made to glitter by the liberal sprinkling of tiny spangles sold for the purpose. This effect was to be seen on a large scale at the pantomime. Away down in Leith Street there was a shop where one could purchase cardboard sheets of figures that lent themselves to various stage productions. All one had to do was to cut them out, and affix a wire or thin stick to each. You could walk them on to the stage easily enough, and often put them through their several contortions and antics with acceptance, though they were inclined to be stilted in movement. If they were easy to walk on, they were as difficult to walk off. When obliged to withdraw, they sometimes assumed an ungainly gait, as their tiny heels tripped against the floor of the stage. Only after much practice could one ensure their backing out with requisite decorum.

With Andrew as stage-manager, chief mechanic, chief electrician, foreman scene-shifter, and producer of the more intricate noises-off, we had one or two quite remunerative performances. Our most successful productions were *Ali Baba & The Forty Thieves* and *Aladdin & His Wonderful Lamp*. The cave scene in the latter was superb—all Andrew's handiwork! A touch of the melodramatic was introduced when Sunny Jim, neatly cut out of a cardboard box that once contained Quaker Oats, strutted across the stage at half-time, to review the audience through his monocle. His entry was the recognised sign that the collection was about to be taken, in order to defray overhead charges and running expenses— marionettes, candles, electric batteries and bulbs, the cost of installing innovations from time to time, and of staging new productions. Performances were held in the spacious hall of our home at Leamy. Even the Colonel favoured us with his presence on occasions, though he always had difficulty in concealing his boredom. Our hall was not so excellent a place as the wash-house attached to Barrie's birthplace at Kirriemuir, which, together with the actual house where he was born, became the property of the National Trust a few years ago. In this wash-house, which was the original of the home built for Wendy in the Never Never Land, Barrie began his theatrical career at the age of seven. Of the first play he staged here, we know little, except that in the final scene there was a life-and-death struggle between two performers, which ended when one of them pitched the other into the boiler. Charges for admission to the wash-house theatre varied. They usually were so many preens (pins), a bool (marble) or a peg-top or peerie. Admission to *our* show, however, was by cold coin of the realm—a penny for adults, and a halfpenny for all under sixteen. No credit was given.

Though I displayed so little aptitude for lessons, I did feel that, if allowed to develop this theatre (the sole rights in which, together with all accessories, the over-generous Andrew eventually transferred to me for the princely sum of a florin!) I might stage some good plays. Indeed, I now had visions of myself as a producer of some standing in years to come. But no! The Colonel would have none of this. My adaptation of *Aladdin & His Wonderful Lamp*, for anything as puerile as a toy theatre, must be extirpated until I had mastered the intricacies of Euclid. Any partiality I exhibited for the histrionic, not even excepting the use of my hands when explaining the dramatic, had to be eradicated, as though it were some foul canker. To fritter away the precious hours on a toy theatre when one's distracted father was faced with the problem of having to meet increasing school-fees for a son not quite all there, was gruelling to a degree. Are you surprised, then, that one day, while I was absorbed in the final rehearsal of a new production, he strode in to put his crashing foot through my theatre? That was Colonel John MacGregor, Honorary Bard of the illustrious Clan Gregor, at his worst, at his most fiendish. He certainly carried through the destruction of one's youthful dreams with damnable thoroughness. But, so far as it affected *me*, such temper and intolerance were never what punishers call *salutary*. On the contrary, they merely intimidated and embittered me. And I could not but perceive an element of poetic justice when, in endeavouring to shake his foot free from the splintered stage, the footlights, that by now had set alight the scenery upon which I had expended so much time and toil, singed his gaiters and knicker-bockers, and bespattered them with spluttering candle-grease!

The Victorian craze for the toy-theatre, or Juvenile Drama, as it was then termed, was wearing off by this time. Yet it is worth recalling that, about the middle of the nineteenth century, half a hundred London publishers did brisk business in issuing sheets of characters and scenery in miniature, ready to be cut out, coloured, and mounted, and introduced eventually on the parlour table in a little rococo theatre. Juvenile Drama was then one of the most popular forms of pastime and domestic entertainment. No sooner had some melodrama achieved success on the London stage than publishers set to work on versions in miniature. Hundreds were employed in designing these sheets, and in colour-ing, fantastically, the more expensive of them. Of all this I had come to know something through Aunt Dorothy's readings by the fireside at Cnocnamoine, so that, by the time I became sole proprietor of Andrew's theatre, I was aware of my participating, not in some silly child's-play, as the Colonel fancied, but in art and craft of ancient and honourable standing. Ah! I hear Aunt Dorothy in my reflective ear now, so vivifying R. L. S.'s essay, *A Penny Plain & Twopence Coloured*, that I resolved to seek out the very shop whenever I returned to Auld Reekie. "Ma laddie, *I* remember the shop where R. L. S. used to linger with empty pockets, wishing he had the toy-theatre that stood in the window, and some of the plays and sheets that went with it." But, as I was soon to discover, the shop had gone long since—the stationer's situated, as he tells us, at a corner of the wide thoroughfare linking the city of his childhood with the sea.[1] This thoroughfare could have been none other than Leith Walk; and I was not entirely disappointed in my quest when I saw, in a window near at hand, a few survivors exposed for sale. For all I knew, these premises were the successor to the stationer's of Stevenson's and Aunt Dorothy's time. Displayed in that window were forest scenes,

[1] This corner-shop, owned by one, Jas. L. Smith, bookseller and stationer, "was dark and smelt of Bibles". It stood at the junction of Union Street with Antigua Street, on the main highroad between Auld Reekie and Leith, facing Baxter's Place, where, at Number One, lived Stevenson's grandfather, Robert Stevenson, builder of the Bell Rock Lighthouse. 'Old Mr. Smith him-self, worn out with my eternal vacillation, once swept the treasures from before me, with the cry: "I do not believe, child, that you are an intending purchaser at all!" ' Thus wrote R.L.S.

Situated in Greenside, close by—at 11, Greenside Street, to be precise—was W. & H. Robinson's, a shop no less celebrated in R.L.S.'s time for Skelt's model theatrical equipment.

skies fraught with lightning, exterior and interior views of dark and foreboding caves, armed banditti ready to take the stage, ships of every description, from smacks to dreadnoughts (not forgetting some in dire distress), pirates, and masked highwaymen. This odd and dusty assortment may even have been remnant from the days of Skelt, at one time doyen of the Fraternity of Juvenile Drama.

This recalls our dealings with Miss Scott, a wee body, auld and grey, who kept the shop half-hidden from the main thoroughfare of Bruntsfield Place, in a protruding corner of Gillespie Crescent. In the days when James Gillespie's School occupied the site of the present Blind Asylum, but a hundred yards away, her establishment constituted the Gillespie children's tuck-shop. In her window she exhibited at all times a vast variety of inferior sweetmeats; while some additional interest in it arose from its seasonal display of articles specially designed for boys. Peeries[1], variegated marbles, miniature cricket-bats, pistols, giant squibs, suckers, and suchlike all found their inviting way into her window in meet season.

We dwellers on the South Side of Auld Reekie, however, knew Miss Scott's chiefly because it supplied us with requirements for the toy-theatre. Here one could buy, for a penny or two, characters and scenery. Her pictorial reproduction of an orchestra was in constant demand. So, too, was the proscenium, available in sections. Miss Scott rendered to the youthful populace, at one end of Edinburgh, the service Robinson's rendered at the other. Robinson's, of course, is gone; and Miss Scott sleeps well with her ancestors. Gone, likewise, is the funny, wee shop that once stood at the top of Morrison Street, and was approached by a short staircase of stone, and had an iron balcony enabling one to examine the contents of the window without danger of falling into the 'area' below. Its site is now occupied by a fish-&-chip shop. But, if you would see precisely what Skelt's productions were like, visit the Edinburgh Room at the Central Library, in George IV. Bridge. There you will find quite a collection of them, together with the corresponding booklets of the words.

*   *   *   *   *   *   *

In wild competition with the ordinary theatres in Auld Reekie were Pringle's Palace, in Grove Street, and the Operetta House, in Chambers Street, both of which are defunct. These institutions catered for louder and more licentious audiences. For many an

---

[1] *Peerie*: a peg-top; the game of top-spinning.

Edinburgh citizen, the go-as-you-please competition at the Operetta House, on Friday nights, was the peak of the week's existence. Both for performers and for audience, it was a night of unmitigated riot. The professional performer usually receives a fair hearing because the public has the notion that, when a man is paid for his work, he must be reasonably good at it. At the Operetta House, however, the amateur performer was there by reason of his conceit, to be assessed by the public without either fear or favour. No sooner were the doors opened than the crowds raced down the gangways to scramble for their favourite places. A strategic position was essential to the full enjoyment of the show. A seat too near the stage put one in as much danger as the performer, whereas a seat too far back placed the performer out of reach. A nicety in judgment, therefore, was required to secure the best results. The stage jutted out into the auditorium, while the orchestra of three lay ensconced in an alcove at the side, under the lower gallery. As there was no orchestra pit in front of the stage, nothing but the footlights intervened between performer and audience. The house was packed from floor to ceiling by the time the lights were lowered, and notices giving the details of the impending competition were flashed upon a rather grubby screen. These announcements were crudely scrawled on slides. The final one bluntly stated that "No giving the berry is allowed". It was instantly greeted by a barrage of the biggest 'berries' the Scottish Capital was capable of producing. This led to the swift withdrawal of the slide, as though the management regretted having anticipated behaviour as unseemly. The screen was then hoisted to its dusty home among the 'flies', and the stage lighting switched on to reveal, in the gaudiest of colours, a quiet country lane. In a trice one noticed the manager hovering uncomfortably about the wings, aware of the reception with which any remarks from *him* must needs be greeted. Shouting and shrill whistling, supplemented by a plenteous supply of 'berries', marked his attempt to read the list of entrants. Above the barracking he might be heard to yell the name of the first, before escaping to the wings again.

The first competitor, usually a young woman, then emerged to take up a position on the stage so disadvantageous from the audience's viewpoint that the manager was obliged to push her forward a step or two. Now well and firmly rooted to the boards, she cast a timid glance toward the orchestra. Piano, fiddle, and drum then struck up an introductory bar or two of *Annie Laurie*. Fidgetting the while with her pink blouse, or tugging at her tweed skirt, she would at last get going. Soon the audience was displaying its approval by joining lustily in the last verse. She had given the old song 'big licks', and in traditional Operetta House style; and it was doubtful now whether subsequent competitors had any chance of a prize against one who had opened the evening's proceedings so agreeably, in this colourful country lane.

The next turn might be contributed by a navvy attired in his workaday clothes—cord trousers with straps round the knees; broad leather belt, studded with regimental badges, encompassing his not inconsiderable middle; Kirkcaldy stripe shirt with several patches in it; silk muffler of red magnificence wound round his thick neck, its ends tucked under his braces. I remember one such competitor who strode confidently to the edge of the stage, and, before the orchestra was ready, started off with *When Irish Eyes Are Smiling*. However, with a little encouragement from the audience, the orchestra caught up on him. Suddenly the singer forgot his words. But the orchestra just played on while he scratched his brow in endeavouring to remember them. The audience, now tired of prompting him, readily took over the song. The louder it sang, the louder did the navvy bellow. Showers of coppers, intermixed with orange peel, then descended on the stage. The competitor manfully stood his ground until the pennies, striking the metal shields of the footlights, produced a metallic ring that warned him of the danger in which he was. With slow, backward steps, but continuing to sing with unflinching courage, he retreated toward the rear of the stage, up and down the front of which small children now scrambled to collect such coppers as they could. At this point a youth might slip down a pillar, from the upper gallery to the lower, to aim, from better vantage, a cabbage at the retreating songster. Navvy and cabbage usually reached the wings about the same time. Amid howls of good-natured derision, the former returned to the footlights to take his bow, embracing the cabbage as though he had been presented with it by way of bouquet.

Such ongoings were quite common at the Operetta House on Friday nights. This 'rough house', this veritable Donnybrook, attracted a fearsome crowd up till the time that the cinema so largely ousted 'variety' in the provinces.

*   *   *   *   *   *   *

An institution that for several years, at Christmas-time, held Edinburgh audiences enthralled was Poole's Myriorama, staged in the Synod Hall. This type of entertainment, now almost obsolete, was intermediary between the magic lantern and the cinematograph. It consisted of the most ambitious representations of anything from active volcanoes to naval battles, all of which were produced in 'flats' of cardboard, canvas, or ply-wood. The subtle use of lighting and of bright colours certainly coöperated in some realistic displays. Who has forgotten the dreadnought that, to the patriotic strains of *Rule, Britannia*, steamed across the stage against a fixed back-cloth, with great waves undulating so irresistibly in the foreground that you felt at any moment the sea-blue canvas containing them might burst with ridiculous consequences? Naval scenes were always a distinctive feature of the Myriorama. For these, two hefty lads were employed, each season, behind the scenes, in order to supply the war-vessels with the necessary motion. After much practice, they acquired the knack of pushing the great, lumbering things across the stage, one at a time, and at an even speed. For all their skill and heaving prowess, nevertheless, a pause or a jerk, a stagger or a sudden burst of acceleration, occasionally disturbed the illusion, and brought forth from the audience a chorus of disapproving groans. A third employee, likewise concealed, but not always in synchrony, pulled Christmas crackers with furious diligence, to represent the firing of the dreadnought's guns. This was made to appear the more real by the puffs of smoke now seen to emerge from its bulwarks. Meanwhile Mr Poole, standing in evening dress by the side of the stage, gave us a running commentary, referring at intervals to some written matter spread under a reading-lamp that, to picturesque advantage, set off his fine head and shoulders. He was immensely proud of his Myriorama, and never more so than when, at the close of the last war, he staged, with such wholehearted approbation, a submarine banging into the Mole at Zeebrugge on St George's Day. Upon my conscience, that was a sublime bit of collision, adequately supported by the fiercest flash-ings of fireworks, and the most deafening noises-off. Do you wonder that we regarded the Poole family and its Myriorama as an integral part of our Edinburgh life? The richly illustrated pro-gramme gave patrons a synopsis of the proprietor's commentary, and became a souvenir in many a home. Families preserved these programmes from year to year, as a record of the weird spectacles they had seen. The performance was sustained (to use a word so beloved of the entertainment world) by the introduction of a couple of music-hall 'shorts'; and I was unexpectedly transported to my youth when, during a recent sojourn in Auld Reekie, a friend, in looking for something else, turned out of a drawer an old Myriorama programme prefaced by the likeness of the coloured coon, who, to concertina accompaniment, sang so agreeably.

* * * * * * *

Christmas was the season when Moss's unique Carnival came to that immense roofed space known as the Waverley Market. To this festival went almost every Auld Reekie youth, as part of the year's routine. The lure of the Carnival was irresistible when the powerful Hackenschmidt was appearing there each night, offering the reward of a thousand pounds to anyone who could throw him. Hackenschmidt's prowess soon fired the imagination of Edinburgh's manhood, so that even the merest schoolboy, boasting his strength, was immediately taunted with having studied the technique of this giant showman. But the part of the Carnival which interested me most was that devoted to Pepper's Ghost, and to other optical illusions, such as the turning of Lot's wife into a pillar of salt. Years later, I saw Pepper's Ghost at a cheap gaff in Paris, and thought it very poor in comparison with our Edinburgh version.

After the death of Sir Edward Moss, the Waverley Market Carnival was taken over by one, Lumley, a wellknown sports promoter and outfitter in Auld Reekie. When Lumley's Carnival closed down, its more spectacular side-shows went to Evans's Carnival, where they might now be seen so much more cheaply—indeed, for a penny or two. This medley was assembled on an open space at Tollcross. Admission to it was free; and it continued a week or two further into January than did the more select and expensive show at the Waverley Market. The glare from its booths and merry-go-rounds and brightly illumined caravans lit up the sky of nights, thus apprizing citizens of its arrival before the wind wafted its jingle-jangle to their ears. It was here I taught myself to shoot, so that, when I joined up, I was already more than self-confident in the matter of rifles and targets. At Evans's Carnival the good shot had the pleasure of knowing that, standing behind him, was a crowd of admiring spectators which increased as he knocked clay pipes out of the jaws of grimacing figures, or shattered those little celluloid balls that bobbed on perpendicular water-jets.

* * * * * * *

When the roller-skating rink in Fountainbridge was converted into the picture-house known as the Coliseum, we had, within easy reach of us, everything one could have desired in the way of films, and at prices that appear ridiculously low nowadays. The huge floor-space of the rink had been divided into three parts. At the back were the fourpenny seats. In front were the twopenny benches. Between these were the best seats, at sixpence, upholstered in scarlet plush. They tipped up, and were ostentatiously partitioned off from the fourpenny ones behind, and the twopenny ones in front. Like those behind, and in contradistinction with the cheapest, all of which were at ground level, they were terraced just sufficiently to ensure that those seated in front of you were at a slightly lower level. And what a difference this made, as one realised after experience of the hard, front benches. There was no upstairs, simply because the height of the roof did not permit. The programme was changed every Monday and Thursday, thus attracting most of its patrons twice weekly. Children under fourteen were allowed in at half-price. At Saturday matinées the least expensive seats cost but one penny to a child. It often looked as though every child under that age within several miles' ambit turned up at these matinées. No sooner were the lights lowered and the first picture thrown on the screen than there began the most disorderly hurdle-race imaginable. Over the barriers separating the twopenny and fourpenny seats from the cushioned sixpenny swept the rabble to occupy such of the best seats as might be unoccupied, the uproar completely drowning the orchestra for a moment or two. The result was that, at the end of the show, not a few of those who had entered by the cheapest door left by the dearest. I cannot deny that on occasions my brother and I took part in this wild scrimmage, though, to all intents and purposes, the fourpenny seats, which we occupied at half-price, were as good as the plush ones, and perhaps better situated in relation to the screen. When finances were low, and we had no objection to rubbing shoulders with hoi polloi—with the 'keelies'—we attached ourselves to the main queue, and eventually fought our way to the best of the cheapest seats, wherefrom, I do declare, we saw, *for a penny*, some of the finest Wild West films ever made.

In the Coliseum's orchestra we took a personal interest. It consisted of no more than a trio—a middle-aged lady and two middle-aged men. Yet, as occasion demanded, it could create as much noise as was required. Now and again, it was augmented to the proportions of a quartette by the appearance of a fellow with a violin, who looked like a friend of the family, as it were, and perhaps gave his services free. Indispensable to the musical programme was the tall and lean lady pianist, whose very thick eyeglasses betrayed her extreme shortsightedness. But, my word! she could thump out Arthur Joyce's *Septembre*, and such waltzes as *The Pink Lady*, with amazing vigour. And you should have heard her tear her way through the more strenuous passages from Boieldieu's *Caliph of Bagdad*! That, in itself, was well worth the money!

The orchestra's chief claim to remembrance arose from its partiality for the more popular excerpts from Wagner. But its *pièce de résistance* was Coleridge-Taylor's *Petite Suite de Concert*. This it rendered twice nightly, five nights a week, and thrice on Saturdays, for at least three years. Over two thousand times in three years! Surely a record in lack of enterprise! The opening movement—*Le Caprice de Nannette*—strummed with emphasis on the resounding piano, became the recognised signal that the principal film was about to be shown. Then, the plaintive strains of the *Démande et Réponse* movement accompanied, invariably, the love scene, making it the more languorous. Its introduction was preceded by a moment so silent that one could hear the film whirring from one spool to the other in the operator's apartment. In the meantime, the intent orchestra watched the screen for the cue. Its entry was timed to the fraction of a second. No other piece of music was ever permitted to take the place of the *Démande et Réponse* when mawkish love-making occupied the screen at the Coliseum.

Gradually the Wild West vogue wore off and, consequently, this popular place of entertainment had to allow itself to be converted into the *Palais de Danse*. A very different public now usurped the floor-space, on which had scrimmaged so many of us who were youthful before the last war. In accompanying a party of friends to this dance-hall on a solitary occasion, I saw how appropriate was Clemenceau's very French comment on our post-war dancing: "*Les figures si tristes, et les derrières si gais!*"

*   *   *   *   *   *   *

Auld Reekie in those days boasted three circuses, and at least two menageries. The most famous of the former was Bostock & Wombwell's, which, at the opening of the present century, came once a year to its customary stance in the Grassmarket. How well I remember the day I discovered that monster marquee there! When, in traversing the Lothian Road, I pass by the end of the King's Stables Road, whence it runs down into the Grassmarket, I always recall that discovery, and imagine I hear the roaring of hapless lions, and the howling of unfortunate wolves, in the centre of that spacious thoroughfare, that I see the red hangings, and the tile-hatted band blaring forth *Men of Harlech* from a wobbly wagon, and smell sawdust and wild beasts serving, in their innocence, a life sentence.

On a patch of waste ground where Iona Street branches off from Leith Walk, Lord George Sanger's Circus assembled at stated times, complete with swing-boats, merry-go-rounds, rifle-ranges, laughing mirrors, halls of horror, a maze, a cake-walk, dwarfs and giants and other human freaks, and a helter-skelter down which one slid on a mat. By the time we arrived in Auld Reekie, however, the huge tent wherein equestrian displays took place had become sere and yellow. Yet, the circus was advertised widely throughout the city by means of huge, colourful posters depicting, in the crudest manner, the most lurid scenes, usually inset among terrifying reproductions of carnivorous animals. Only once, in youth, did I venture as far afield for entertainment; and I recollect the occasion vividly, for, on arrival, I found the neighbourhood in a state of panic. A tiger had got loose! Everything was suspended until the wretched and, doubtless, terrified creature was impounded once more, since no one quite knew where it might turn up.

The Misses Sanger gave to the circus its *locus standi*. Stout, elderly sirens they were, with names appropriate to archduchesses. They dressed in short ballet skirts, and were tightly corsetted. They bowed to right and to left, and waved flat, flabby arms elegantly, while ploughing their way into a ring ankle-deep in tan.

Grandest of all the circuses in the days of youth was Cooke's, in the Fountainbridge. This was a place of magic and surprise. What with its blatant band that blared as the lights went on, and the immaculate John Henry Cooke, doyen of the ring, entered, wreathed in smiles and blandishments, and bowing heavily, bearing whip and white gloves and a very prominent floral display in his button-hole; what with the clowns, whose middle-quarters bulged so much as to suggest a gastronomic capacity as vast as it was comic; what with its jugglers, who sent piles of plates whizzing up into the air, never allowing one of them to fall and get broken; what with the acrobats who, on purpose, swung so dangerously near us as to call forth shrieks of apprehension from the more timid—well, Bertram Mills's show at Olympia was a modest affair by comparison. Mills never produced, out of hats, such rabbits as did the magicians at Cooke's. When it came to the haphazard borrowing of watches from members of the audience, the smashing of them to smithereens in our very sight, *before restoring them, intact*, we were indeed mystified.

One must not forget to mention 'the daring young man on the flying trapeze', nor the aquatic spectacle, preparatory to which a considerate management provided those seated near the fringe of the ring with waterproof sheets to keep laps and legs dry. To be given a sheet was half the thrill of the show. It lent to one a sense of personal participation in the performance.

As for the display of horsemanship (remembering Dick Turpin's furious ride to York) we could not imagine anything more thrilling in the whole wide world. Than horses and more horses and still more horses, we asked for nothing else. The clowns' capers and the acrobats' antics we regarded as mere stop-gaps until the ring was a-whirl once more with galloping steeds.

Cooke did much to give to the circus a better tone than it had enjoyed hitherto. His first circus, situated in Grindlay Street, where now stands the Lyceum Theatre, had already acquired a status which the ordinary travelling circus could never hope to achieve. When he removed to Fountainbridge, he won instant popularity by introducing novelties, such as open competitions, for which he gave substantial prizes. He presented silver cups at the end of the season, for instance; and even a pony or a pig might be included among his awards.

In later years, by which time the site of Cooke's Circus had become that of a rather second-rate picture-house known fancifully as the Palladium, it was pathetic to see John Henry in the vicinity of Leven Street and Barclay Place—he lived in retirement close at hand, in Gillespie Crescent—having his circumscribed walk each forenoon, but not before he had purchased at a local florist's a red carnation for his button-hole. Though now old and enfeebled, he was still as spruce as in the zenith of his equestrian splendour. There he toddled in his top-hat, frock-coat, and pearl-grey waistcoat, the ensemble the better set off by the neatness of his neck-wear, by the carnation, by his spotless gloves and gilded walking-stick. Nothing but memories now remained of his pristine glory. He resembled an attenuated philosopher who had stepped down from an ancestral picture-frame to await, yet again, his translation to a sphere we wist not of.

*   *   *   *   *   *   *

I would not have you think from the foregoing that I am the least in sympathy with the circus as popularly understood, for, after vivisection, there is no institution through which animals suffer so much. For this statement, both as regards domesticated and wild animals, there is abundant evidence. Most of us remain ignorant of the barbarities mankind inflicts upon captive and performing animals. Yet, there are many who, in their inmost hearts, are aware, but satisfy conscience with the platitude that *it's all done by kindness*. Kindness, forsooth! Though I write freely here of the circuses of boyhood and youth, today, if I happen to be present at an entertainment into which an animal turn is introduced, I rise and leave, temporarily, in conformity with the pledge of the Jack London Club, and at the same time lodge some protest with the management.

> '*Twould ring the bells of Heaven*
> *The wildest peal for years,*
> *If Parson lost his senses,*
> *And people came to theirs,*
> *And he and they together*
> *Knelt down in angry prayers*
> *For tamed and shabby tigers,*
> *And dancing dogs and bears,*
> *And wretched, blind pit-ponies,*
> *And little, hunted hares.*

CHAPTER XX

THE GREAT LAFAYETTE

FEW OCCURRENCES of serious import stirred our douce city. If I were to enumerate those that did, I would have to include some that might appear ludicrous to those accustomed to cities where really important things happen. We were *en fête*, as it were, for very little. For instance, you can have no idea of the significance attached to Harry Lauder's coming through from the West (from Glasgow or, maybe, from Dunoon) to christen the lion cubs at the Marine Gardens, by the seaside at Portobello! A visit from royalty could not have thrown us and our newspapers into greater civic excitement. Incidentally, while the subject of this chapter was being burned to death at one of our theatres, Harry Lauder was attracting equally large houses at another, tricycling round the stage in the guise of an errand-boy, his cheek bulging with an outsize in bull's-eyes.

One recalls, too, the flutter caused by the appearance on staid Princes Street of the first hobble skirt in our city. Even now, before my mind's eye, there passes the natty mannequin who, twice daily at least, had the courage—nay, the impropriety, the temerity—to defy our sense of decorum by disporting herself in so unseemly a garment among those whose antique habiliments exhibited a long-standing contempt for the vicissitudes of fashion. A brazen hussy, our womenfolk called her. (*Fancy, the likes o' her!*) When we arrived from the North, Edinburgh women were still wearing their skirts down to the ankles; and only by some mis-adventure was a woman's ankle seen on Princes Street by those habitually parading there. In blustery weather, however, things might be a little different, for, much as our women strove to defeat the wind's indiscretion, an ankle was to be seen occasionally. But this was so rare and thrilling a sight, even as late as 1910, that on windy days the naughty roués of the wealthier classes used to beseat themselves with carnal eye at the bow windows of Princes Street's clubs.

Then there was the affair known as the Cameron Case, which produced a stir nigh unprecedented in Auld Reekie. In February,

1911, a certain Lieutenant Cameron, stationed with the Royal Field Artillery at Piershill, was shopping with his wife in Shandwick Place. Cameron entered a shop, leaving his wife outside. Suddenly, there was the most frightful commotion. Mrs Cameron, in a state of hysteria, tottered into the shop with her coat torn open. She declared that a man had attacked her, and wrenched off the pearl necklace she was wearing. The police was summoned. Investigations revealed that the Camerons were in money difficulties, and that the necklace was valued at £6,500. But no one on this fairly busy thoroughfare had witnessed the attack: nor had anyone seen the man described. There was no evidence but Mrs Cameron's that she had been robbed, and none but hers and her husband's that she was wearing the necklace at the time. The upshot was that the insurance company refused to recognise the claim.

Was there ever an incident that set Auld Reekie more truly by the ears? It remained the sole topic of discussion for several months. Was Lieutenant Cameron acting in collusion with his wife, or had she deceived him? That was the moot point with us all. Anyhow, seventeen days after the alleged robbery, both were arrested. On June, 3rd, husband and wife were sentenced to three years' penal servitude, having been found guilty on the charge of attempt to defraud the insurers.

Ah! I well remember the verdict! It precipitated father into abysmal gloom and despondency. That anyone bearing the name of Cameron should have done such a thing, bringing disgrace on a Highland clan that had acquitted itself so estimably, first, for James, and then for Charles Edward, his ill-starred son!

If, however, there be one event more memorable than another, it is that which took place on the 9th of May, 1911. About 11 p.m. on that date, fire devastated the Empire Theatre, in Nicolson Street, toward the close of the second house, while The Great Lafayette was engaged in *The Lion's Bride*, one of the more elaborate of his thaumaturgics. A burst of flame rose from the middle of the scenery, and soon engulfed the stage. The illusionist himself was among the seven persons who lost their lives. For the most part, they were members of his own company. Four others were seriously injured. When morbid curiosity brought me to the scene early the following morning, the fire brigade was still pouring water on smouldering ruins, and recovering charred remains.

You may imagine the sensation this tragedy occasioned in our Capital. It was a long time since our newsvendors, dashing through the city with sensational posters, had had so dramatic a cry. The wording of those posters I visualise clearly: "Edinburgh Theatre Disaster—The Great Lafayette among the Dead." Accounts of what happened were as varied as they were numerous. At one moment our city was overcast with gloom: at another, feverish with rumour.

The fate of Lafayette's African lion, and of the horse on which he rode to rescue the maiden from the jaws of the latter, but heightened the tragedy. Our newspapers liked the romantic and fanciful story that Lafayette would have been saved, had he not rushed back through the flames to shoot the lion and rescue the horse. Then there was much discussion as to the way in which the fire-proof curtain was held to have saved members of the orchestra and audience from being victims, and much speculation as to whether Lafayette, somewhat unhinged by the death of his dog, Beauty, but a few days previously, had not put the theatre on fire, and thrown himself suicidally into the vast conflagration of his own making. What Edinburgh schoolboy at the time did not share my own satisfaction from giving further currency to the fantastic report that, in a moment of frenzy, The Great Lafayette, with the revolver he carried lest the lion escaped, had fired at one of the arc-lamps high above the stage, with the result that "the electricity came pouring down on the stage like golden rain"? And who has forgotten how the fire-curtain stuck while being lowered, and the orchestra played on, undismayed, until the flames swept forward to singe the hair and whiskers of some of its members? Never did ship go down amid such reputed heroism.

The explanation seems to be that the fire originated through the fusing of an electric wire, which set alight the highly inflammable tinsel decorations forming so indispensable a feature of his show.

While what actually befell Lafayette has been open to speculation, it is now generally conceded that the lives of himself, and those of his company on the stage with him at the time, would not have been lost, but for his insistence, contrary to regulations, on having all doors leading to the stage locked during performances, so as to prevent intruders from discovering the secrets of his illusions. Consequently, when fire broke out on the stage, he tried to escape by a pass door, forgetting it had been secured by his own order. Smoke and flame soon enveloped the stage. Overcome by fumes when making for some alternative way of escape, he fell, unconscious, on the boards.

* * * * * * *

One of the first bodies recovered, and believed by the remainder of the company, and also by the doctors summoned to the scene, to have been Lafayette's, afterwards turned out to be that of John W. Bell, his double, known professionally as C. E. Richards. In the meantime, this body had been sent through to Glasgow for cremation, since Edinburgh had no crematorium at that time. It was not until late the same evening, after the cremation had taken place, that another body, charred beyond recognition, was discovered among the debris by Lafayette's solicitor, Mr Alfred Nisbet, of Walter Maskell & Nisbet, East Dulwich, who by this time had arrived from London. Mr Nisbet, whom I happen to know, and to whom I am indebted for many of these details, tells me that he found it lying under the stage while investigating the ruins. It had fallen there through a trap-door immediately above. He was able to identify such as remained of it by a ring on one of the fingers. As the most elaborate funeral arrangements had been made for Sunday, 14th, and the double's body had been cremated in error, Mr Nisbet, in his capacity as Lafayette's legal representative, was in a sorry quandary. Special authority had to be obtained from the Sheriff of Edinburgh and the Lothians, therefore, to permit of the immediate removal of Lafayette's body to Glasgow for cremation, in order to ensure the return of the ashes in time. From Mr Nisbet's evidence, the Sheriff was satisfied that the body he had found was Lafayette's. This enabled W. T. Dunbar & Sons, the wellknown Edinburgh funeral directors, to rush it through to the Glasgow crematorium by car during the night, and have the ashes back in Edinburgh in the early hours of Sunday morning.

* * * * * * *

A few days earlier, as I have mentioned, the dog, Beauty, had died at the Caledonian Hotel. She had been staying there with her master in his somewhat expensive suite of rooms, and had succumbed to a fit of apoplexy. To this animal Lafayette was more attached than to any human being. The morning she died, Messrs Dunbar were telephoned for. At an interview in the hotel, Lafayette gave them instructions for Beauty to be embalmed, and

Above : The Embalmed Beauty

Below : Beauty in her coffin, together with the casket containing the ashes of Lafayette

The Great Lafayette and Beauty

enclosed thereafter in an elaborate coffin. For the embalming, the services of a professor of the Royal College of Surgeons had to be engaged, as Lafayette refused to countenance its being done by a veterinary surgeon. That same day, at the undertakers' suggestion, Lafayette proceeded with them to Piershill Cemetery, where he purchased a piece of ground on the grassy, flower-fringed mound situated immediately in front of the entrance gates to this famous Edinburgh burial-place, and at that time overhung by a wych-elm.

After Beauty had been embalmed, she was placed, lying full out on her side, in an oak casket lined with zinc, and beautifully finished in silk. Her head reclined on a silk cushion; and a silken quilt was spread over her. The casket, which had a glass lid to it, was to lie in one of the undertakers' private mortuaries until the burial took place. Each day, and each evening after his show at the Empire, Lafayette visited this mortuary to see his embalmed Beauty. The death of this dog affected him acutely; and one remembers the sensation it caused in our city.

Beauty was to have been buried at Piershill Cemetery on Tuesday, May, 10th; but, owing to the tragedy at the Empire, her interment had to be postponed until the following day. Four days later—on Sunday, May, 14th, to be precise—The Great Lafayette was buried, like a conqueror, at the spot he had purchased there. The casket containing the embalmed Beauty was opened, so that the casket containing her master's ashes might be placed between her paws. Beauty's casket was then re-sealed. A vast procession, starting from Messrs Dunbar's premises in Lothian Road, stretched more than a mile through our city. The funeral car, drawn by four black horses, was followed by the magician's own private car, behind which walked his negro attendant. Thereafter came seven coaches filled with wreaths, and fourteen more for the principal mourners, most of whom were members of the theatrical profession, and had come to Edinburgh from all over the country. In addition, there was at least a mile of horse-cabs. (Taxis, you may remember, were comparatively scarce in the Scottish Capital in 1911.) In the first of the mourners' coaches, and accompanied by a friend, sat the chief mourner, in the person of *another* dog belonging to The Great Lafayette.

The crowds witnessing the funeral procession were amazing. They lined the pavements all the way between the undertakers' and the cemetery gates, a distance of over three miles. Local newspapers described the funeral as the greatest free show Edinburgh had had for many a year. With the curiosity of boyhood, I found myself one of the vast concourse that reached the cemetery.

Not long afterwards, two memorial stones were placed under that wych-elm in Piershill Cemetery. Inscribed on the larger and upright one are the words:—

SACRED
TO THE MEMORY
OF
THE GREAT LAFAYETTE
BORN
25 · FEBRUARY · 1871
DIED
9 · MAY · 1911

This stone, you will observe, gives no clue as to the illusionist's origin or identity.

At the base of it lies a large, recumbent slab:—

DEDICATED
TO THE
LOVING MEMORY OF
MY DEAREST
BEAUTY

with the words, "The Great Lafayette", reproduced from his signature, in the bottom righthand corner.

Even yet, when passing down the Portobello road, I find my eyes drawn unconsciously toward the circular mound beyond the cemetery gates at Piershill. Though the wych-elm is gone, the mound, surmounted by its large, upright tombstone, can be seen quite easily from the road, and more easily still from the upper deck of a tramcar. In my boyhood days, Lafayette and Beauty had the entire mound to themselves. However, when in Edinburgh recently, I found that several other tombstones now denote burials which have since taken place round its perimeter.

Eighteen months after the Empire Theatre fire, there came to the King's Theatre at Edinburgh, under the direction of an actress named Lalla Selbini, a company, many of whom had been associated with Lafayette. Lalla Selbini, who was described as

the only successor to The Great Lafayette, had returned to our
city with *The Lion's Bride*. She had been the dead magician's
principal understudy.

*   *   *   *   *   *   *

Will Goldston, a fellow-illusionist, tells me that The Great
Lafayette was a most unsociable man, and that he drilled his
company as if composed of soldiers under military discipline.
He insisted that its members should salute him on the street.

It would be an exaggeration to claim that he was the greatest
of music-hall artists, though he is said to have commanded one of
the greatest salaries. But he was, indubitably, one of the most
mysterious and amazing members of his profession. Born at Los
Angeles in 1871, Ignatius Neuburger (for that was his real name)
was sent to Germany to study art, but seems to have devoted
most of his time to giving entertainments, and answering demands
for his services at amateur theatricals and the like. Eventually
he returned to America, where he became a bank clerk, an occupation he found so boring that he decided to go on the variety stage.
In 1892 he had saved enough money to enable him to revisit
Europe, where he now came into contact with Sir Edward Moss,
whose estimate of his capacity as an artist likely to draw packed
houses was anything but encouraging at the outset. By 1900,
however, he was going over 'big', as the Americans say, breaking
all records at the London Hippodrome. Though still a good way
from obtaining the sensational salary of later years, he put up at
the Hotel Cecil, where he had engaged a special suite of rooms
for Beauty. Each day, Beauty was taken for a drive in a landau.
No care, no expense, no request, however ridiculous, must be
withheld where Beauty was concerned. At night-time she was
served with a regular *table d'hôte* meal, which included soup as
well as a sweet. Little wonder she died of apoplexy! Tradition
says that no dog in Christendom had so much lavished upon it.
At a home the magician subsequently had in Torrington Square,
her likeness adorned the front of the building, with the saying,
"The more I see of men, the more I love my dog", inscribed
underneath. A brass plate by the front door bore the names,
"The Great Lafayette & Beauty". The house, furthermore,
contained a room regarded primarily as the dog's. To this private
apartment was attached her bathroom. I have been told in
London that Lafayette's cheques, specially designed and printed

for him, depicted the dog seated beside two bags of gold, with the words, "My Two Best Friends", thereunder. A portrait of Beauty was also printed on his theatrical contracts. The dog's collar— so we had been assured in Edinburgh as school-children, anyway —was studded with gold plates, edged with diamonds. On each plate was engraved the signature of the proprietor of such of the world's principal music-halls at which Lafayette had appeared. All part of showmanship, of course, to which was added the bewitching touch of the Almighty Dollar. "I have no friend save Beauty", he is accredited with having said on innumerable occasions. No one ever alluded to Beauty as a *dog*, without incurring her master's extreme resentment.

Lafayette died intestate. A day or two before his tragic death, and consequent, doubtless, upon Beauty's, he had destroyed his will, with the intention of making a new one, which, alas! he did not live to do. After the tragedy, there turned up in Edinburgh a Mr Alfred Neuberger, brother of The Great Lafayette, of whose existence no one, hitherto, seemed to have known. Mr Neuberger, one presumes, inherited what he left. Lafayette's solicitor tells me that he was not so fabulously wealthy as was popularly supposed— certainly not so far as his assets in *this* country were concerned, though he may have had some money in America, about which we know nothing on this side. And, while on the subject of money, it may be of passing interest to know that he paid all his bills by cheque, even when the sums involved were no more than a few pence.

Lafayette's funeral expenses exceeded £600. The undertakers had to bring an action in the courts to obtain these expenses, since Mr Alfred Neuburger refused to pay anyone. The Sheriff, in granting Messrs Dunbar's claim for them, made the observation that, in ordinary circumstances, he would have considered them excessive, but not necessarily so for the burial of a showman of Lafayette's standing. In the course of obtaining Letters of Administration, Somerset House had required the deposit by Lafayette's solicitor of £800 as security for any further estate duty that might accrue. Out of this sum the undertakers' account was ultimately paid in full.

CHAPTER XXI

ROUND THE WORLD WITH THE COLONEL

IT REMAINED one of the family's observances that, while the Colonel was in process of divesting himself of some of his learning or philosophy, his offspring paid heed to what he had to say as though he were expected to deliver himself of something divinely inspired. He was swift to regard as a personal affront the occasional admission that we could not follow him. While this might have been due to obtuseness on our part, it might also have arisen from a lack of clarity in his didactic methods. Of course, any hint that it was the latter riled a man so confident that he possessed the faculty for making everything as plain as the proverbial pikestaff. Like the scholarly Bentley, of Trinity College, he could be formidable in retort on such occasions. "Are we then to wait until your mud has settled?" Bentley once asked when, at the conclusion of a protracted argument, someone had the temerity to confess himself more confused than ever. The rebuff was worthy of Colonel MacGregor, except that he would have added to sarcasm a dash of profanity and despair.

"Are you there?" he might enquire, if I happened to be seated somewhere in the same room, but not necessarily in view, as he sat ruminating in his armchair, and it suddenly occurred to him that an account of one of his experiences in foreign climes might well bear repetition.

"Yes, father," I would reply, perhaps with a touch of indifference, cognisant of the sort of thing he wanted to say, partly by way of disseminating knowledge and of broadening my mind, but mainly for the purpose of impressing upon me how exemplary a father I had.

"Come *nearer*, won't you? You know I'm a little deaf. Well, now, did I ever tell you of my plight in the Atlantic Ocean, aboard the waterlogged *City of Paris*, then the largest ship afloat?" (The emphasis on 'nearer' was a warning of what might ensue if his audience showed a deficiency either in deference to the narrator, or in disciplined advertence to what he had to say.)

"Yes, of course, father! *Hundreds* of times!"

"*Hundreds* of times, did I hear you say?"

"Well, father, I mean that—that—that—th——."

"Sit down, then, and never mind what you mean, for you will have to hear me tell it at least once again. Pay attention, now!"

Thereupon he would proceed along lines so familiar to me that I could have recited every word in anticipation, and mimicked all the rhetorical tricks he employed when carrying us back with him into his glorious and adventurous past. For all that, his mind, so crammed with apt allusion, so rich in anecdote, reached beyond that of the greater proportion of his educated contemporaries. He was certainly more extensively travelled, and more widely read, than many who were notable for their scholarship. A catholicity of tastes and interests he regarded as of the very essence of being. Was there ever a man who knew so much about so many things? Yet, he was inclined to be uncharitable and intolerant when it came to dealing with those whose circumstances had denied to them the opportunity of journeying to distant horizons. I remember how scathingly he spoke of those who taught geography at Watson's. "What do *they* know about geography? I don't suppose they've ever been out of Scotland in their lives." In a sense, there was something to be said for this view. In another sense, there was as little support for it as for the view that it was within the competency only of a Roman, born and bred a citizen of the Eternal City, to teach Latin.

* * * * * * *

It must be accredited largely to the Colonel's dissertations on those parts of the world he had visited that I felt a confidence with geography as with no other subject, although, as you may remember, he deeply deplored my aptitude in this field when academic society placed a much greater value on mathematics. I had picked up from him many a thing, of which the masters at Watson's knew nothing. What knew it of Penhom-Penh, in the heart of Cambodia, for instance, or of the Cocos Islands, but what they had derived from writings such as his?

I recall an afternoon Iain and I sat on the hearth-rug whilst father treated us to one of his peripatetics on the exploits of the Burmese monarch, Alompra, always a favourite topic with him. "This talented soldier," he would continue, "founded the last Burmese dynasty. He spent years in driving the—the what, Iain?"

"The Peguans, father."

"Clever boy! The Peguans, out of the country. Then he turned his attention to the conquest of—of what, Alasdair?"

(Here a painful pause would occur while I searched my empty head for knowledge it never had.)

"The conquest of what, Iain?" he would proceed.

"Siam, of course, father!"

"Splendid, my boy! It is clear to you and me that your brother hasn't shown sufficient interest to read his own father's books."

"But *I've* read them, father!"

"Quite obviously you have, my boy. That's why you know a thing or two."

Such topics readily brought the Colonel's eyes to the huge enlargement of a photograph he had taken many years before, and of which he was very proud. It occupied a position in the study enabling him to gaze at it from his armchair, when meditating on his glowing past. Taken during his official residence at Aden, it represents types of nine castes or countries selected from among the prisoners at the great penal settlement there. He entitled it the Millennium Brotherhood. In the centre of the group sits the Colonel, himself, in the rôle of a Highland cateran disguised as an Arab chief. When circumnavigating the world with him in his study, 'The Brotherhood', as we children called it, never failed to command its share of attention, since he always was loth to omit Arabia from any periplus on which we embarked.

Iain's knowledge about the world increased daily. His storage capacity knew no bounds. If he were not absorbing information from father's ever-readiness to discourse on his own travels and experiences, he was doing so through his obsession for foreign stamps. He was, for a time, the most zealous philatelist among the schoolboy population of Auld Reekie, continually writing away for stamps and stamp catalogues, as prompted by advertisements in magazines and newspapers. His stamp-collecting kept him in constant touch with the larger world, and with those peoples and places about which the Colonel spoke so authoritatively. Catalogues of things other than stamps used to arrive for him too. He was enjoying the phase through which so many juveniles go— that of receiving communications by post. A boy will often answer an advertisement merely for the satisfying experience of having the postman deliver something addressed to him. This, he feels, immediately places him on a par with the adult members of the household. I remember, in this connection, a contemporary at

Watson's, who replied to the advertisement of a firm of organ-builders. His letter of enquiry looked so promising from a sales point of view that, a few days later, a deputation of four gentlemen from Birmingham arrived in Edinburgh, and waited upon the lad on his father's doorstep, seeking an interview. They may have imagined that their correspondent represented some kirk-session. The father was infuriated with his son. Yet, the latter's part in this was innocent enough.

*　　*　　*　　*　　*　　*　　*

Notwithstanding my backwardness, the Colonel's accounts of his journeyings in outlandish lands did quicken my youthful imagination. They included his experiences when wandering with a kodak about the Gizeh Pyramids, or among the ruins of Palmyra and of rock-hewn, rose-red Petra. Then, there were his excursions to venerable shrines and temples throughout the world —to the Temple of Darius, at Persepolis; to the Golden Temple at Amritsar; to the Great Temple at Thebes; to yet another at Karnak. There were the pagodas of Burma, chief among them Shwe-Dagon, the glittering glory of Rangoon. He used to tell us of a visit he once made to this shrine at the full moon of Tasaung-mon, the Festival of Lights, when myriads of the devout buy candles to burn before the shrine of Buddha, in this Land of Lotus Blossom. The Colonel knew Rangoon when it was much more primitive than it is to-day, although, even then, transport methods in this centre of population were becoming sufficiently European to necessitate the strict observance of the municipal by-law excluding elephants from the principal thoroughfares after 7 a.m.

There were also his tales of forgotten Angkor Wat, about which he had written a certain amount, and some faded photographs of which lay among the more precious of his eastern treasures. His account of how, when exploring Indo-China, he accidentally came upon those mighty ruins at nightfall was one of the most entrancing things to which his children had ever listened. His photograph album, worn with use and travel, certainly enshrined memories of an adventurous career. It contained, among much else, photographs he had taken of the Stone Colossus on Easter Island, of the Great Wall of China, of the rocketing geysers of New Zealand, of the caves among the Blue Mountains, of King Theebaw's residence at Mandalay. He often spoke to us of the oriental glitter of Theebaw's Golden Palace, and of its astonishing mirrors. Victorians may recall that the latter attracted much attention, when Mandalay was taken in the Burmese War. But the crown and crown jewels of the deposed Theebaw, so extravagant with the rubies for which Burma had been renowned, were never found.

King Theebaw's doings were a fertile source of interest in our home. They were matters upon which father could speak with authority. In 1879 Theebaw excited horror by executing several members of the Burmese royal family. Disorder now became rampant in the country. Open defiance of Great Britain led to the ultimatum of 1885, and the advance of a British force to Mandalay and Ava. The ex-King was deported to Ratnigiri; and Upper Burma was formally annexed. So long had Theebaw been in detention that, when he died in 1916, his existence was almost forgotten.

The mirrors of his Golden Palace, by the way, had been imported by a certain Malcolm MacKenzie, who made a considerable part of his fortune in Mandalay. MacKenzie died in Edinburgh a month or two before the ex-King, and at an advanced age. The Colonel and he had known one another all their days. Both hailed from Lewis; and I rather think they were related in some way—distant cousins.

This chapter would assume proportions too compendious, were I to set out all the wonderful things and peoples father had seen in the world, and the experiences he had survived by way of typhoon, blizzard, sand-storm, and shipwreck. Added to these were his adventures of forest and jungle. "Do tell us again, father," Iain might urge, "about the tiger that stalked you in Bengal!" Details of this we could have read in a back-number of a wellknown magazine for boys, illustrated with drawings, one of which depicted our father, wearing a sun helmet, emerging cautiously from dense undergrowth with rifle at the cock, to find a tiger crouching round the corner, ready to spring at him. The contribution, I seem to remember, was entitled *The Tightest Corner I was ever In.* It formed the first of a series of hair-raising articles by army officers. We read and re-read it, until we knew it by heart. But we much preferred to have him relate the incident by word of mouth, when he was at liberty to elaborate as he pleased. Among the other adventures, of which he used to tell when in communicative mood, was a lone camel ride across the Arabian Desert.

His description of the wretched pariah dogs, fighting for such scraps as came their way, wrung the hearts of his children, who could not comprehend how men were so thoughtless and cruel. (To the degrading cruelties displayed everywhere around us, almost every day of the Christian year, we still exhibit a callous indifference. "Horrible, flayed carcases of brutes, dripping blood," writes H. G. Wells, "are hung for sale in the public streets"; and even at this time of day such a spectacle is abhorrent but to the merest fraction of the populace. Yet, most people declare that war is hateful to them!)

Depressing touches about pariahs and lepers and the like were counterbalanced by the Colonel's vivid descriptions of the more daring ways of mankind. For example, we loved to hear of his sojourn among the Sea Dyaks of Borneo, with their curious idols. And few things delighted us more than to have him recount his experiences when accompanying some Burmese to the lofty cliffs of the Tenasserim, or of the Mergui Archipelago, to collect edible nests, a delicacy for which this region is so famous. Swiftlets, as you probably know, are the birds responsible for these highly-prized nests. The commerce in them is still quite considerable. They are particularly sought after by the Chinese. But I cannot say that father's boosting of birds'-nest-soup gave members of his family any great desire to partake of it.

There is an odd coincidence I might mention in conclusion. The Colonel has recorded in one of his books[1] a peculiar feature relating to the Great Mekong River and Telé-Sap, the Great Lake of Indo-China. He noted that, in the dry season, the Mekong flows out of the lake, whereas, at the height of the rainy season, it flows *into* the lake. Shortly after the publication of this book of his, it was brought to his notice that, about a hundred years earlier, another Hebridean from the same parish had made the identical discovery in the case of Lake Athabasca and the Peace River. That Hebridean was Sir Alexander MacKenzie, who gave his name to one of the world's great rivers. Confusion existed among travellers as to whether the river empties into the lake, or the lake into the river. MacKenzie showed both to be correct, though not simultaneously, of course. During high-water, the river flows into the lake: at other times, the direction of flow is reversed.

[1] *Through the Buffer State.*

CHAPTER XXII

BOOKS! BOOKS! BOOKS!

THOSE PARTS of the home the Colonel allocated to himself were stacked with books—books, books, books, books, moving up and down again, as it were, like the marching boots of Kipling's ballad. To him, a room without books was as a room without a window. Stacked with books, it was as a place inhabited by peoples of all the centuries. He did much to make his children realise that the world of books is the most remarkable, and at the same time the most abiding, of the many worlds man creates. No other survives the turmoil of the ages. Nations rise and fall. Civilizations flourish and perish, and their monuments wither and decay. Continents grow old and cold. But in books there remains something imperishable, something timeless, and yet of the essence of Time itself.

While this was the perspective given to us by the Colonel throughout our lives with him, so far as books were concerned, it was a happy coincidence that I should have spent so many impressionable years in Edinburgh, a city in which, despite the contrary influences of the ledger and the countinghouse, one finds so general an appreciation of good literature. It was the right setting for books in every sense, from the assessment of their contents, to the actual manufacture of them—to the printing and binding.

You may estimate the intellectual atmosphere in which the Colonel was anxious to rear us when I add that he was constantly impressing upon us the verity of Bacon's apothegm: "Reading maketh a full man; conference a ready man; and writing an exact man." This sentiment, always ready to lip when in affable mood, was designed to give to our home a commendable tone. It was with considerable relish he used to reiterate it, laying particular emphasis on the final phrase, when I, his erstwhile backward son and the anxiety of his days, took to the pen and redeemed myself in his sight. For many a year, however, no other member of the household, apart from father and Iain, showed much interest in the printed word.

The variety of books in father's library was enormous; and he knew the contents of wellnigh every volume in his possession. Of this his children were often made aware by his quoting a recondite passage. To his catholicity of taste in reading must be ascribed, in large measure, the diversity of his knowledge. I still remember my surprise at his discoursing, freely and authoritatively, on the law of the conservation of energy, and the method of determining the mechanical equivalent of heat, as established by Joule. A professional physicist could not have explained these matters more simply. What was there, from physics to paraheliotropism, from Hindustani to Gaelic orthography, about which he did not know something? When, however, it came to examining me on the multitudinous subjects, upon which he would embark in the hope of instilling into me a smattering from his own vast store, I was disposed to the view that, as in Macaulay's case, his information was greater than humanity required.

* * * * * * *

The guns of the Great War had scarcely begun their booming across the Channel when our household was reduced by one. The younger of its bookish inmates was smuggled away by Mabel. (Father preferred the stronger terms of *kidnapped* and *stolen*.) While I was luxuriating in the lap of lovingkindness at Aunt Dorothy's, that fateful August in 1914, did not Mabel arrive in Auld Reekie, hurry through some legal formalities, and carry Iain off by stealth? You can imagine father's worry and suspense when you learn that the lad was gone a couple of days before he knew what had happened. The Edinburgh police were still searching for Iain when there came a last-minute letter from him, intimating a voluntary change of guardianship, as he was in a position to do in Scotland at the age of fourteen. The only other member of the family who knew of this abduction was Jessie. But she was sworn to secrecy. In any case, she would have been too fearful to tell her father where Iain and his mother were staying, lest he went forth to retrieve the one and to murder the other, thus completely wrecking a plan that, as it soon turned out, proved a blessing in disguise. By the time Iain's communication reached the Colonel, it was already too late for him to have done anything. The laddie was safely over the Border, if not actually having his first supper somewhere in London. The suddenness, with which this *coup d'état* was effected, staggered father. It left him dumb and stupefied for several days. The breach it created between him and his younger son was never wholly closed, though allowance was made for the fact that Iain was little more than fourteen when his abduction took place, and was under some measure of influence. So, while the bookish boy went south to be converted into a soldier and a gallant English gentleman, and at the same time endued with those attributes sought in their sons by parents who consign them to institutions like the Imperial Service College and Woolwich, the booby lad remained behind with his father, and eventually returned from the Great War to look after him for the remaining years of his life.

Perhaps Iain's heart, for all his bookishness, was more in tune with Mars than with the Muses. In reflecting on his clandestine translation to brighter prospects south of the Tweed, and the relief his departure afforded me, I am reminded of how De Quincey (as he tells in the passage describing his introduction to the world of strife) managed to rid himself of his bullying and imperious elder brother. A certain academician, living in Hammersmith, pronouncing favourably on the lad's promise of excellence, took charge of him as a pupil at a fee of a thousand guineas. And that was the last the terrified Thomas ever saw of his brother, King of Tygrosylvania and scourge of Gombroon, since he died of typhus shortly afterwards, thus concluding their fratricidal feud. The skilful application of a little gold-dust in this way, as De Quincey remarks, brought to a close a state of hostility that, otherwise, might have assumed Carthagenian longevity. There was little hope of my being relieved of Iain in a manner so fortuitous, if also expensive! But, as you have seen, he went in the end; and this separation granted me permanent respite from his warfare. All his wit and brains and early promise would seem to have been stultified by this precipitate change of environment.

Anyhow, his transference from Watson's to an English public school halved the bookish personnel in the home. This did not mean a decline, however, in the zeal of our learnéd father, who, like so many parents and school teachers, still sought to satisfy his own aspirations in me. How many there are who, showing reluctance to allow us develop our personalities, strive to mould us to their own imperfect patterns! I wonder how far this explains the Colonel's fervent ambition for his children! He would have had us continually panting after things unobtainable to the vast majority of mankind. He believed that nothing on earth was beyond our reach, if only we stuck conscientiously to our lessons, and at the same time appreciated how exemplary a father we had behind us. To him, nothing was more ignoble than sloth. Every one of the unforgiving minutes had to be filled to bursting-point. We had to live intelligently every waking moment; and I am not sure that he would not also have directed our dreams, had he but known how. "No idling, now!" he would say when it looked as though we were having a rest from mental pursuits. But, whatever else he may have had in view for Iain and me, I must say how grateful I am that never for a moment did he entertain the notion—so prevalent among Scottish parents—that either of us should wag his head in a pulpit. Prominence in some great and important sphere, won through excellence in mathematics, was what *he* really desired for us. Well, Iain has got where he is largely through mathematics; and I have got where I am without any, despite our father's claim that this was preëminently the field in which to train both intellect and character to cope with life's conflict. I deal with this conflict quite satisfactorily in my own way, and am just as able as any mathematician to resist the insidious influences of indolence and complacency which he feared were bound to overwhelm anyone as backward, conventionally, as I was for some years. My feeble assurance that one day I would be able to provide for myself, and not have to fall back on Iain's charity for a maintenance allowance (!!) produced ridicule and scorn. And how long would it be ere he could feel that I might be competent to earn my own living? After all, *he* couldn't live for-ever; and what would happen to me when he was gone? It was certainly time I realised how hopeless a fellow I was. And think of the disgrace it would be to other members of the family, and especially to the pushing Iain, if it became known that they had a ne'er-do-weel brother! (I ought to mention, parenthetically, that father and Iain had discussed this contingency; and there was a period during which the sedulous Iain envisaged his having to provide for me. But he assured our parent that he wouldn't promise a standard of life for me much above the bare subsistence level!)

In the mind of such a father, then, a constant striving was essential; and, the more laudable the objective, the better he was pleased. If he saw no wheel within reach, to which one's shoulder might be placed, a wheel had to be invented. If no stone remained unturned, something had gone wrong with the world, and there was no rest until an unturned stone had been found. If there were no brass tacks at hand, to which one ought to be getting down, you may be sure the Colonel could produce the requisite minimum. In practice, this meant that I had to resort to a text-book and indulge in a spell of bewilderment by setting myself a knotty, little problem. Father was never more delighted, and I seldom more distraught, than when he found me engaged with something like this: *A man stands at a distance of 85 feet from the top of a building, and observes that the angles of elevation of the top and bottom of a flag-staff on its roof are 56° and 54°, respectively. What is the length of the flag-staff?* My excursions into trigonometry would never have helped *me* to arrive at the answer. In any event, I have always had a suspicion that the world is already over-populated with those to whom such problems are elementary.

The Colonel gave to mathematics the credit Sydney Smith bestowed upon the Classics. Substitute the word, mathematics, where this reverend gentleman has Latin and Greek,[1] and you have the argument constantly proffered by way of inciting me to proficiency in all branches of mathematics—pure, mixed, or applied. "*They inure children to intellectual difficulties, and make the life of a young student what it ought to be, a life of considerable labour. . . . They at least secure a solid and vigorous application at a period of life which materially influences all other periods.*"

Of course, they do, if you happen to be made that way! But I ask myself where all these mathematics have got us! From reliable accounts, they have enabled us, on the one hand, to fly at terrific speeds and altitudes in the heavens, and smash one another's lives and countries to bits: on the other, they have taught us how to bring each other down from these lofty regions with a good, hearty smack, if not already consumed by raging conflagration while hurtling earthward. Without the mathematicians, in subtle coöperation with the physicists, how could the Christian nations, with their partiality for high explosive, have kept one another's hospitals, mortuaries, and lunatic asylums so well stocked? No, they couldn't possibly have done so! And that would have been a pity, speaking nationally, rather than rationally.

Distinction in scientific calculations was, in our father's view, the greatest honour mankind could enjoy—except, perhaps, in the realm of literature. Ah! this was just where he and I fell into agreement in later years, and found one another tolerable. But

---

[1] See his essay, *On the Study of Latin and Greek.*

literature was so overcrowded, and so precarious, he would point out, that he still favoured a career based on figures and formulæ. Nowadays, of course, it is increasingly difficult to make a name for oneself in anything of a serious nature, and correspondingly easy to do so, if one be disposed to caterwaul at the microphone, or undertake to drive a particular make of car along the Great Wall of China, *preferably backwards*, on a single wheel if possible, and in less time than it took some other lunatic.

While on the topic of Latin and Greek, it is not inappropriate to mention that, during the latter part of my school career, the Colonel insisted on a Classical, rather than a Modern and Commercial, bias. He revered the Classics as much as he abhorred business. His preference, therefore, was readily explained; and it was a preference for which I have had reason to be grateful in my more enlightened years. Though my serious tuition in Latin and Greek concluded with my going to the war, I still try to retain a working knowledge of these languages and of Classical literature. See with what amplitude they have enriched the world's pages! Who was it wrote that these two ancient tongues, as mere inventions—as pieces of mechanism—are incomparably more beautiful than any of our modern languages, and that their mode of signifying time and case by terminations, instead of by auxiliary verbs and particles, would, of itself, stamp their superiority?

The Scots, of course, have been renowned for their Latinity since the days of George Buchanan. That is to say, for about four centuries. And I number among my friends Scots who write Greek as easily and accurately as most Englishmen write English. The *dead* languages, Latin and Greek are usually called by the moderns. Dead, forsooth! How can two languages, which have got themselves so fundamentally mixed up with all the living tongues of Europe and America, be described as *dead*? They must be more alive today than ever, as the Colonel was constantly impressing upon me when refuting the imputation. But, whether he decided that my later education should be Classical, because of his own love for the Classics, or because he found that the alternative curriculum embraced subjects like book-keeping and shorthand, I cannot say. There are times when I deplore my ignorance of modern languages; but even what I remember of Latin alone helps me very materially with at least three of the most important of them. Yet, I should prefer to be without any than never to have discovered how Rome and Greece have flooded the world with imperishable thoughts and illustrious images. Woe betide civilization if ever its varying educational curricula exclude the Classics! That, assuredly, would be its end.

It is of interest to myself that I should have lived long enough to arrive at this conclusion, for, considering the severity of my schooling at George Watson's, I find that I was in much the same position and condition as Henry Cockburn when, toward the close of the eighteenth century, he suffered like tribulation at Auld Reekie's High School. "Out of the whole four years of my attendance," he wrote, "there were probably not ten days in which I was not flogged, at least once. . . . Oh! the bodily and mental weariness of sitting six hours a day, staring idly at a page, without motion and without thought, and trembling at the gradual approach of the merciless giant. I never got a single prize, and once sat *booby* at the annual public examination. The beauty of no Roman word, or thought, or action, ever occurred to me; nor did I ever fancy that Latin was of any use except to torture boys."

* * * * * * *

Apart from the shelves containing medical and scientific treatises, and, of course, the very sacred shelf devoted exclusively to copies of the Colonel's own publications and unpublished MSS., his library was of an informative and stimulating character. As might be expected of the books belonging to one so energetic in mind and body, it embraced few anodynes, if indeed any. Numerous among them were reference books, apropos which we were taught to appreciate that well-known sentiment expressed long ago by an anonymous Latin writer: "To know where you can find anything, that, briefly, is the biggest part of learning."[1]

The twelve principal books perpetually in use, and upon which he reared his family, were the following:

I. *The Bible.* You already know the place this ancient library, this greatest of human documents, occupied in our lives, so that I need not dilate upon it here, beyond reminding you that its story was fundamental.

II. *The Shorter Catechism.* And was there ever a better introduction to logic for young people? It had been drafted mainly by Englishmen, with some formidable Scottish representation, at the Westminster Assembly. But the English found it too difficult for them; and so the Scots alone adopted it. This minute publication,

---

[1] *Scire ubi aliquid invenire possis, ea demum maxima pars eruditionis est.*

available in waistcoat-pocket proportions at any reputable stationer's in the Scotland of my boyhood and youth, and for a halfpenny, has done more for basic education north of the Tweed than have all our bureaucratic enactments. It opens with the question, *What is man's chief end?* Listen to the answer! *Man's chief end is to glorify God, and to enjoy Him forever.* Can you formulate a sounder philosophy with which to embark upon life?

In many a Scottish home during my early years, *The Shorter Catechism* constituted a challenge thrown down before us when we were still little more than infants. A piece of good, sound logic, precisely compiled by men of integrity. Consider for a moment its definition of God. *God is a Spirit, Infinite, Eternal, and Unchangeable in His being, wisdom, power, holiness, justice, goodness, and truth.* There's clarity and profundity for you!

III. *Cruden's Concordance,* which we hurriedly consulted to refresh the memory on some point likely to emerge at question-time, during family-worship under the Colonel's direction. A last-minute appeal to this monumental work prevented many a squall.

IV. *Chambers's Twentieth Century Dictionary.* All through life I have retained affection and esteem for this concise piece of scholarship; and at times I recall the pride with which I read and re-read a letter from the late Charles Edward Stuart Chambers (then chairman of the publishing house of W. & R. Chambers) thanking me for a list of omitted words, together with their meanings and derivations. I had submitted these for possible inclusion in future editions; and I am happy in the knowledge that several of them are now incorporated. So I like to preen myself now and again with the notion that I may have had even some infinitesimally small part in offering to the world, in its present form, this achievement in accuracy and authenticity. Excepting the Bible, nothing in the realm of the printed word was accorded so much attention in our home as this celebrated Dictionary. The household's copy got so worn by constant reference to it, that, every year or two, it had to be replaced with a new one. In those days the Colonel wrote voluminously and, therefore, had occasion to consult it a great deal. The other member of the family using it extensively, I need hardly say, was Iain, the bookworm. But there was a lucid period in my school-days, during which I bound and obliged myself to learn three new words from it every day. I kept up this resolve for some months before departing to the war. Whether this was to any purpose or not, I must leave it to my readers to decide.

Only once has my faith in this most admirable publication been shaken. While consulting it on the origin of 'by Jingo' (a phrase father continually used) I was surprised to find it attributed to the popular music-hall song of 1878, conveying the Russophobes' threat of intervention on behalf of the Turks:

> *We don't want to fight; but, by Jingo, if I do,*
> *We've got the ships, we've got the men, and got the money too!*

Quite by accident (since I was still more booby than bookish) I had spotted the phrase when idly looking through *The Great Hoggarty Diamond*, published forty years earlier. Father happened to be reading it at the time; and I, in turning over the pages somewhat perfunctorily, chanced to see it. "I'll tell you what, Brough," wrote Thackeray, "I'm of age; and, if you don't pay me my salary, I'll arrest you—by Jingo, I'll have you in quod, or my name's not Bob Swinney!"

To the origin as given in *Chambers's*, I now drew the Colonel's attention. "Here's a pure case of parachronism, father!" I observed, with an unusual accession of confidence.

"Splendid word, my son! You appear to be making some intelligent use of your Greek."

There followed a few minutes' silence while I referred to *Brewer's Dictionary of Phrase & Fable*, the next volume on the list of family foundation-stones. But *Brewer* appeared to corroborate *Chambers's*. So I thought I had better search speedily in Thackeray. I found the passage just quoted, and promptly pointed it out to my father.

"So you're not entirely devoid of brains after all," he mumbled, not so much by way of encouraging *me*, as of making such private admission to himself as he felt, in conscience, my discovery warranted.

"But you're too late for the Indian Civil now!" he added, with more than audible emphasis.

V. *Brewer's Dictionary of Phrase & Fable*, a brand-new copy of which he gave me as a birthday present to celebrate my 'by Jingo' triumph, and in the hope that I might now acquire an interest in literature, and appreciate what it had meant to him in his latter years. That birthday gift is by my elbow now.

VI. *Bartlett's Familiar Quotations*, a work which, as he frequently reminded me, had long since been accepted as indispensable to every scholar and to every writer—"a book for every library and every household", as is stated in the preface to the tenth edition. *Bartlett's* was seldom out of father's hands; and I like to linger idly through this great tome I inherited from him, conning his own marginal annotations, and the passages he marked.

VII. *Roget's Thesaurus of English Words & Phrases.* All my life I have been familiar with this monument in verbal classification, and had acquired an ease with it long before it came into more general use among crossword devotees.

VIII. Scott's *Rob Roy,* and his

IX. *Lady of the Lake.* From what I have told you about our devotion to clan matters, you will have gathered that certain of the works of Sir Walter Scott occupied a position in the home secondary only to the Scriptures. "What has Scott not done for every one of us?" father used to ask, quoting with measured dignity the words of Dr. John Brown. "Who else ever, except Shakespeare, so diverted mankind, entertained and entertains a world so liberally, so wholesomely?"

X. *Through the Buffer State,* the Colonel's own best-seller, being an account of his lone wanderings in the Land of the White Elephant, illustrated with photographs taken by himself.

XI. A ponderous tome—ponderous in every sense of the word—written by our clanswoman, Miss Murray MacGregor of Mac-Gregor. Its exact title I now forget. It consisted, in the main, of genealogical tables and the like, setting forth our royal lineage!!

XII. Robert Chambers's *Book of Days,* that stupendous compendium of exact scholarship which, in later years, was to constitute for me the 'open sesame', where the world of letters was concerned.

If a thirteenth were required of me, I would answer with Homer, or perhaps with Herodotus, since the Colonel was resolved that no child of his should be untutored where matters relating to Ancient Greece were involved. Indeed, we were carefully nurtured on the glories of Greece and Rome. In subsequent years their thoughts and allusions were to become almost as intertwined with our young lives as were those affairs pertaining to the MacGregors and their ancient and honourable descent. Father was insistent that we should know at least *something* of Greece's contribution to world culture—to religion and philosophy, to astronomy and mathematics, to natural science, to medicine, to literature, to architecture, and to political thought. We were still quite young when we could boast a fair smattering of all this. And a very excellent background it was, as I have had reason to find in my more academic moments. Stories like that of Thermopylæ had been instilled into us long before we could read. At an early age we were as familiar with the mellifluous names of illustrious Greeks as with the characters of the Bible, though I doubt whether we could have spelt the more difficult of them. But, of a truth, we *pronounced* them properly. The Colonel saw to that! The valour of Leonidas and his three hundred Spartans, in face of the illimitable host assembled against them by King Xerxes, threw into the shadow all the achievements of modern armies. So, too, did the conduct of Themistocles at Salamis.

* * * * * * *

Included in another category, and regarded as of secondary importance, were other works of reference, chief among which was *Whitaker's Almanack*. For practical purposes, the Colonel found this omniscient publication indispensable. It kept him right on matters of phenomena, especially those connected with the heavenly bodies, in whose movements he took a deep interest. And he consulted it eagerly for exact figures when he suspected that government and other public officers, as also the bishops, were being paid more than they were worth! That England's two archbishops then received, between them, something like £24,000 a year, was one of the monstrous disclosures for which he was indebted to *Whitaker*!

Except for the Bibles stacked on the study mantelpiece, the foregoing volumes formed a small library in themselves, set aside from the remainder of the family's books. We were expected to know something about each of them, both as regards their bibliography and what they contained. At any moment father was liable to wake up from his muse, and rattle off some questionnaire, so as to ascertain whether we were appreciative of his efforts to impart to us a little of his vast learning. Do you wonder that we sometimes marvelled "that one small head could carry all *he* knew"?

It was singular that in the matter of authorship I was to be more successful than my father, who had striven so fruitlessly, as he imagined, to make something of me. From the outset of my career in this sphere, royalty returns began to reach me regularly, whereas publishers were usually worrying him for the payment of costs entailed, in excess of the usual percentage allowed, in effecting corrections. When he gleefully awaited the receipt of royalties to the tune of, say, twenty or thirty pounds, in respect of the sales of some particular work of his, he usually received, instead, a statement of accounts showing how, by his insistence on major alterations after the type had been set, he had incurred a debt of twice that amount. His incurable predilection for such alterations, and for lengthy interpolations at the most awkward places, rendered publishing an arbitrary undertaking for him—a sorry disillusionment. It, therefore, remained a mystery to him how *I* was able to handle my publishing without any such shocks.

True, he had had a bad spell at the hands of pirates and plagiarists. As I write, there also lies before me correspondence relating to the extensive pirating, especially in Canada and the United States, of his short stories. One particular story—*The Capture of Boh Yoh*—had been widely plagiarised in the New World, as well as in the Old, and spread like wildfire across the prairies. Throughout the earlier part of my life with him, he appeared to have been conducting a prodigious correspondence with the editors of various American publications, from whom he occasionally received a cheque in respect of the violation of his copyright. I well remember the storm that broke in the home when it was discovered that the first story included in a Christmas Annual for boys was *A Donkey-boy of Cairo*, copied word for word from an Indian paper, without his permission, though actually stating that it was his. The Society of Authors (his membership of which he retained for over half a century) now came to his assistance, and procured for him some financial recognition.

This was by no means the only occasion on which that admirable institution lent him aid. Early in the present century, he found himself at loggerheads with the Religious Tract Society on the question of its rates of payment. "Dear Sirs", runs a letter in my possession, "I received the enclosed cheque and receipt-form this morning, and I return them, as there must surely be some mistake in paying for a story like *A Peer of the Realm*, of 4,000 words, £1 : 11 : 6, or at the rate of 7/6 per thousand words. As this rate would beat the sweating process of the lowest class catchpenny London dreadful, I find it difficult to believe that it has got the sanction of a professedly religious society. Far from furthering the cause of religion, it is more calculated to bring religion into contempt; and I hope you will not think £1 : 11 : 6 per thousand words, or six guineas in all, too much for so good and so long a story, published in a respectable paper like yours. Will you kindly let me know?—Yours, faithfully, John MacGregor."

As this failed to produce any improvement, the help of the Author's Society was again invoked; and I still have in my possession the copy of a letter father afterwards wrote to the secretary, thanking him and his committee for the promptitude with which they obtained for him adequate payment.

Apropos the pirating of his writings, a few weeks after his death, in 1932, there came to me, from Kawene, Ontario, a letter worthy of inclusion here, without comment:

My dear Mr MacGregor,
    I hope you will pardon an old Western prospector for intruding, and bringing to mind something that happened some twenty-nine years ago. Perhaps, your late lamented father, Colonel MacGregor, spoke of it.

At any rate, I was stationed at Tache, on the main line of the Canadian Pacific Railway, some 200 miles east of Winnipeg, when I had occasion to bring to Colonel MacGregor's notice, through the courtesy of the Editor of the *Oban Times*, a story which appeared in the *Winnipeg Telegram*, presumably by an American author.

I was convinced that I had read the same story in an English magazine, and that Colonel MacGregor was the real author. I shall never forget how grateful he was to me; and I still have the bright and racy letters I afterwards received from him. To Mrs MacGregor also I am indebted for some beautiful letters and for photographs of you all. These I greatly appreciated. For two years an interesting and instructive correspondence was kept up; and then I had occasion to leave the district for other parts of Canada. But, through all these years, I never forgot Colonel and Mrs MacGregors' courtesy; and I assure you, Sir, that up to the time I read of Colonel MacGregor's death, I was wondering whether he were still to the fore, and, if so, where he lived.

The service I rendered, of course, was an insignificant one. I had hoped Colonel MacGregor would have demanded his rights, and brought this spurious author to see the error of his ways. The copyright laws, I understand, were then in a deplorable state, and nothing could be done.

The distinguished author of *Luinneagan Luaineach* and *Through the Buffer State* is, alas! no more; and an old backwoodsman begs to offer his sincere and heartfelt sympathy.

'Tis an old story now. Yet, it brings one back to other days, when we, who are Old Timers, were in our prime, and dreamt dreams of Eldorado, and hopes were high.

Believe me, Sir, I beg to remain
Yours sincerely,
Thomas S. Campbell.

*   *   *   *   *   *   *

Among the smaller and more specialised works father kept on a shelf at his elbow was a slender volume, foolscap-8vo in size, containing eighty pages of linen paper, finely finished. Printed in 8-point type on the righthand pages only, and arranged in alphabetical order, are lists of phonetic finals—literally thousands of them. It had taken him thirty years or more to put together this somewhat unique work. In 1892, as is shown by a note on the title-page in his own handwriting, he had had this one solitary copy privately printed for him in Bombay. The last page, in conformity with statutory requirements, bears the printer's imprint in the usual way. Most of the lefthand pages of this volume, all of which were blank originally, are covered with additions and minute corrections, made in ink by the compiler himself. Some of these are so neat and small that anyone lacking excellent eyesight would require a magnifying-glass to distinguish them. So, in this manner, just like Roget's classical compilation, this rhyming counterpart—this veritable dictionary of rhymes—was being constantly amended, added to, and generally brought up to date with the accession to our language of new words.

The neatness of the whole work surprises me yet, although I have been familiar with it ever since I knew what a book looked like. Somehow or other, it never occurs to one that one's own father could have been so painstaking, so meticulous. When he grew old (as, alas! some of us are destined to do) I often found it difficult to believe that this selfsame person, now largely confined to an armchair, had once been as alert, and as accurate in all that concerned the printed word.

This thesaurus of phonetic finals father regarded as indispensable when writing poetry, or when versifying. (There's more than a subtle difference between the two, you know, though comparatively few seem to be able to distinguish the one from the other!) In his latter years, when age and circumstance obliged him to live a life more sedentary, literature, which hitherto had been his chief recreation, now became the all-absorbing interest of his days. This little book, so neatly enclosed in darkgreen boards, was now in constant use. Consequently, it got a little tattered. Year by year, it went on growing in content; and, when the supply of unrecorded finals diminished, he began to fill its blank fly-leaves with parallel rows of words that are homographic, and words that are homonymous, and with prefixes that change the quantity and quality of words without changing the rhymes. On one of the fly-leaves he had written the following note, explanatory of this precious volume:—"A trans-Atlantic writer, denouncing the practice of authors' revealing the methods by which they work, is 'shocked to find that Tennyson makes it a constant practice to employ the services of a rhyming dictionary'. He would be more shocked still, if he knew that Byron, apparently the most impetuous and extempore of poets, did the like. This unnecessary indignation probably arises from the popular idea that all the great poems are inspired, and from the disinclination to believe that genius can be 'an infinite capacity for taking pains'. The notion that poems are thrown off like fragments of diseased bone is a very common one, but not correct."

For years, as I have said, this treasury, home-made from start to finish, stood on a shelf by father's elbow. As it became more and more tattered, no one was allowed even to dust it. Not that this mattered much: it remained too steadily in use to gather dust. And heaven succour the member of the family who, without the express permission of owner and compiler, removed it for an instant from its wonted place! On one occasion, when contemplating a verbal alteration in a poem of my own, I stealthily withdrew it for a few moments, while father dozed in his armchair. He suddenly woke to find it gone! Fortunately for me, I was seated at a table near at hand, and thus could explain, instantly, its temporary displacement. In mitigation of my offence, I pleaded that I could not very well have interrupted his nap to refer to a book I had every intention of replacing ere he wakened. My plea was successful, in that it resulted in some slight modification of the disciplinary measures enforced to ensure its safety and immediate availability. As a munificent concession, I was to be permitted to refer to it henceforth, provided it never left the room, and was always replaced exactly where I had found it—precisely between two specified volumes, its spine an agreed fraction of an inch from the edge of the bookshelf.

"Look at the title-page and end-papers!" father commanded in gruff tones. "What in the name of God possessed the little devil to mutilate my labour of a lifetime?"

On turning to end-papers and title-page, I discovered that, in a wayward moment, Margaret, then a child at school, had scribbled her name backwards, several times, in indelible pencil, upon them. When appending her father's name in like fashion, she had just got as far as the second g in MacGregor, when he entered and caught her. Loud lamentations followed. The study was placed out of bounds to Margaret for several weeks.

Before me lies this slender, fragile thing, so lovingly compiled by hands that have been dead these twelve years, and by eyes that no longer see as ours do. . . .

As a final word, let me make an odd admission. I had read little or nothing by the time I was twenty-six, though I had written my first two books. Yet, somehow, I had assimilated much of literature indirectly, it being surely remarkable how we become familiar with the greatest authors, without necessarily reading a page of them. There are so many avenues through which their thoughts and their very words permeate society, and impinge upon our everyday existence. With a father like mine, and the twelve books, which I have enumerated, in perpetual use—in endless circulation, one might say—it was not altogether surprising that, eventually, I should have drifted into authorship.

But that's another story, and a story for another book.

INDEX

239

PRINTED IN GREAT BRITAIN BY RICHARD CLAY AND COMPANY, LTD., BUNGAY, SUFFOLK.